New England Pet Friendly Hotels

Connecticut, Maine, Massachusetts,
New Hampshire, Rhode Island, Vermont

A Bed & Pet® Guide

By Milo Maxwell
As told to Laurence A. Canter

Bed & Pet® Publications

Host Milo Corporation

This publication is designed to provide accurate information in regard to the subject matter covered, as of the time this was written. It is sold with the understanding that the information concerning hotel pet policies, fees, and descriptions is subject to change at any time. This book is intended only as a reference.

ISBN 978-0615536019

How to use this guide

Sample Listing

★★★↲ ♥ 🛏 🎾

Milo's Favorite Hotel B&B
1234 First Street
Pet City MA 05814
(617) 123-4567
$119 - $309
SAVE –B&P Discount Available

Pet Policy: Dogs only, up to 80 lbs. Daily pet fee of $10 per pet. Pet amenities include personalized dog dish and dog room service menu with tasty canine treats prepared by our chefs.

Features: Number of rooms: 15, Number of floors: 3, Wireless Internet, Free breakfast, Multilingual staff, Free newspapers in lobby, Concierge desk, Smoke-Free property, Tennis courts, Free parking, Full service Health Club.

Note the following details within each hotel listing:

Special Feature Icons

🛏	Bed & Breakfast	🏌	Golf Course
🎾	Tennis Courts	⛵	Marina
♥	Romantic	⛷	Skiing nearby

Star Ratings

★★ 1 to 5 stars (higher is better)
Nothing negative should be implied to those shown as *Not Rated.* This means only that insufficient reviews were available for a reliable rating. Ratings have been compiled as an average from a variety of reputable sources but obviously are very subjective. They are shown here just to give you a comparative point of reference to the degree of 'luxury' and service you may expect at a given property. Full reviews are available for each hotel on the BedAndPet.com website.

Rates & Discounts

Rates listed are the hotel's standard published rates. If **SAVE –B&P Discount Available** appears below the rate, Bed & Pet® has negotiated discounted rates and last minute specials for the property. To get the best rate you must either book online at BedAndPet.com or by telephone,
> Using promo code 102350:
> U.S. and Canada: 1-800-780-5733
> Europe: 00-800-11-20-11-40

Pet Policies

Pet policies listed are the most current information available, however policies and fees do change. You may wish to verify the current policy. Some of the smaller New England properties have seasonal pet policies and rates.

Connecticut

Avon

Also see the following nearby communities that have pet friendly lodging:
Simsbury - 5 miles, Farmington - 5 miles, Hartford - 8 miles, New Britain - 10 miles,
Windsor - 10 miles.

★★★★

Avon Old Farms Hotel
279 Avon Mountain Rd
Avon CT 06001
(860) 677-1651
$139 - $189
SAVE –B&P Discount Available

Pet Policy: Pets up to 50 lbs accepted. Please contact us for details regarding this policy. You can reach us by calling (860) 677-1651.

Features: Business Center, Airport transportation (free), 2 Restaurants, Room service (limited hours), Photocopy machines, Suitable for children, Fax machine, Library, Video library, Piano, Multilingual staff, Picnic area, Nearby fitness center (discount), Pick up service from train station, RV and truck parking, Conference Room(s), Accessible bathroom, Handicapped parking, In-room accessibility, Wireless Internet, Concierge desk, Fireplace in lobby, Dry cleaning/laundry service, Bar/lounge, Number of rooms: 150, Number of floors: 3, Elevator, Air-conditioned public areas, Patio, Coffee in lobby, Poolside bar, Free breakfast, Parking (free), 24-hour front desk, Porter/bellhop, Meeting rooms (small groups), Sauna, Outdoor pool - seasonal, Wedding services, Area shuttle (free).

★★★

Residence Inn by Marriott
55 Simsbury Rd
Avon CT 06001
800-331-3131
$149 - $190
SAVE –B&P Discount Available

Pet Policy: Pets allowed, $100 per stay cleaning fee.

Features: Number of suites: 100, Number of floors: 3, Elevator, Conference room(s), Business services, Coffee in lobby, Free breakfast, Parking (free), Free newspapers in lobby, Picnic area, 24-hour front desk, Meeting rooms (small groups), Outdoor pool - seasonal, Dry cleaning/laundry service, Air-conditioned public areas.

Berlin

Also see the following nearby communities that have pet friendly lodging:
New Britain - 4 miles, Cromwell - 5 miles, Meriden - 6 miles, Southington - 6 miles, Rocky Hill - 6 miles, Farmington - 9 miles.

★★★

Best Western Plus New England Inn & Suites
2253 Berlin Tpke
Berlin CT 06037
(860) 828-3000
$89 - $90
SAVE –B&P Discount Available

Pet Policy: Pets may be accepted. Please contact the hotel directly for full details and reservations.

Features: Indoor pool, Number of rooms: 57, Number of floors: 2, Elevator, Air-conditioned public areas, Fireplace in lobby, Laundry facilities, Free breakfast, Parking (free), Multilingual staff, Free newspapers in lobby, 24-hour front desk, Business center, Wireless Internet, Meeting rooms (small groups), Smoke-free property, Breakfast service, Coffee in lobby, Business services, Fitness facilities.

★★

Days Inn Berlin Meriden
2387 Berlin Turnpike
Berlin CT 06037
(860) 828-4181
$51 - $79
SAVE –B&P Discount Available

Pet Policy: Pets accepted, $10 per stay.

Features: Dry cleaning/laundry service, Free breakfast, Parking (free), Barbecue grill(s), Airport transportation (additional charge), Arcade/game room, Conference room(s), Air-conditioned public areas, Wireless Internet, Business services, Coffee in lobby, Restaurant(s), Number of rooms: 68, Number of floors: 2, Multilingual staff, Free newspapers in lobby, 24-hour front desk, Wireless Internet, Meeting rooms (small groups), Outdoor pool - seasonal, Fitness facilities, RV and truck parking.

Bethel

Also see the following nearby communities that have pet friendly lodging:
Danbury - 4 miles, Brookfield - 7 miles, Ridgefield - 8 miles .

★★

Days Inn Bethel - Danbury
18 Stony Hill Road
Bethel CT 06801
(203) 743-5990
$55 - $84
SAVE –B&P Discount Available

Pet Policy: Dogs accepted, $10 per night.

Features: Parking (free), Number of rooms: 44, Free breakfast, RV and truck parking,

★★
Microtel Inn & Suites
80 Benedict Rd
Bethel CT 06801
(203) 748-8318
$59 - $114
SAVE –B&P Discount Available

Pet Policy: Pets accepted, $11 per day fee.

Features: Conference Room(s), Business services, Dry cleaning/laundry service, Number of rooms: 78, Number of suites: 30, Number of floors: 2, Coffee in lobby, Free breakfast, Parking (free), Free newspapers in lobby, Wireless Internet.

Branford

Also see the following nearby communities that have pet friendly lodging
East Haven - 5 miles, New Haven - 8 miles, North Haven - 9 miles, Hamden - 10 miles.

★★
Baymont Inn and Suites
3 Business Park Dr
Branford CT 06405
(203) 488-4991
$74 - $129
SAVE –B&P Discount Available

Pet Policy: Pets accepted, $20 per pet per night. May not leave pets alone in room.

Features: Number of rooms: 58, Number of floors: 2, Self-parking (free), 24-hour front desk, Wireless Internet, Meeting rooms, Indoor pool, Conference room(s), Sauna, Nearby fitness center (discount), Free breakfast, Laundry facilities, Coffee in lobby.

★★
Days Inn & Conference Center
375 E Main St
Branford CT 06405
(888) 339-7813
$63 - $109
SAVE –B&P Discount Available

Pet Policy: Pets accepted, $15 per pet per night.

Features: Restaurant(s) Restaurant, Number of floors: 2, Parking (free), Outdoor pool - seasonal, Restaurant(s)

Bridgeport

Also see the following nearby communities that have pet friendly lodging:
Stratford - 3 miles, Shelton - 8 miles.

★★★
Holiday Inn Bridgeport
1070 Main St
Bridgeport CT 06604
(203) 334-1234
$90 - $169
SAVE –B&P Discount Available

Pet Policy: Pets welcome, $15 per night plus $50 damage deposit. Pets not allowed in pool or food areas. Must be in leash or crated when outside the room, and may not be left alone in the room.

Features: Indoor pool, Restaurant(s), Room service (limited hours), Gift shop, Number of rooms: 226, *Continued on next page*

7

Days Inn – Branford
Continued from previous page

Number of floors: 9, Elevator, Conference room(s), Secretarial services, Air-conditioned public areas, Breakfast available (additional charge), Multilingual staff, Front desk (limited hours), Wireless Internet, Meeting rooms (small groups), Accessible bathroom, Handicapped parking, In-room accessibility, Dry cleaning/laundry service, Business center, Bar/lounge, Parking (additional charge) $6 Per Day, Fitness facilities.

Brookfield

Also see the following nearby communities that have pet friendly lodging:
Bethel - 7 miles, Danbury - 7 miles.

★★
Newbury Inn
1030 Federal Road
Brookfield CT 06804
(203) 775-0220
$79 - $139
SAVE –B&P Discount Available

Pet Policy: Pets accepted, $100 refundable damage deposit required.

Features: Parking (secure), Number of rooms: 46, Number of floors: 2, Conference room(s), Air-conditioned public areas, Free breakfast, Nearby fitness center (free), Picnic area, 24-hour front desk, Wireless Internet, Business center

---

Cromwell

Also see the following nearby communities that have pet friendly lodging:
Rocky Hill - 3 miles, Berlin - 5 miles, New Britain - 7 miles, Glastonbury - 8 miles, Meriden - 8 miles.

★★★♩
Crowne Plaza Cromwell
100 Berlin Rd
Cromwell CT 06416
(860)-635-2000
$99 - $184
SAVE –B&P Discount Available

Pet Policy: Pets up to 50-pounds are welcome at the Crowne Plaza Cromwell hotel. No more than two pets may occupy a single room. Please note that a $50 non-refundable deposit will be charged per stay.

Features: Accessible bathroom, Handicapped parking, Dry cleaning/laundry service, Restaurant(s), Concierge services, Gift shops or newsstand, Number of rooms: 215, Number of floors: 4, Elevator, Business services, Air-conditioned public areas, Breakfast available (additional charge), Wireless Internet, Health club, Parking (free), Multilingual staff, 24-hour front desk, Porter/bellhop, Conference room(s), Sauna, Indoor pool, Bar/lounge, Room service (limited hours), Spa Tub.

★★★/

Quality Inn
111 Berlin Rd
Cromwell CT 06416
(860) 635-4100
Rates from $99
SAVE –B&P Discount Available

Pet Policy: Pet accommodation: $25/night per pet. Pet Limit: Maximum of two pets per room, 30 pounds or less.

Features: Number of rooms: 77, Number of floors: 4, Business services, Coffee in lobby, Free breakfast, Parking (free), Meeting rooms Fitness facilities.

★★

**Super 8 Motel -
Cromwell/Middletown**
1 Industrial Park Rd
Cromwell CT 06416
(860) 632-8888
$65 - $105
SAVE –B&P Discount Available

Pet Policy: Pets accepted, no fee, but advanced approval required. Please contact hotel directly for pet approval and reservation.

Features: Business services, Free breakfast, Elevator, Conference room(s), Coffee in lobby, Wireless Internet (additional charge), Parking (free), Free newspapers in lobby, 24-hour front desk.

Danbury

Also see the following nearby communities that have pet friendly lodging:
Bethel - 4 miles, Brookfield - 7 miles, Ridgefield - 8 miles.

★★★

Danbury Plaza
18 Old Ridgebury Road
Danbury CT 06810
(203) 794-0600
Rates from $89
SAVE –B&P Discount Available

Pet Policy: Pets welcome, no additional fee. Limit 2 per room.

Features: Bar/Lounge, Conference Room(s), Health Club, Shoe Shine, Restaurant(s), Room service (limited hours), Gift shop, Number of rooms: 242, Number of floors: 10, Air-conditioned public areas, Pool table, Wireless Internet, Parking (free), Multilingual staff, Free newspapers in lobby, 24-hour front desk, Porter/bellhop, Security guard, Meeting rooms (small groups), Wedding services, Indoor pool, Business services, Dry cleaning/laundry service, Smoke-free property.

★★★

Ethan Allen Hotel
21 Lake Avenue Extension
Danbury CT 06811
(203) 744-1776
$99 - $139
SAVE –B&P Discount Available

Pet Policy: Ethan Allen Hotel welcomes your furry friends. There is a $15 per day pet charge. A designated pet walk area, including a pet waste disposal unit is located just outside the rear entrance for your convenience.
Continued on next page

Ethan Allen Hotel – Danbury
Continued from previous page

Features: Gift shop, Wireless Internet, Bar/lounge, Restaurant(s), Room service, Number of rooms: 193, Number of floors: 6, Conference room(s), Air-conditioned public areas, Fireplace in lobby, Patio, Parking (free), Free newspapers, 24-hour front desk, Porter/bellhop, Smoke-free property, Outdoor pool - seasonal, Wedding services, Dry cleaning/laundry service, Fitness facilities, Business center.

★★★

Holiday Inn Danbury-Bethel at Interstate 84
80 Newtown Road
Danbury CT 06810
(203) 792-4000
$80 - $155
SAVE –B&P Discount Available

Pet Policy: Pets up to 75 lbs, $25 per night per pet. Limited to first floor double bed rooms. Pets must not be left alone in room.

Features: Bar/lounge, Restaurant, Room service, Concierge, Business services, Breakfast available, Number of rooms: 114, Number of floors: 4, Parking (free), Wireless Internet, Meeting rooms (small groups), Outdoor pool - seasonal, Handicapped parking, In-room accessibility, Dry cleaning/laundry service, Fitness facilities.

★★☆

La Quinta Inn & Suites Danbury
116 Newtown Road
Danbury CT 06810
(203) 798-1200
$95 - $100
SAVE –B&P Discount Available

Pet Policy: Pets up to 50 lbs accepted, no fee.

Features: Restaurant(s), Number of rooms: 183, Number of floors: 5, Elevator, Conference room(s), Free breakfast, Parking (free), Free newspapers in lobby, 24-hour front desk, Wireless Internet, Meeting rooms (small groups), Accessible bathroom, Handicapped parking, Laundry facilities.

★★☆

Maron Hotel And Suites
42 Lake Avenue Ext
Danbury CT 06811
(203) 791-2200
$89 - $149
SAVE –B&P Discount Available

Pet Policy: Pets are accepted, $25 additional per day. Some restrictions apply so please call if you have further questions.

Features: Free Breakfast, Dry cleaning/laundry service, Restaurant(s), Room service (limited hours), Number of rooms: 87, Number of floors: 3, Elevator, Air-conditioned public areas, Parking (free), Free newspapers in lobby, 24-hour front desk, Wireless Internet.

★★★
Residence Inn Marriott
22 Segar St
Danbury CT 06810
203 797 1256
$109 - $219
SAVE –B&P Discount Available

Pet Policy: Pets allowed, $100 per stay cleaning fee.

Features: Dry cleaning/laundry service, Number of suites: 78, Number of floors: 4, Parking (free), 24-hour front desk, Wireless Internet, Meeting rooms (small groups), Conference room(s), Business services, Indoor pool, Fitness facilities.

★★
Super 8 Danbury Ct
3 Lake Avenue Ext
Danbury CT 06811
(203) 743-0064
$47 - $67
SAVE –B&P Discount Available

Pet Policy: Pets accepted, $20 per pet per night. No size restrictions, limit of 2 pets per room.

Features: Business services, Elevator, Free breakfast, Parking (free), Free newspapers in lobby, 24-hour front desk, Security guard.

Dayville
Also see the following nearby communities that have pet friendly lodging:
Putnam - 4 miles, Moosup - 9 miles.

★★★
Comfort Inn & Suites Dayville
16 Tracy Rd
Dayville CT 06241
(860) 779-3200
$124 - $142
SAVE –B&P Discount Available

Pet Policy: Pets accepted, $15 per night per pet.

Features: Coffee in lobby, Parking (free), Wireless Internet, Bar/lounge, Restaurant, Number of rooms: 78, Number of suites: 17, Number of floors: 3, Elevator, Business services, Air-conditioned public areas, Fax machine, Laundry facilities, Free breakfast, 24-hour front desk, Fitness facilities, Indoor pool.

East Hartford
Also see the following nearby communities that have pet friendly lodging:
Hartford - 3 miles, Glastonbury - 5 miles, Windsor - 6 miles, Rocky Hill - 8 miles.

★★
Econo Lodge
490 Main St
East Hartford CT 06108
(860) 569-1100
$52 - $119
SAVE –B&P Discount Available

Pet Policy: Pets accepted , $10 per night plus $50 refundable damage deposit.

Features: Coffee in lobby, Gift shops or newsstand, Number of rooms: 83, Number of floors: 2, Parking (free), 24-hour front desk, Wireless Internet, Air-conditioned public areas, Business services, Free breakfast.

★★★♩
Hartford Plaza Hotel
100 E River Drive
East Hartford CT 06108
(860) 528-9703
$89 - $99
SAVE –B&P Discount Available

Pet Policy: The Hartford Plaza allows pets up to 125 pounds. Pets must not be left unattended in guest rooms at any time. Additional fees may apply if there is damage to the rooms.

Features: Bar/lounge, Restaurant(s), Gift shop Number of rooms: 215, Number of floors: 8, Breakfast available, Parking (free), Free newspapers in lobby, 24-hour front desk, Porter/bellhop, Security guard, Wireless Internet (additional charge), Meeting rooms (small groups), Wedding services, Accessible Handicapped parking, In-room accessibility, Health club, Medical assistance available, Indoor pool, Business center, Room service, Concierge services.

★★★
Ramada East Hartford
363 Roberts Street
East Hartford CT 06108
(860) 528-9611
$79 - $99
SAVE –B&P Discount Available

Pet Policy: Pets accepted, $35 per night per pet. Limit 2 per room, no size restrictions.

Features: Restaurant(s), Number of floors: 5, Elevator, Conference room(s), Air-conditioned public areas, Coffee in lobby, Parking (free), Free newspapers in lobby, 24-hour front desk, Wireless Internet, Accessible bathroom, Handicapped parking, In-room accessibility, Dry cleaning/laundry service, Business center, Room service (limited hours), Indoor pool, Bar/lounge, Concierge services, Fitness facilities, Airport transportation (additional charge)

East Haven

Also see the following nearby communities that have pet friendly lodging: New Haven - 4 miles, Branford - 5 miles, North Haven - 9 miles, Hamden - 9 miles.

★★
Quality Inn East Haven
30 Frontage Rd
East Haven CT 06512
(203) 469-5321
$89 - $104
SAVE –B&P Discount Available

Pet Policy: Quality Inns charge a fee of $10.00 per night per pet and may require a $50 refundable damage deposit. Quality Inns accept any well-behaved pets with a maximum of 3 per room, but dogs are limited to 50 pounds. They do not currently require a veterinarian certificate. Pets may not be left alone in the room unless in a cage.

Features: Business center, Wireless Internet, Number of rooms: 80, Number of floors: 2, Business services, Parking (free), Outdoor pool - seasonal, Free breakfast, Coffee in lobby.

East Windsor

Also see the following nearby communities that have pet friendly lodging:
Windsor Locks - 4 miles, Windsor - 5 miles, Enfield - 5 miles, Vernon - 8 miles.

★★★

Clarion Inn & Suites
161 Bridge St
East Windsor CT 06088
(860) 623-9411
$79 - $94
SAVE –B&P Discount Available

Pet Policy: Pet Charge: $25 for 1 - 3 nights, plus $25 each additional 1-3 nights. Pet limit: 2 pets per room 50 lbs or less.

Features: Accessible bathroom, Restaurant(s), Free breakfast, Outdoor pool - seasonal, Dry cleaning/laundry service, Restaurant(s), Fax machine, Bar/lounge, Airport transportation (free), Fitness facilities, Number of rooms: 111, Number of rooms: 120, Number of floors: 2, Conference room(s), Suitable for children, Air-conditioned public areas, Patio, Pool table, Wireless Internet, Parking (free), Free newspapers in lobby, 24-hour front desk, Business center, Meeting rooms (small groups), Billiards, Wedding services, Room service, Area shuttle (free), Luggage storage.

★★★

Holiday Inn Express
260 Main St
East Windsor CT 06088
860-627 6585
$87 - $111
SAVE –B&P Discount Available

Pet Policy: Medium size pets accepted, $35 per pet per stay. Limit 2 per room and may only stay on first floor.

Features: Business Center, Accessible bathroom, Handicapped parking, In-room accessibility, Airport transportation (free), Number of rooms: 116, Number of floors: 2, Conference room(s), Air-conditioned public areas, Coffee in lobby, Free breakfast, Parking (free), Multilingual staff, Free newspapers in lobby, 24-hour front desk, Wireless Internet, Dry cleaning/laundry service, Fitness facilities.

For best rates, book reservations at BedAndPet.com
Or call:
U.S. & Canada – 1-800-780-5733
Europe - 00-800-11-20-11-40
Please enter Promo Code 102350 when requested by phone

Enfield

Also see the following nearby communities that have pet friendly lodging: East Windsor - 5 miles, Windsor Locks - 6 miles, Springfield - 9 miles, Windsor - 9 miles, West Springfield - 10 miles.

★★★

Holiday Inn Enfield Springfield
1 Bright Meadow Blvd
Enfield CT 06082
(860) 741-2211
$92 - $179
SAVE –B&P Discount Available

Pet Policy: Pets up to 50 lbs, $50 per stay.

Features: Airport transportation, Number of rooms: 176, Room service, Wireless Internet, Restaurant, Accessible bathroom, Handicapped parking, Indoor pool, Outdoor pool, Laundry facilities, Fitness facilities.

★★

Motel 6 Hartford - Enfield
11 Hazard Ave
Enfield CT 06082
(860) 741-3685
$65 - $89
SAVE –B&P Discount Available

Pet Policy: Well-behaved pets stay free. Animals that pose a health or safety risk may not remain onsite, and include those that, in our managers' discretion, are too numerous for any one room, cause damage to our property or that of other guests, are too disruptive, are not properly attended, or demonstrate undue aggression. All pets must be declared at check-in.

We will not service a room with an unattended pet. If your unattended pet prevents our staff from servicing your room, you may be asked to vacate the property.

Pets must be attended to and under control at all times. Pets should not be left alone in a room or automobile. If unavoidable circumstances require a pet to remain in a room while the owner is offsite, the pet must be secured in a crate. Pets must be on a leash or securely carried outside of guest rooms. Please clean up after your pet.

Features: Wireless Internet, Business services, Coffee in lobby, Laundry facilities, Parking (free).

★★

Red Roof Inn Enfield
5 Hazard Avenue
Enfield CT 06082
(860) 741-2571
$69 - $84
SAVE –B&P Discount Available

Pet Policy: One well-behaved family pet per room is welcome. No fee.

Features: Parking (free), 24-hour front desk, Wireless Internet.

★★
Super 8
1543 King St
Enfield CT 06082
(860) 741-3636
Rates from $62
SAVE –B&P Discount Available

Pet Policy: Guests can arrange to bring pets by contacting the property directly.

Features: Coffee in lobby, Free breakfast, Laundry facilities, Parking (free), Free newspapers in lobby, 24-hour front desk, Business center, Wireless Internet, Airport transportation (free)

Farmington

Also see the following nearby communities that have pet friendly lodging:
New Britain - 5 miles, Avon - 5 miles, Hartford - 8 miles, Berlin - 9 miles, Rocky Hill - 9 miles, Southington - 9 miles, Simsbury - 10 miles.

★★★
Centennial Inn Hotel
5 Spring Lane
Farmington CT 06032
(860) 677-4647
$119 - $165
SAVE –B&P Discount Available

Pet Policy: Pet Friendly: $20 per day or $175 per month (per pet, 2 maximum/suite)

Features: Dry cleaning/laundry service, Gift shop, Airport transportation (additional charge), Conference room(s), Air-conditioned public areas, Free breakfast, Parking (free), Picnic area, Meeting rooms (small groups), Outdoor pool - seasonal, Designated smoking areas, Wireless Internet, Business center, Outdoor pool, Barbecue grill(s).

★★★
Extended Stay Deluxe Hartford - Farmington
1 Batterson Park Rd
Farmington CT 06032
(860) 676-2790
$104 - $105
SAVE –B&P Discount Available

Pet Policy: One pet is allowed in each guest room. A $25 per day non-refundable cleaning fee (not to exceed $150) will be charged the first night of your stay. Weight, size and breed restrictions may apply. Please contact the hotel directly with inquiries.

Features: Number of rooms: 91, Number of floors: 3, Business services, Air-conditioned public areas, Wireless Internet (additional charge), Free breakfast, Parking (free), Nearby fitness center (free), Front desk (limited hours), Laundry facilities.

★★★
Homewood Suites by Hilton Hartford-Farmington
2 Farm Glen Blvd
Farmington CT 06032
(860) 321-0000
$109 - $299
SAVE –B&P Discount Available

Pet Policy: Pets up to 75 lbs. Pet fee: $150.

Features: Accessible bathroom, Handicapped parking, Dry cleaning/laundry service, Indoor pool, Gift shop, Number of rooms: 121, Number of floors: 3, Elevator, Suitable for children, Barbecue grill(s), *Continued on next page*

15

Homewood Suites by Hilton Hartford-Farmington
Continued from previous page

Free breakfast, Grocery, Health club, Parking (free), Free newspapers in lobby, 24-hour front desk, Wireless Internet, Meeting rooms (small groups), Business center, Wireless Internet, Coffee in lobby, Conference room(s), Fireplace in lobby, Picnic area, Air-conditioned public areas, Area shuttle (free).

★★☆ 🛏

The Farmington Inn & Suites
827 Farmington Ave
Farmington CT 06032
(860) 677-2821
$119 - $149
SAVE –B&P Discount Available

Pet Policy: Pets up to 100 lbs accepted, $25 per night plus a $100 refundable damage deposit. At The Farmington Inn, we know that pets are part of the family and we welcome them to our pet friendly hotel in Connecticut with treats and maps of pet friendly walking trails. Pets must be quiet, especially at night.

Features: Accessible bathroom, Handicapped parking, Business center, Coffee in lobby, Dry cleaning/laundry service, Airport transportation (free), Restaurant, Room service (limited hours), Number of rooms: 72, Number of floors: 2, Air-conditioned public areas, Fireplace in lobby, Video library, Free breakfast, Parking (free), Free newspapers in lobby, 24-hour front desk, Porter/bellhop, Security guard, Meeting rooms (small groups), Health club, Wireless Internet.

Glastonbury
Also see the following nearby communities that have pet friendly lodging:
East Hartford - 5 miles, Rocky Hill - 5 miles, Hartford - 6 miles, Cromwell - 8 miles.

★★★

Homewood Suites by Hilton
65 Glastonbury Blvd
Glastonbury CT 06033
(860) 652-8111
$116 - $259
SAVE –B&P Discount Available

Pet Policy: Pets up to 100 lbs. Fee $15 per day per pet.

Features: Dry cleaning/laundry service, Number of floors: 6, Parking (free), 24-hour front desk, Wireless Internet, Shopping on site, Business center, Outdoor pool, Fitness facilities, Luggage storage.

Greenwich

Also see the following nearby communities that have pet friendly lodging:
Stamford - 7 miles.

★★

**Howard Johnson Hotel
Greenwich**
1114 East Putnam Avenue
Greenwich CTO 6878
(203) 637-3691
Rates from $79

Pet Policy: Pets accepted. Please contact hotel directly for current fees, restrictions and pet reservations.

Features: Floors: 3, Restaurant, Daily bus to Mogegan Sun Casino ($22 per person round trip).

★★★★

**The Delamar Greenwich
Harbour**
500 Steamboat Rd
Greenwich CT 06830
(203) 661-9800
$269 - $349
SAVE –B&P Discount Available

Pet Policy: Dogs up to 100 lbs are accepted, $50 per night pet fee, a portion of which is donated to Adopt a Dog. Our sophisticated pets may browse the Pet Services Menu that lists special services, such as walking, grooming, and local pet activities. The hotel has seven pet friendly rooms that are reserved specifically for animal lovers. Your pampered pooch will receive a comfortable bed, food and bowls with bottles of mineral water.

Features: Conference Room(s), Dry cleaning/laundry service, Fitness facilities, Bar/lounge, Restaurant, Room service, Number of rooms: 82, Number of floors: 4, Coffee in lobby, Library, Spa services on site, Shoe shine, Free newspapers, Porter/bellhop, Limo or Town Car service, Parking, Wireless Internet.

Groton

Also see the following nearby communities that have pet friendly lodging:
New London - 3 miles, Mystic - 4 miles, Waterford - 6 miles, Stonington - 7 miles, Niantic - 9 miles.

★★★

Ramada Groton
156 Kings Hwy
Groton CT 06340
(860) 446-0660
$55 - $164
SAVE –B&P Discount Available

Pet Policy: Pets up to 50 lbs accepted, $15 per night per pet, limit 2 per room.

Features: Bar/lounge, Laundry facilities, Indoor pool, Room service, Concierge, Beauty services, Breakfast, Restaurant, Number of rooms: 69, Number of suites: 4, Number of floors: 3, Coffee in lobby, Pool table, Wireless Internet, In-room accessibility, Business center, Full-service health spa.

17

Hamden
Also see the following nearby communities that have pet friendly lodging:
North Haven - 2 miles, New Haven - 6 miles, East Haven - 9 miles,
Branford - 10 miles.

★★★
Clarion Hotel And Suites
2260 Whitney Ave
Hamden CT 06518
(203) 288-3831
$119 - $419
SAVE –B&P Discount Available

Pet Policy: Pets accepted, $50 pet stay. Limit 2 pets per room.

Features: Restaurant, Number of rooms: 103, Number of floors: 4, Parking (free), 24-hour front desk, Wireless Internet, Indoor pool, Poolside bar, Business center, Fitness facilities.

Hartford
Also see the following nearby communities that have pet friendly lodging:
East Hartford - 3 miles, Glastonbury - 6 miles, Windsor - 7 miles, Rocky Hill - 7 miles,
Farmington - 8 miles, Avon - 8 miles, New Britain - 8 miles.

★
Americas Best Value Inn
100 Weston Street
Hartford CT 06120
(860) 724-0369
$41 - $49

Pet Policy: Small pets accepted. No fee listed but please contact hotel directly to confirm.

Features: Golf nearby, Number of rooms: 109, air conditioned, cable tv, smoking permitted.

★★★★
Crowne Plaza Hartford Downtown
50 Morgan St
Hartford CT 06120
(860) 549-2400
$150 - $209
SAVE –B&P Discount Available

Pet Policy: Pets up to 15 lbs. Fee $50.

Features: Restaurant(s), Number of suites: 5, Number of floors: 15, Business services, Free newspapers in lobby, Accessible bathroom, Handicapped parking, Outdoor pool, Wireless Internet, Bar/lounge, Room service, Self-parking (additional charge), Fitness facilities, Number of rooms: 350, Conference room(s).

★★
Days Inn Hartford
207 Brainard Rd
Hartford CT 06114
(860) 247-3297
$55 - $129
SAVE –B&P Discount Available

Pet Policy: Pets accepted, $10 per pet per day.

Features: Number of rooms: 67, Number of floors: 3, Elevator, Free breakfast, Parking (free), 24-hour front desk, Wireless Internet.

★★★★↓
Hilton Hartford
315 Trumbull St
Hartford CT 06103
(860) 728-5151
$103 - $199
SAVE –B&P Discount Available

Pet Policy: Pets up to 75 lbs, $75 per stay. Pet bed and limited bowls available.

Features: Sauna, Currency Exchange, Business services, Indoor pool, Bar/lounge, Restaurant(s), Gift shops or newsstand, Number of rooms: 392, Number of floors: 22, Elevator, Conference room(s), Fireplace in lobby, Parking (additional charge), Laundry facilities, Coffee shop, Multilingual staff, Room service, 24-hour front desk, Wireless Internet (additional charge), Concierge desk, Fitness facilities

★★★↓
Holiday Inn Express Hartford Convention Center Are
185 Brainard Rd
Hartford CT 06114
(860) 525-1000
$85 - $129
SAVE –B&P Discount Available

Pet Policy: Pets accepted, $25 per day fee plus $50 damage deposit.

Features: Accessible bathroom, Handicapped parking, In-room accessibility, Dry cleaning/laundry service, Concierge services, Number of rooms: 129, Number of floors: 3, Elevator, Conference room(s), Air-conditioned public areas, Health club, Parking (free), Multilingual staff, 24-hour front desk, Porter/bellhop, Wireless Internet, Meeting rooms (small groups), Outdoor pool - seasonal, Business center, Free breakfast, Fitness facilities.

★★★↓
Holiday Inn Express Hartford-Downtown
440 Asylum St
Hartford CT 06103
(860) 246-9900
$108 - $145
SAVE –B&P Discount Available

Pet Policy: Pets accepted with $50 per stay additional cleaning fee.

Features: Accessible bathroom, Dry cleaning/laundry service, Parking (additional charge), Fitness facilities, Bar/lounge, Restaurant, Room service, Number of floors: 9, Conference room(s), Suitable for children, Coffee in lobby, Free breakfast, Free newspapers, Business center, Wireless Internet.

★★★
Homewood Suites Hartford Downtown
338 Asylum St
Hartford CT 06103
(860) 524-0223
$179 - $219
SAVE –B&P Discount Available

Pet Policy: Pets up to 50 lbs. Fee: $50 per pet per stay.

Features: Bar/lounge, Number of floors: 10, Conference room(s), Coffee in lobby, Self-parking, Free newspapers in lobby, Meeting rooms, Business center, Free breakfast, Laundry facilities, Parking charge $16 Daily, Fitness facilities.

19

Not Rated
Oakwood At Hartford 21
221 Trumbull Street Bldg. 1
Hartford CT 06103
(860) 525-2121
$125 - $172

Pet Policy: Pets accepted, $10 per day to a maximum of $300.

Features: Number of floors: 36, Concierge services, 24 hour fitness center, Well- furnished extended stay apartments with full kitchens, Separate dining and living room areas, Microwave, Toaster, Wireless Internet, Cable/satellite TV. Laundry facilities. Minimum 30 day stay may be required.

★★★
Residence Inn By Marriott Hartford Downtown
942 Main St
Hartford CT 06103
(860) 524-5550
$191 - $289
SAVE –B&P Discount Available

Pet Policy: Pets allowed, $100 per stay cleaning fee.

Features: Laundry Facilities, Dry cleaning/laundry service, Number of suites: 120, Number of floors: 8, Coffee in lobby, Free breakfast, Free newspapers in lobby, 24-hour front desk, Business center, Wireless Internet, Meeting rooms (small groups), Parking garage (additional charge), Fitness facilities.

Ivoryton

Also see the following nearby communities that have pet friendly lodging:
Old Saybrook - 4 miles.

★★★★
The Copper Beech Inn
46 Main Street Middlesex
Ivoryton CT 06442
(860) 767-0330
$227 - $362
SAVE –B&P Discount Available

Pet Policy: 1 dog allowed to stay at any one time, $85 additional fee per stay. Since we only allow ONE dog on the property at any time, you must confirm your reservation directly with the Guest Services prior to booking your room. No other pets are accepted.
Pets may not be left unattended in the room unless they are quiet and comfortably crated.

Any damages to room and/or property will be the financial responsibility of the pet owner. Any resulting billing adjustments for complaints about barking or other misbehaving will be the financial responsibility of the pet owner. Dogs must be on a leash and accompanied by an owner at all times when on the property. Pets are only permitted in The Carriage House. Please clean up after your pet by using the provided pet waste bags when using common areas. We have some old towels to lend you to wipe off the dog. Please clean dirty and/or wet paws, at least, before letting your dog in the

The Copper Beach Inn
Continued from previous page

room. Please do not allow your dog on the bed or furniture. Please be sure and register your pet at check in. Failure to register pets will incur an automatic $100 charge to your account.

Features: Number of restaurants 2, Dry cleaning/laundry service, Number of rooms: 22 Suitable for children, Parking (free), Wireless Internet, Conference room(s), Wedding services, Free breakfast, Laundry facilities.

Litchfield
Also see the following nearby communities that have pet friendly lodging:
Torrington - 5 miles.

Not Rated
Tollgate Hill Inn
571 Torrington Road
Litchfield CT 06759
(860) 567-1233
$115 - $225

Pet Policy: Well behaved pets welcome in certain rooms for an additional $25 per night.

Features: Small fridge and fireplaces available in some units, air conditioned. No in room accessibility features available, so if handicapped and require them, please book elsewhere.

Manchester
Also see the following nearby communities that have pet friendly lodging:
Vernon - 5 miles, Glastonbury - 6 miles, Hartford - 8 miles, Windsor - 8 miles,

★★
Baymont Inn And Suites
20 Taylor Street
Manchester CT 06040
(860) 643-1864
Rates from $64
SAVE –B&P Discount Available

Pet Policy: Pets accepted, $10 per pet per night.

Features: Elevator, Laundry facilities, Free breakfast, Business center, Meeting rooms (small groups),Free Internet, Conference room(s), Arcade/game room, Parking (free), Fitness facilities.

Not Rated
Clarion Suites Manchester
191 Spencer St
Manchester CT 06040
(860) 643-5811
$109 - $170
SAVE –B&P Discount Available

Pet Policy: Pets accepted, $10 per pet per night. Limit 2 pets per room.

Features. Fitness facilities, Business center, Meeting rooms, Wireless Internet, Free breakfast, free manager reception, Free parking, Library, Laundry facilities, Number of rooms: 104, all units have kitchens with microwaves, fridge, coffee makers, air conditioning, Cable TV, Housekeeping.

★★
Extended Stay America
Hartford - Manchester
340 Tolland Tpke
Manchester CT 06040
(860) 643-5140
$69 - $94
SAVE –B&P Discount Available

Pet Policy: One pet is allowed in each guest room. A $25 per day non-refundable cleaning fee (not to exceed $150) will be charged the first night of your stay. Weight, size and breed restrictions may apply. Please contact the hotel directly with inquiries. Please Note: Signature rooms do not currently accommodate pets, with the exception of handicap accessible rooms.

Features: Laundry facilities, Number of rooms: 104, Number of floors: 3, Coffee in lobby, Parking (free), Nearby fitness center (free), Front desk (limited hours), Wireless Internet (additional charge).

★★★
Residence Inn By Marriott
Hartford Manchester
201 Hale Rd
Manchester CT 06040
(860) 432-4242
$128 - $169
SAVE –B&P Discount Available

Pet Policy: Pets allowed, $75 per stay cleaning fee.

Features: Barbecue grill(s), Smoke-free property, Dry cleaning/laundry service, Wireless Internet, 24-hour business center, Number of suites: 96, Number of floors: 3, Air-conditioned public areas, Coffee in lobby, Grocery, Parking (free), Free newspapers in lobby, Picnic area, 24-hour front desk, Outdoor pool - seasonal, Fitness facilities, Free reception.

Meriden

Also see the following nearby communities that have pet friendly lodging:
Berlin - 6 miles, Southington - 6 miles, Cromwell - 8 miles, New Britain - 9 miles.

★★
Candlewood Suites Meriden
1151 E Main St
Meriden CT 06450
(203) 379-5048
$55 - $85
SAVE –B&P Discount Available

Pet Policy: Pets allowed with nonrefundable fee. Up to $75 for 1-6 nights and up to $150 for 7+ nights. Each pet must weigh less than 80lbs. Record of complete and up-to-date vaccinations required.

Features: Business services, Accessible bathroom, Handicapped parking, In-room accessibility, Dry cleaning/laundry service, Number of floors: 4, Elevator, Photocopy machines, Suitable for children, Coffee in lobby, Fax machine, Parking (free), Multilingual staff, Free newspapers in lobby, Wireless Internet, Air-conditioned public areas, Fitness facilities, On-site car rental, Shopping on site, 24-hour front desk, Luggage storage.

★★
**Extended Stay America
Hartford - Meriden**
366 Bee St
Meriden CT 06450
(203) 630-1927
$74 - $84
SAVE –B&P Discount Available

Pet Policy: One pet is allowed in each guest room. A $25 per day non-refundable cleaning fee (not to exceed $150) will be charged the first night of your stay. Weight, size and breed restrictions may apply. Please contact the hotel directly with inquiries.

Features: Laundry facilities, Number of rooms: 104, Number of floors: 3, Suitable for children, Barbecue grill(s), Coffee in lobby, Parking (free), Nearby fitness center (free), Wireless Internet (additional charge).

★★★
Hawthorn Suites-Meriden
390 Bee St
Meriden CT 06450
203-634-7770
$84 - $129
SAVE –B&P Discount Available

Pet Policy: Pets up to 25 lbs, $15 per pet per night.

Features: Dry cleaning/laundry service, Outdoor pool, Barbecue grill(s), Picnic area, Business center, Number of suites: 106, Number of floors: 3, Elevator, Air-conditioned public areas, Fireplace in lobby, Patio, Coffee in lobby, Free breakfast, Grocery, Parking (free), Free newspapers in lobby, 24-hour front desk, Wireless Internet, Meeting rooms (small groups), Smoke-free property, Outdoor pool - seasonal, Tennis on site, Fitness facilities.

★★
**Red Carpet Inn and Suites
Meriden**
1696 N Broad St
Meriden CT 06450
(203) 235-2877
$59 - $94
SAVE –B&P Discount Available

Pet Policy: Pets up to 25 lbs accepted, $15 per night.

Features: Number of rooms: 30, Number of floors: 3, Meeting rooms (small groups), Free breakfast, 24-hour front desk, Air-conditioned public areas, Parking (free), RV and truck parking.

Milford
Also see the following nearby communities that have pet friendly lodging:
Stratford - 4 miles, Shelton - 6 miles, Bridgeport - 7 miles.

★★
Mayflower Motel Inn
219 Woodmont Rd
Milford CT 06460
(888) 880-6854
Rates from $59
SAVE –B&P Discount Available

Pet Policy: Pets accepted, no fee, no size restriction. Limit of 2 pets per room.

Features: Parking (free), 24-hour front desk, Laundry facilities, Wireless Internet, RV and truck parking

★★
Red Roof Inn Milford
10 Rowe Ave
Milford CT 06460
(203) 877-6060
$65 - $75
SAVE –B&P Discount Available

Pet Policy: One well-behaved family pet is permitted. Service animals are always welcome. Pets must be declared during guest registration. In consideration of all Red Roof guests, pets must never be left unattended in the guestroom.

Features: Wireless Internet, Number of floors: 3, Conference room(s), Parking (free), Coffee in lobby, Handicapped parking, In-room accessibility.

★★★
Residence Inn by Marriott
62 Rowe Avenue
Milford CT 06460
(203) 283-2100
$99 - $169
SAVE –B&P Discount Available

Pet Policy: Pets allowed, $100 per stay cleaning fee.

Features: Number of rooms: 74, Number of floors: 3, Elevator, Business services, Coffee in lobby, Grocery, Parking (free), Free newspapers, Wireless Internet, Meeting rooms, Outdoor pool - seasonal, Dry cleaning/laundry service, Fitness facilities.

Mystic

Also see the following nearby communities that have pet friendly lodging:
Stonington - 3 miles, Groton - 4 miles, New London - 7 miles,
North Stonington - 7 miles, Waterford - 10 miles.

★★★↴
Comfort Inn Mystic
48 Whitehall Ave
Mystic CT 06355
(860) 572-8531
$99 - $189
SAVE –B&P Discount Available

Pet Policy: Pet Accommodation: $75.00 stay Pet Limit: maximum 1 pet per room, up to 50 pounds.

Features: Coffee in lobby, Accessible bathroom, Handicapped parking, Number of rooms: 120, Number of suites: 2, Number of floors: 2, Business services, Free breakfast, Parking, Free newspapers, Security guard, Meeting rooms, Wireless Internet, Dry cleaning/laundry service, Concierge.

★★
Econo Lodge Mystic
251 Greenmanville Ave
Mystic CT 06355
(860) 536-9666
$69 - $159
SAVE –B&P Discount Available

Pet Policy: Pet Accommodation: 10.00 per night per pet. Pet Limit: 2 pets per room up to 50 lbs. in designated rooms. Call hotel directly for pet room types and reservations.

Features: Accessible bathroom, Handicapped parking, Parking, Wireless Internet, Free breakfast, Number of rooms: 54, Number of floors: 2, Business services, Coffee in lobby, Free newspapers in lobby, Meeting rooms, Outdoor pool – seasonal.

★★★↓
Hampton Inn & Suites Mystic
6 Hendel Dr
Mystic CT 06355
(860)-536-2536
$109 - $379
SAVE –B&P Discount Available

Pet Policy: Pets accepted, no fee. Pet room restricted to first floor.

Features: Dry cleaning/laundry service, Indoor pool, Supervised child care/activities, Gift shops or newsstand, Number of rooms: 92, Elevator, Business services, Free breakfast, Parking (free), Business center, Meeting rooms (small groups), Fitness facilities, Free reception.

★★★
Residence Inn by Marriott Mystic Groton
42 Whitehall Ave
Mystic CT 06355
(860) 536-5150
$189 - $329
SAVE –B&P Discount Available

Pet Policy: Pets allowed, $100 per stay cleaning fee.

Features: Dry cleaning/laundry service, Number of rooms: 128, Number of floors: 3, Parking (free), Multilingual staff, Free newspapers in lobby, Wireless Internet, Meeting rooms, Coffee in lobby, Barbecue grill(s), Fireplace in lobby, Grocery, Free breakfast, Indoor pool, Suitable for children, Fitness facilities.

★★★
Residence Inn Marriott Mystic
40 Whitehall Avenue
Mystic CT 06355
(860) 536-5150
$161 - $429

Pet Policy: Pets allowed, $100 per stay cleaning fee.

Features: Continental breakfast, free manager receptions,. Indoor Pool, Whirlpool spa, Exercise facility and outdoor sports court,. Jacuzzi tubs in select units,. Furnished apartments with full kitchens, dining and living areas..

Naugatuck

Also see the following nearby communities that have pet friendly lodging:
Southbury - 8 miles.

★★
Comfort Inn Naugatuck
716 New Haven Rd
Naugatuck CT 06770
(203) 723-9356
$95 - $115
SAVE –B&P Discount Available

Pet Policy: Pets up to 25 lbs accepted, $10 per pet per night. Limit 2 per room.

Features: Number of rooms: 50, Number of floors: 3, Business services, Coffee in lobby, Free breakfast, Wireless Internet, Meeting rooms, Parking (free), Fitness facilities.

New Britain

Also see the following nearby communities that have pet friendly lodging:
Berlin - 4 miles, Farmington - 5 miles, Rocky Hill - 6 miles, Cromwell - 7 miles, Southington - 7 miles, Hartford - 8 miles, Meriden - 9 miles, Avon - 10 miles.

★★★
La Quinta Inn & Suites New Britain/Hartford South
65 Columbus Blvd
New Britain CT 06051
(860) 348-1463
$65 - $82
SAVE –B&P Discount Available

Pet Policy: Cats and dogs up to 50 pounds are accepted. Housekeeping services for rooms with pets require pet owner be present or pet must be crated. No fees or deposits are required.

Features: Number of floors: 6, Laundry facilities, Parking, Free newspapers, Wireless Internet, Conference room(s), Accessible bathroom, Business center, Breakfast, Fitness facilities.

New Haven

Also see the following nearby communities that have pet friendly lodging:
East Haven - 4 miles, Hamden - 6 miles, North Haven - 6 miles, Branford - 8 miles.

★★
Econo Lodge Conference Ctr
100 Pond Lily Ave
New Haven CT 06525
(203) 387-6651
$49 - $69
SAVE –B&P Discount Available

Pet Policy: Pets accepted, $10 per night per pet.

Features: Accessible bathroom, Wireless Internet, Number of rooms: 125, Number of floors: 2, Business services, Free breakfast, Parking (free), Meeting rooms, Sauna, Indoor pool, Fitness facilities.

Not Rated
Farnam Guest House
616 Prospect Street
New Haven CT 06511
(203) 562-7121
Rates from $149

Pet Policy: We have a resident very mellow, male cat named Wilson and we can accommodate some pets, generally under 15 lbs. $20 fee per night. Please call directly for pet approval.

Features: Free breakfast, Wireless Internet, Free parking, Guest kitchen and laundry facilities, Free Wall Street Journal.

★★★
La Quinta Inn & Suites
400 Sargent Dr
New Haven CT 06511
(203) 562-1111
$91 - $110
SAVE –B&P Discount Available

Pet Policy: Pets up to 50 lbs accepted, no fee.

Features: Accessible bathroom, Dry cleaning/laundry service, Wireless Internet, Business center, Airport transportation, Restaurant, Number of rooms: 158, Number of floors: 8, Breakfast, Parking, Smoke-free property, Outdoor pool - seasonal, Fitness facilities.

★★★★
Omni New Haven Hotel at Yale
155 Temple St
New Haven CT 06510
(203) 772-6664
$158 - $309
SAVE –B&P Discount Available

Pet Policy: Dogs and cats up to 25 lbs accepted, $50 per stay per pet, maximum of $100 per stay.

Features: Business Center, Meeting rooms, Parking garage (fee – Valet is available), Wedding services, Bar/lounge, Restaurant(s), Number of rooms: 306, Number of floors: 19, Conference room(s), Wireless Internet, Porter/bellhop, Doorman/doorwoman, Security guard, Concierge, Dry cleaning/laundry service, Fitness facilities, Room service.

★★★
Premiere Hotel and Suites
3 Long Wharf Dr
New Haven CT 06511
(800) 488-4771
$148 - $239
SAVE –B&P Discount Available

Pet Policy: Pets accepted, any size, $75 per stay. Limit 2 per room.

Features: Coffee in Lobby, Business Services, Accessible bathroom, Handicapped parking, Meeting rooms, Smoke-free property, Free newspapers in lobby, 24-hour front desk, Airport transportation (free), Outdoor pool, Wireless Internet, Number of rooms: 112, Number of floors: 2, Laundry facilities, Free breakfast, Parking (free), Fitness facilities.

Not Rated
The Study At Yale
1157 Chapel Street
New Haven CT 06511
(203) 503-3900
$159 - $374

Pet Policy: Pets allowed up to 40 lbs, $50 per night

Features: Number of rooms: 124, Number of suites: 8, Wireless Internet, In room safe, Restaurant, Fitness Center, Turn down service, Valet parking (additional charge), Concierge.

New London
Also see the following nearby communities that have pet friendly lodging:
Waterford - 3 miles, Groton - 3 miles, Mystic - 7 miles.

★★★
Hotel Latitude 41
269 N Frontage Road
New London CT 06320
(860) 442-0631
$108 - $138
SAVE –B&P Discount Available

Pet Policy: Pets accepted, $10 per pet per night, limit 2 per room.

Features: Dry cleaning/laundry service, Room service, Parking (free), Multilingual staff, Free breakfast.

★★
Red Roof Inn Mystic - New London
707 Colman Street
New London CT 06320
(860) 444-0001
$69- $119
SAVE –B&P Discount Available

Pet Policy: Red Roof's Pet Policy: One well-behaved family pet is permitted unless they are prohibited by state law or ordinance. Service animals are always welcome. Pets must be declared during guest registration. In consideration of all Red Roof guests, pets must never be left unattended in the guestroom.

Features: Business services, Wireless Internet, Number of floors: 2, Air-conditioned public areas, Coffee shop, Parking (free), Free newspapers in lobby, 24-hour front desk.

North Haven
Also see the following nearby communities that have pet friendly lodging:
Hamden - 2 miles, New Haven - 6 miles, East Haven - 9 miles, Branford - 9 miles.

★★★
Holiday Inn North Haven
201 Washington Avenue
North Haven CT 06473
(203) 239-6700
$93- $149
SAVE –B&P Discount Available

Pet Policy: Pets allowed. $50 deposit.

Features: Sauna, Business Center, Restaurant(s), Number of rooms: 140, Number of suites: 3, Number of floors: 2, Elevator, Parking (free), 24-hour front desk, Wireless Internet, Meeting rooms, Accessible bathroom, Handicapped parking, Indoor pool, Dry cleaning/laundry service, Room service (limited hours), Bar/lounge, Fitness facilities.

North Stonington
Also see the following nearby communities that have pet friendly lodging:
Stonington - 6 miles, Mystic - 7 miles.

★★✦
Cedar Park Whirlpool Suites
85 Norwich Westerly Rd
North Stonington CT 06359
(860) 535-7829
$69 - $249
SAVE –B&P Discount Available

Pet Policy: Pets accepted with a fee at check in. Please contact hotel directly for policy details and pet reservations.

Features: Free Breakfast, Accessible bathroom, Handicapped parking, In-room accessibility, Airport transportation (free), Number of rooms: 66, Number of floors: 2, Business services, Air-conditioned public areas, Patio, Barbecue grill(s), Coffee in lobby, Parking (free), Picnic area, 24-hour front desk, Wireless Internet.

Norwalk

Also see the following nearby communities that have pet friendly lodging:
Stamford - 7 miles.

★★
Econo Lodge Norwalk
469 Westport Avenue
Norwalk CT 06851
(203) 847-5827
$71- $91
SAVE –B&P Discount Available

Pet Policy: Pet accommodation: $15.00/night per pet, Pet limit: 1 pet per room 25 lbs or less

Features: Number of rooms: 50, Free breakfast, Wireless Internet, RV and truck parking, Number of floors: 2, Fax machine, Self-parking.

★★★
Four Points by Sheraton Norwalk
426 Main Ave
Norwalk CT 06851
(203) 849-9828
$79 - $179
SAVE –B&P Discount Available

Pet Policy: Pets up to 25 lbs accepted, no additional fee. Limit 2 pets per room.

Features: Accessible bathroom, Handicapped parking, Dry cleaning/laundry service, Bar/lounge, Restaurant(s), Concierge services, Number of rooms: 127, Number of floors: 4, Conference room(s), Business services, Parking (free), Room service, 24-hour front desk, Porter/bellhop, Wireless Internet, Fitness facilities, Smoke-free property.

★★
Homestead Norwalk - Stamford
400 Main Ave
Norwalk CT 06851
(203) 847-6888
$91 - $176
SAVE –B&P Discount Available

Pet Policy: We gladly welcome one pet per guest room. A $25 per day non-refundable cleaning fee (not to exceed $150) will be charged the first night of your stay. Weight, size and breed restrictions may apply. Please contact the hotel directly with inquiries.

Features: Number of rooms: 131, Number of floors: 3, Elevator, Air-conditioned public areas, Parking (free), Wireless Internet (additional charge), Nearby fitness center (discount), Laundry facilities.

Not Rated
Oakwood At Merritt River
399 Main Avenue
Norwalk CT 06851
(602) 687-3322
$155 - $200

Pet Policy: Pets accepted, $10 per day to a maximum of $300.

Features: Extended stay furnished apartments, Concierge services, Business Center, Elevator, Free parking, Outdoor pool, In room accessibility, Restaurant, Tennis courts.

Old Saybrook

Also see the following nearby communities that have pet friendly lodging:
Ivoryton - 4 miles.

★★
Days Inn Old Saybrook Ct
1430 Boston Post Rd
Old Saybrook CT 06475
(860) 388-3453
$71 - $159
SAVE –B&P Discount Available

Pet Policy: Dogs welcome. Please contact our hotel front desk for our pet policies as they sometimes change seasonally.

Features: RV and truck parking, Wireless Internet, Coffee in lobby, Free breakfast, Parking (free), Newspapers, Business center, Concierge, Laundry facilities.

★★
Econo Lodge Inn and Suites
1750 Boston Post Rd
Old Saybrook CT 06475
(860) 399-7973
$99 - $189
SAVE –B&P Discount Available

Pet Policy: Pet accommodation: $30/stay . Pet limit: 2 pets per room, 35 lbs or less.

Features: Wireless Internet, Outdoor pool, Number of floors: 3, Number of rooms: 44, Coffee in lobby, Free breakfast, Parking, Newspapers, Business center.

★★
Knights Inn Old Saybrook
7 N Main St
Old Saybrook CT 06475
(860) 388-3463
$71 - $108
SAVE –B&P Discount Available

Pet Policy: Pets accepted, $10 per night per pet.

Features: Free breakfast, Wireless Internet, Parking (free), Room service, 24-hour front desk, Luggage storage.

★★
Liberty Inn
55 Springbrook Road
Old Saybrook CT 06475
(860) 388-1777
$79 - $129
SAVE –B&P Discount Available

Pet Policy: Accepts large pets, up to 125 lbs, $15 per night, up to maximum of $100 per stay.

Features: Number of rooms: 25, Number of floors: 2, Laundry facilities, Free breakfast, Parking (free), Concierge, Wireless Internet, Handicapped parking.

★★★⛵
Saybrook Point Inn And Spa
2 Bridge Street
Old Saybrook CT 06475
(860) 395-2000
$349 - $599

Pet Policy: Dogs up to 25 lbs accepted, $50 first night, $25 each additional night. When making your reservation, let us know your special guests name and breed so we can prepare our special amenities to include welcome treats, a souvenir bandana, and a custom-made doggie day bed. Dog sitting can be

Saybrook Point Inn And Spa
Continued from previous page

arranged at a rate of $11/hour with a $30 minimum. Please take your dog with you when you leave the property. Please do not leave dogs unattended. We encourage you to make plans with us prior to arrival so pet sitting or other assistance can be arranged.

Features: Marina, Indoor and outdoor heated pools, Full health club, Hot tub, Sauna and steam room, Free shuttle service, Use of bicycles, Restaurant, Wireless Internet, Bar/Lounge, Miniature golf, Business Center.

Ridgefield

Also see the following nearby communities that have pet friendly lodging:
Danbury - 8 miles, Bethel - 8 miles.

★★
Days Inn Ridgefield Us
296 Ethan Allen Hwy - Route 7
Ridgefield CT 06877
(203) 438-3781
$71 - $119
SAVE –B&P Discount Available

Pet Policy: Well-behaved pets are welcome, $20 per night.

Features: Restaurant, Coffee in lobby, Parking (free), Free newspapers in lobby, Concierge desk, Wireless Internet, Bar/lounge, Laundry facilities, Business center, Fitness facilities.

Rocky Hill

Also see the following nearby communities that have pet friendly lodging:
Cromwell - 3 miles, Glastonbury - 5 miles, New Britain - 6 miles, Berlin - 6 miles, Hartford - 7 miles, East Hartford - 8 miles, Farmington - 9 miles.

★★
Howard Johnson Express
1760 Silas Deane Highway
Rocky Hill CT 06067-1302
(860) 529-3341
$60 - $84
SAVE –B&P Discount Available

Pet Policy: Pets accepted, no size limit. $10 per pet per day.

Features: Shopping on site, Conference room(s), Business services, Free breakfast, Parking (free), Free newspapers in lobby, Limo or Town Car service.

★★★
Residence Inn By Marriott
680 Cromwell Ave
Rocky Hill CT 06067
(860) 257-7500
Rates from $120
SAVE –B&P Discount Available

Pet Policy: Pets allowed, $100 per stay cleaning fee.

Features: Indoor pool, Number of rooms: 96, Number of floors: 3, Free breakfast, Parking (free), Free newspapers in lobby, Fitness facilities, Restaurant, Dry cleaning/laundry service, Tennis on site, Snack bar/deli.

★★
Super 8 Rocky Hill
1499 Silas Deane Hwy
Rocky Hill CT 06067
(860) 372-4636
Rates from $69
SAVE –B&P Discount Available

Pet Policy: Pets accepted, $10 per pet per night. Limit 2 per room.

Features: Fitness facilities, Business center, Free breakfast, Restaurant(s), Parking (free), Room service, 24-hour front desk.

Shelton
Also see the following nearby communities that have pet friendly lodging:
Milford - 6 miles, Stratford - 6 miles, Bridgeport - 8 miles.

★★
Homestead Shelton - Fairfield County
945 Bridgeport Ave
Shelton CT 06484
(203) 926-6868
$96 - $111
SAVE –B&P Discount Available

Pet Policy: We gladly welcome one pet per guest room. A $25 per day non-refundable cleaning fee (not to exceed $150) will be charged the first night of your stay. Weight, size and breed restrictions may apply. Please contact the hotel directly with inquiries.

Features: Number of rooms: 140, Number of floors: 3, Coffee in lobby, Parking (free), Nearby fitness center (free), Wireless Internet, Laundry facilities.

★★★
Residence Inn by Marriott Shelton-Fairfield County
1001 Bridgeport Ave
Shelton CT 06484
(203) 926 9000
$169 - $189
SAVE –B&P Discount Available

Pet Policy: Pets allowed, $100 per stay cleaning fee.

Features: Number of rooms: 96, Number of floors: 2, Coffee in lobby, Parking (free), Newspapers in lobby, Nearby fitness center (free), Wireless Internet, Meeting rooms, Smoke-free property, Outdoor pool - seasonal, Dry cleaning/laundry service.

Simsbury
Also see the following nearby communities that have pet friendly lodging:
Avon - 5 miles, Windsor - 8 miles, Windsor Locks - 8 miles, Farmington - 10 miles.

Not Rated
Iron Horse Inn
969 Hopmedow St - Rte 10
Simsbury CT 06070
(860) 658-2216
$75 - $85

Pet Policy: Accepts pets up to 40 lbs, $15 per night additional fee, limit 1 per room.

Features: Microwave, Fridge, Private balcony, Laundry facilities, Free coffee in lobby, Wireless Internet, Outdoor pool – seasonal.

★★★ 🏃

Simsbury 1820 House
731 Hopmeadow St
Simsbury CT 06070
(860) 658-7658
$128 - $169
SAVE –B&P Discount Available

Pet Policy: Pets up to 100 lbs accepted, $20 per night plus a $100 refundable security deposit. At Simsbury 1820 House, we know that pets are part of the family and we welcome them to our pet friendly hotel in with treats and maps of pet friendly walking trails. Pets must be quiet especially at night.

Features: Year Built 1820, Free Breakfast, Conference Room(s), Number of rooms: 33, Number of floors: 3, Air-conditioned public areas, Fireplace in lobby, Coffee in lobby, Free newspapers in lobby, Wedding services, Airport transportation (free), Video library, Parking (free), Nearby fitness center (free), Wireless Internet, 24-hour business center.

Southbury

Also see the following nearby communities that have pet friendly lodging:
Naugatuck - 8 mile.

★★★✦

Crowne Plaza Southbury
1284 Strongtown Rd
Southbury CT 06488
(203) 598-7600
$99 - $139
SAVE –B&P Discount Available

Pet Policy: The hotel is pet friendly and offers nearby walking paths. A pet fee of $25.00 per night will be added to the rate. Service animals are welcomed.

Features: Indoor pool, Restaurant, Room service, Gift shop, Number of rooms: 197, Number of suites: 10, Number of floors: 3, Parking (free), Free newspapers, Porter/bellhop, Concierge, Wireless Internet, Sauna, Accessible bathroom, Handicapped parking, Area shuttle, Fitness facilities, Business center, Bar/lounge, Airport transportation (free).

★★★✦ 🏃 🎾🏌

Heritage Hotel
522 Heritage Rd
Southbury CT 06488
(203) 264-8200
$109 - $159
SAVE –B&P Discount Available

Pet Policy: Dogs up to 25 lbs accepted, $25 per stay. Nice walking areas nearby.

Features: Accessible bathroom, Handicapped parking, Dry cleaning/laundry service, 2 Restaurants, Number of rooms: 163, Number of floors: 3, Parking, Business center, Wireless Internet, Full-service health spa, Concierge, Bar/lounge, Indoor pool, Golf course on site, Tennis on site, Room service, Meeting rooms, Steam room, Smoke-free property, Billiards, Ski storage, Massage - treatment room(s), Sauna, Outdoor pool - seasonal, Wedding services.

Southington
Also see the following nearby communities that have pet friendly lodging:
Berlin - 6 miles, Meriden - 6 miles, New Britain - 7 miles, Farmington
- 9 miles.

★★ 🐾
Days Inn Southington
30 Laning St
Southington CT 06489
(860) 628-0921
$61 - $103
SAVE –B&P Discount Available

Pet Policy: Dogs only, $25 per stay.

Features: Number of floors: 2, Fax machine, Parking (free), 24-hour front desk, Restaurant(s), Free breakfast, Free newspapers in lobby, RV and truck parking, Room service (limited hours), Wireless Internet, 24-hour business center.

★🏅 🐾
Knights Inn Southington
462 Queen St
Southington CT 06489
(860) 621-0181
$44 - $65
SAVE –B&P Discount Available

Pet Policy: Pets accepted, $10 per night per pet.

Features: Shopping on site, Business services, Air-conditioned public areas, Free breakfast, Parking (free), Free newspapers in lobby, 24-hour front desk, Outdoor pool – seasonal.

★★★ 🐾
Residence Inn by Marriott Southington
778 West St
Southington CT 06489
(860) 621 4440
$169 - $170
SAVE –B&P Discount Available

Pet Policy: Pets allowed, $100 per stay cleaning fee.

Features: Grocery, Dry cleaning/laundry service, Meeting rooms (small groups), Wireless Internet, Indoor pool, Number of suites: 94, Number of floors: 4, Free newspapers in lobby, Parking (free), Fitness facilities.

Stamford
Also see the following nearby communities that have pet friendly lodging:
Norwalk - 7 miles, Greenwich - 7 miles.

★★
Americas Best Value Inn
1209 E Main St
Stamford CT 06902
(203) 325-2655
$68 - $103
SAVE –B&P Discount Available

Pet Policy: Pets accepted, $10 per night.

Features: Restaurant, Number of rooms: 80, Number of floors: 2, Handicapped parking, Coffee in lobby, Laundry facilities, Free breakfast, Parking (free), 24-hour front desk, Business center, Wireless Internet.

★★
Amsterdam Hotel
19 Clarks Hill Ave
Stamford CT 06902
(203) 327-4300
$99 - $259
SAVE –B&P Discount Available

Pet Policy: Pets allowed, $20 per night per pet. Limit 2 pets per room.

Features: Free Breakfast, Gift shop, Number of rooms: 86, Number of floors: 6, Elevator, Coffee shop, Parking (additional charge), Free newspapers in lobby, 24-hour front desk, Wireless Internet, Fitness facilities.

★★★★
Hilton Stamford Hotel & Executive Meeting Center
1 First Stamford Pl
Stamford CT 06902
(203) 967-2222
$84 - $269
SAVE –B&P Discount Available

Pet Policy: Pets up to 75 lbs, $50 per stay. Limit of 2 pets per room.

Features: Dry cleaning/laundry service, Indoor pool, Restaurant(s), Parking (additional charge), Number of rooms: 484, Coffee in lobby, Wireless Internet, Shoe shine, Multilingual staff, Free newspapers in lobby, 24-hour front desk, Porter/bellhop, Security guard, Fitness facilities, Room service (limited hours), Bar/lounge, Business center.

★★★★
Holiday Inn Stamford
700 Main St
Stamford CT 06901
(203) 358-8400
$108 - $304
SAVE –B&P Discount Available

Pet Policy: Pets under 15 lbs accepted, $49 per stay cleaning fee.

Features: Handicapped parking, In-room accessibility, Dry cleaning/laundry service, Bar/lounge, Indoor pool, Restaurant(s), Room service (limited hours), Gift shop, Number of rooms: 380, Number of floors: 9, Elevator, Conference room(s), Secretarial services, Parking (additional charge), Pool table, Multilingual staff, Porter/bellhop, Limo or Town Car service available, Wireless Internet, Fitness facilities.

★★★
La Quinta Inn & Suites Stamford/New York City
135 Harvard Avenue
Stamford CT 06902
(203) 357-7100
$89 - $119
SAVE –B&P Discount Available

Pet Policy: Pets accepted, no fee. Limit 2 per room.

Features: Accessible bathroom, Handicapped parking, Indoor pool, Dry cleaning/laundry service, Wireless Internet, Restaurant(s), Number of rooms: 158, Number of floors: 8, Elevator, Business services, Air-conditioned public areas, Free breakfast, Parking (free), Free newspapers in lobby, Room service, 24-hour front desk, Fitness facilities.

Not Rated
Oakwood At Parc Grove
180 Broad Street
Stamford CT 06905
(888) 444-8170
$180 - $200

Pet Policy: Pets accepted, $10 per day to a maximum of $300.

Features: Extended Stay, completely furnished apartments, Fully equipped kitchens, Outdoor pool, Fitness center, Indoor sports court, business center. No accessibility features available so if handicapped and require them, you should book elsewhere. Minimum stay of 30 days may be required.

★★★★
Stamford Marriott Hotel & Spa
243 Tresser Blvd
Stamford CT 06901
(203) 357-9555
$118 - $319
SAVE – B&P Discount Available

Pet Policy: Pets accepted, $49 per stay cleaning fee.

Features: Indoor pool, Restaurant(s), Gift shop, Number of rooms: 506, Number of floors: 16, Conference room(s), 24-hour front desk, Business center, Bar/Lounge, Parking garage (additional charge, Valet available), Dry cleaning/laundry service, Room service (limited hours), Fitness facilities, Wireless Internet, Full-service health spa, Massage - spa treatment room(s), Outdoor pool - seasonal, Smoke-free property.

★★★★
Stamford Plaza Hotel and Conference Center
2701 Summer St
Stamford CT 06905
(203) 359-1300
$98 - $159
SAVE – B&P Discount Available

Pet Policy: Pets under 25 lbs accepted, $50 per stay fee.

Features: Indoor pool, Bar/lounge, Room service (limited hours), Business center, Dry cleaning/laundry service, Conference room(s), Restaurant(s), Hair salon, Concierge services, Gift shop, Number of rooms: 448, Free newspapers in lobby, 24-hour front desk, Security guard, Area shuttle (free), Parking (additional charge - $10 per day), Wireless Internet.

★★
Super 8 Stamford Greenwich
32 Grenhart Rd
Stamford CT 06902
(203) 324-8887
$75 - $99
SAVE – B&P Discount Available

Pet Policy: Pets accepted, $20 per stay. Limit 2 per room.

Features: Business Center, Area shuttle (free), RV and truck parking, Free breakfast, Parking (free), Multilingual staff, Security guard

Stratford
Also see the following nearby communities that have pet friendly lodging:
Bridgeport - 3 miles, Milford - 4 miles, Shelton - 6 miles.

★★★
Homewood Suites by Hilton
6905 Main St
Stratford CT 06614
(203) 377-3322
$98- $239
SAVE –B&P Discount Available

Pet Policy: Pets up to 75 lbs. $25 per night, to a maximum of $400.

Features: Dry cleaning/laundry service, Free breakfast, Business center, Indoor pool, Fitness facilities, Gift shop, Number of rooms: 135, Number of floors: 3, Business services, Suitable for children, Coffee in lobby, Ski storage, Library, Video library, Parking (free), Free newspapers in lobby, 24-hour front desk, Limo or Town Car service available, Wireless Internet, Meeting rooms.

★★
Rodeway Inn Stratford
10 Washington Pkwy
Stratford CT 06615
(203) 377-6288
$69 - $119
SAVE –B&P Discount Available

Pet Policy: Rodeway Inns charge a fee of $10 per night per pet and require a $50 refundable damage deposit. Max of 2 pets per room. A veterinarian certificate that the pet is on a flea and parasite program and that they are free from parasites is required. Pets may not be left alone in the room unless in a cage.

Features: Free breakfast, Wireless Internet, Handicapped parking, In-room accessibility, Restaurant(s), Number of rooms: 28, Number of floors: 2, Air-conditioned public areas, Parking (free.

Torrington
Also see the following nearby communities that have pet friendly lodging:
Litchfield - 5 miles.

★★★
Quality Inn And Suites
395 Winsted Rd
Torrington CT 06790
(860) 496-8808
Rates from $79
SAVE –B&P Discount Available

Pet Policy: Quality Inns charge a fee of $10 per night per pet and may require a $50 refundable damage deposit. Quality Inns accept any well-behaved pets, up to 50 lbs, with a maximum of 3 per room. Pets may not be left alone in the room unless in a cage.

Features: Meeting rooms, Fitness facilities, Free breakfast, Parking (free), Wireless Internet, Bar/lounge, Indoor pool, Laundry facilities.

★★ 🛏
Yankee Peddler Inn
93 Main St
Torrington CT 06790
(860) 489-9226
$69 - $119
SAVE –B&P Discount Available

Pet Policy: Pets up to 20 lbs, $20 per stay. Pets must remain in pet carrier or cage.

Features: Business Center, Free Breakfast, Bar/Lounge, Restaurant(s), Room service (limited hours), Number of rooms: 60, Number of floors: 3, Air-conditioned public areas, Laundry facilities, Video library, Parking (free), 24-hour front desk, Porter/bellhop, Meeting rooms (small groups), Wedding services, Fitness facilities, Self-parking, Wireless Internet.

Vernon
Also see the following nearby communities that have pet friendly lodging:
East Windsor - 8 miles, Windsor - 10 miles.

★★
Howard Johnson Express Inn -
451 Hartford Tpke
Vernon CT 06066
(860) 875-0781
$48 - $88
SAVE –B&P Discount Available

Pet Policy: Pets accepted, $10 per day per pet.

Features: Business services, Free breakfast, Parking (free), Free newspapers in lobby, 24-hour front desk, Wireless Internet, Outdoor pool - seasonal, Dry cleaning/laundry service, RV and truck parking.

★★
Motel 6
51 Hartford Tpke
Vernon CT 06066
(860) 646-5700
Rates from $59
SAVE –B&P Discount Available

Pet Policy: Well-behaved pets stay free. Animals that pose a health or safety risk may not remain onsite, and include those that, in our managers' discretion, are too numerous for any one room, cause damage to our property or that of other guests, are too disruptive, are not properly attended, or demonstrate undue aggression. All pets must be declared at check-in.

We will not service a room with an unattended pet. If your unattended pet prevents our staff from servicing your room, you may be asked to vacate.

Pets must be attended to and under control at all times. Pets should not be left alone in a room or automobile. If unavoidable circumstances require a pet to remain in a room while the owner is offsite, the pet must be secured in a crate or travel carrier. Pets must be on a leash or securely carried outside of guest rooms. Please clean up after your pet.

Motel 6 – Vernon
Continued from previous page

Features; Wireless Internet, RV and truck parking, Laundry Facilities, Number of floors: 2, Number of rooms: 123, Parking (free), Picnic area, 24-hour front desk, Meeting rooms (small groups), Outdoor pool - seasonal, Wedding services, Coffee in lobby.

Waterford

Also see the following nearby communities that have pet friendly lodging:
New London - 3 miles, Groton - 6 miles, Mystic - 10 miles.

Not Rated
Oakdell Motel
983 Hartford Turnpike
Waterford CT 06385
(860) 442-9446
Rates from $118

Pet Policy: Dog friendly, no fee, but requested to contact motel directly for pet reservations.

Features: Outdoor pool, Family oriented, Continental breakfast.

★★
Rodeway Inn Waterford
211 Parkway North
Waterford CT 06385
(860) 442-7227
$69 - $149
SAVE –B&P Discount Available

Pet Policy: Rodeway Inns charge a fee of $10 per night per pet and require a $50 refundable damage deposit. Max of 2 pets per room. A veterinarian certificate that the pet is on a flea and parasite program and that they are free from parasites is required. Pets may not be left alone in the room unless in a cage.

Features: Number of rooms: 38, Number of floors: 2, Free breakfast, Outdoor pool - seasonal, Parking (free), Wireless Internet, Fitness facilities, Business services, Laundry facilities.

Westport

Also see the following nearby communities that have pet friendly lodging:
North Dartmouth - 6 miles, Somerset - 7 miles, Fairhaven - 9 miles, New Bedford - 9 miles.

★★★
The Westport Inn
1595 Post Road East
Westport CT 06880
(203) 259-5236
$154 - $220
SAVE –B&P Discount Available

Pet Policy: Pets accepted with advanced approval, nightly fee charged up to $40 (depending on season). Please call Inn directly for pet approval.

Features: Dry cleaning/laundry service, Free breakfast, Concierge, Parking, Wireless Internet, 24-hour business center, Number of rooms: 113, Number of suites: 2, Number of floors: 2, Smoke-free property.

Willington

★★
Rodeway Inn Willington
327 Ruby Rd
Willington CT 06279
(860) 684-1400
Rates from $66
SAVE –B&P Discount Available

Pet Policy: Rodeway Inns charge a fee of $10 per night per pet and require a $50 refundable damage deposit. Max of 2 pets per room. A veterinarian certificate that the pet is on a flea and parasite program and that they are free from parasites is required. Pets may not be left alone in the room unless in a cage.

Features: Wireless Internet, Outdoor pool, Gift shop, Number of rooms: 62, Number of floors: 3, Elevator, Free breakfast, Parking (free), 24-hour front desk, Laundry facilities, Fitness facilities.

Windsor
Also see the following nearby communities that have pet friendly lodging:
East Windsor - 5 miles, Windsor Locks - 5 miles, East Hartford - 6 miles, Hartford - 7 miles, Simsbury - 8 miles, Enfield - 9 miles, Vernon - 10 miles, Avon - 10 miles.

★★★
Hyatt Summerfield Suites Hartford North/Windsor
200 Corporate Dr
Windsor CT 06095
(860) 298-8000
$98 - $239
SAVE –B&P Discount Available

Pet Policy: Housebroken dogs up to 25 lbs and cats accepted with $200 per stay cleaning fee. Pet must be crated when left unattended. Guest to provide own crate. Guest may be liable for additional damage fees upon departure.

Features: Nearby fitness center (free), Dry cleaning/laundry service, Wireless Internet, Airport transportation, Indoor pool, Gift shop, Ski storage, Free breakfast, Parking, Smoke-free property, Wedding services, 24-hour business center, Number of rooms: 132, Number of floors: 7, Accessible bathroom, Free reception, Newspapers, Convenience store, Pick up service from train station.

★★★
Residence Inn by Marriott Hartford/Windsor
100 Dunfey Ln
Windsor CT 06095
(860) 688-7474
$169 - $189
SAVE –B&P Discount Available

Pet Policy: Pets allowed, $100 per stay cleaning fee.

Features: Number of rooms: 96, Number of floors: 2, Parking, Newspapers in lobby, Wireless Internet, Smoke-free property, Dry cleaning/laundry service, Conference room(s), Nearby fitness center (free), Coffee in lobby, Outdoor pool, Airport transportation.

Windsor Locks

Also see the following nearby communities that have pet friendly lodging:
East Windsor - 4 miles, Windsor - 5 miles, Enfield - 6 miles, Simsbury - 8 miles.

★★★
Bradley Hotel
383 S Center St
Windsor Locks CT 06096
(860) 623-4400
$52 - $59
SAVE –B&P Discount Available

Pet Policy: Dogs & cats accepted, $25 per night plus $50 refundable deposit. Designated rooms only.

Features: Restaurant, Conference room(s), Coffee in lobby, Pool table, Nightclub, Parking (free), Free breakfast, Wireless Internet, Fitness facilities, Smoke-free property.

★★
Candlewood Suites Windsor Lock
149 Ella Grasso Tpke
Windsor Locks CT 06096
(860) 623-2000
$89 - $129
SAVE –B&P Discount Available

Pet Policy: Pets allowed with $75.00 nonrefundable fee. Each pet must weigh less than 80 lbs. Pet agreement must be signed at check-in. Call hotel for details. Record of complete and up-to-date vaccinations required.

Features: Accessible bathroom, Dry cleaning/laundry service, Airport transportation, Gift shop, Number of floors: 3, Suitable for children, Barbecue grill(s), Parking (free), Business center, Wireless Internet, Area shuttle, Fitness facilities, Indoor pool.

★★
Econo Lodge Inn Suites Airport
34 Old County Rd
Windsor Locks CT 06096
(800) 243-7779
$69 - $79
SAVE –B&P Discount Available

Pet Policy: Pet accommodation: $20 per night, limit 2 pets per room.

Features: Number of rooms: 47, Number of floors: 2, Coffee in lobby, Free breakfast, Parking (free), Wireless Internet, Outdoor pool, Airport transportation (free).

★★★
La Quinta Inn Hartford-Bradley Airport
64 Ella Grasso Tpke
Windsor Locks CT 06096
(860) 623-3336
$74 - $104
SAVE –B&P Discount Available

Pet Policy: Cats and dogs up to 50 pounds are accepted in all guest rooms. Housekeeping services for rooms with pets require pet owner be present or pet must be crated. No fees or deposits are required.

Features: Accessible bathroom, Handicapped parking, Number of rooms: 102, Number of floors: 4, Free breakfast, Health club, Free newspapers in lobby, Meeting rooms, Airport transportation, Parking, Wireless Internet, Business center.

★★☆

Ramada Inn Bradley Airport
5 Ella Grasso Tpke
Windsor Locks CT 06096
860-623-9494
$63 - $79
SAVE –B&P Discount Available

Pet Policy: Pets accepted with fee at check in.

Features: Restaurant(s), Room service (limited hours), Business services, Air-conditioned public areas, Free newspapers in lobby, 24-hour front desk, Outdoor pool - seasonal, Bar/Lounge, Accessible bathroom, Handicapped parking, In-room accessibility, Indoor pool, Valet parking (additional charge), Laundry facilities, Wireless Internet, Fitness facilities.

★★★☆

Sheraton Hartford Hotel at Bradley Airport
1 Bradley International Airport
Windsor Locks CT 06096
(860) 627-5311
$115 - $289
SAVE –B&P Discount Available

Pet Policy: Pets accepted without size limit or fee, limit 2 per room. Sheraton Sweet Sleeper Dog Bed Available.

Features: Restaurant(s), Porter/bellhop, Smoke-free property, Wedding services, Accessible bathroom, Handicapped parking, In-room accessibility, Dry cleaning/laundry service, Free Internet, Fitness facilities, Airport transportation, Self-parking, Indoor pool, Sauna, Business center, Bar/lounge, Concierge desk, Elevator, Conference room(s).

Maine

Auburn

Also see the following nearby communities that have pet friendly lodging:
Hebron 10 miles.

★ 🏃

Executive Inn
170 Center Street
Auburn ME 04210
(207) 784-1331
$57 - $94

Pet Policy: Pets accepted, $15 per pet per night, limit 2 pets per room.

Features: Smoke-free property, Free parking, 24 hour front desk, Wireless Internet, Continental breakfast, Truck & RV parking, Laundry facilities, In room accessibility, Copy service, Wheel chair access, Microwave, Cribs available, Air-conditioned public areas, Picnic area.

★★✦ 🏃

Fireside Inn & Suites Auburn
1777 Washington St. South
Auburn ME 04210
(207) 777-1777
$71 - $99
SAVE –B&P Discount Available

Pet Policy: Pets accepted, $10 per pet per day. Limited pet rooms, please book directly with hotel.

Features: Wireless Internet, Self-parking (free), Dry cleaning/laundry service, Restaurant(s), Concierge services, Number of rooms: 100, Number of floors: 2, Conference room(s), Suitable for children, Air-conditioned public areas, Fireplace in lobby, Patio, Arcade/game room, Pool table, Free breakfast, Free newspapers in lobby, Picnic area, 24-hour front desk, Business center, Meeting rooms (small groups), Outdoor pool - seasonal, Barbecue grill(s), Bar/lounge, Coffee in lobby, Fitness facilities.

★★★ 🏃

Residence Inn Marriott Auburn
670 Turner Street
Auburn ME 04210
(207) 777 3400
$159 - $269
SAVE –B&P Discount Available

Pet Policy: Pets allowed, $75 per stay cleaning fee.

Features: Dry cleaning/laundry service, Number of suites: 100, Number of floors: 4, Business services, Barbecue grill(s), Coffee in lobby, Parking (free), Picnic area, Smoke-free property.

Augusta

★★★
Best Western Plus Civic Center Inn
110 Community Drive
Augusta ME 04330
(207) 622-475
Rates from $129
SAVE –B&P Discount Available

Pet Policy: Pets allowed based on the availability of pet friendly rooms. Up to 2 dogs per room with an 80 pound weight limit. Additional pet types (cats, birds, etc.) may be accepted at the hotel's discretion. Pet rate is $10 per day with a $100 per week maximum.

Features: Restaurant, Number of rooms: 102, Number of floors: 2, Free newspapers in lobby, Room service, Meeting rooms (small groups), Accessible bathroom, Handicapped parking, Outdoor pool, Business services, Dry cleaning/laundry service, Wireless Internet, Self-parking (free), Bar/lounge, Fitness facilities.

★★
Comfort Inn Civic Center
281 Civic Center Dr
Augusta ME 04330
(207) 623-1000
$130 - $140
SAVE –B&P Discount Available

Pet Policy: Pets accepted, $10 per night per pet. Pets must be registered with front desk at check-in .

Features: Wireless Internet, Indoor pool, Number of rooms: 99, Number of suites: 5, Number of floors: 3, Business services, Coffee in lobby, Free breakfast, Parking (free), Swimming pool - children's, Free newspapers in lobby (M-F), Dry cleaning/laundry service, Fitness facilities.

★★
Econo Lodge Inn & Suites
390 Western Ave
Augusta ME 04330
(207) 622-6371
Rates from $69
SAVE –B&P Discount Available

Pet Policy: Pets up to 50 lbs accepted, limit 2 per room.

Features: Restaurant, Free breakfast, Outdoor pool, Laundry facilities, Fridge and Microwave available, Parking (free), Coffee makers, Free newspapers, Smoke-free property.

★★★
Quality Inn & Suites Maine Evergreen Hotel
65 Whitten Rd
Augusta ME 04330
(800) 228-5151
$99 - $124
SAVE –B&P Discount Available

Pet Policy: Quality Inns charge a fee of $10 per night per pet and may require a $50 refundable damage deposit. Any well-behaved pets are accepted with a maximum of 3 per room, but dogs are limited to 50 pounds. Pets may not be left alone in the room unless in a cage.

Features: Accessible bathroom, Free breakfast,

Quality Inn & Suites Maine Evergreen Hotel
Continued from previous page

Business services, Computer station, Wireless Internet, Outdoor pool, Number of rooms: 76, Number of floors: 3, Elevator, Self-parking (free), Laundry facilities, Fitness facilities, Gift shop, Coffee in lobby.

★★★
Senator Inn & Spa
284 Western Ave
Augusta ME 04330
(207) 622-5804
$99 - $139
SAVE –B&P Discount Available

Pet Policy: Pets accepted, $12 per pet per night. Pets not allowed in spa areas.

Features: Free breakfast, Wireless Internet, Dry cleaning/laundry service, Bar/lounge, Indoor pool, Restaurant(s), Room service (limited hours), Number of rooms: 124, Number of floors: 2, Elevator, Air-conditioned public areas, Parking (free), Free newspapers in lobby, 24-hour front desk, Business center, Full-service health spa, Massage - treatment room(s), Meeting rooms (small groups), Steam room, Smoke-free property, Outdoor pool - seasonal, Sauna, Beauty services, Shopping on site, Garden.

Bangor

Also see the following nearby communities that have pet friendly lodging:
Orono - 7 miles.

★★
Best Western White House Inn
155 Littlefield Ave
Bangor ME 04401
(207) 862-3737
$125- $270
SAVE –B&P Discount Available

Pet Policy: Pets are welcome when accompanied by their parents. There is a $10 fee per pet, max charge of $20/day or $100/week (please contact us if you have any questions). We have a back field with a walking path where you're welcome to walk your dog.

Features: Accessible bathroom, Handicapped parking, Parking (free), Fitness facilities, Bar/lounge, Number of rooms: 77, Elevator, Suitable for children, Coffee in lobby, Free breakfast, Free newspapers in lobby, Wireless Internet, Outdoor pool - seasonal, Business center, Dry cleaning/laundry service.

★★
Comfort Inn Bangor
750 Hogan Rd
Bangor ME 04401
(207) 942-7899
$119 - $130
SAVE –B&P Discount Available

Pet Policy: Pet friendly, $10 per stay.

Features: Gift shops, Number of rooms: 96, Number of floors: 2, Elevator, Self-parking, Free newspapers, Smoke-free property, Wireless Internet, Fitness facilities, Conference room(s), Airport transportation (free), Coffee in lobby, Arcade/game room, Free breakfast, Business services.

★★
Days Inn Bangor
250 Odlin Rd
Bangor ME 04401
(207) 942-8272
$72 - $123
SAVE –B&P Discount Available

Pet Policy: Dogs only, $10 per stay.

Features: Indoor pool, Restaurant(s), Shopping on site, Conference room(s), Air-conditioned public areas, Coffee in lobby, Arcade/game room, Free breakfast, Parking (free), Free newspapers in lobby, 24-hour front desk, Concierge desk, Business services, Dry cleaning/laundry service, Smoke-free property, Wireless Internet.

★★
Econo Lodge Inn & Suites
327 Odlin Road
Bangor ME 04401
(207) 945-0111
$81 - $135
SAVE –B&P Discount Available

Pet Policy: Pets accepted, $10 per stay.

Features: Gift shops or newsstand, Wireless Internet, RV and truck parking, Coffee in lobby, Indoor pool heated, Free breakfast, Laundry facilities, Number of rooms: 117, Elevator.

★★★
Fairfield Inn By Marriott Bangor
300 Odlin Rd
Bangor ME 04401
(207) 990-0001
$138 - $179
SAVE –B&P Discount Available

Pet Policy: Pets allowed, $20 additional cleaning fee.

Features: Sauna, Indoor pool, Dry cleaning/laundry service, Number of rooms: 153, Number of floors: 3, Elevator, Conference room(s), Air-conditioned public areas, Free breakfast, Parking (free), Free newspapers in lobby, 24-hour front desk, Smoke-free property, Coffee in lobby, Fitness facilities, In-room accessibility, Suitable for children, Fireplace in lobby, Handicapped parking, Meeting rooms (small groups), 24-hour business center, Accessible bathroom, Wireless Internet, Currency exchange, Business center.

★★
Fireside Inn & Suites Bangor
570 Main Street
Bangor ME 04401
(207) 942-1234
$99 - $129
SAVE –B&P Discount Available

Pet Policy: A Fireside Inn Bangor welcomes pets and we offer comfortable accommodations for their owners. To insure your pet's comfort, the comfort of other pets, and of all our guests, we have a few guidelines that we ask your pet to follow: Pets shouldn't be left alone in their room. Even well-behaved pets do act up when their master leaves them alone. Pets should be kept on a leash when not in their room (unless, of course, you have a goldfish). When you walk your pet, please do your part to help keep our grounds clean. There is a perfect dog walking area behind the hotel, toward

Fireside Inn & Suites Bangor
Continued from previous page

the waterfront.

When asked if we allow dogs at our hotel, here's what we generally reply: "Dogs are welcome in this hotel. We've never had a dog that smoked in bed and set fire to the blankets. We've never had a dog who stole the towels, played the TV too loud or had a fight with his traveling companion. We've never had a dog who got drunk and broke up the furniture. So, if your dog can vouch for you, you're welcome, too!"

Features: Bar/lounge, Wireless Internet, Dry cleaning/laundry service, Restaurant(s), Gift shops or newsstand, Number of rooms: 51, Number of floors: 2, Business services, Air-conditioned public areas, Coffee in lobby, Video library, Free breakfast, Parking (free), 24-hour front desk.

★★★
Four Points by Sheraton Bangor Airport Hotel
308 Godfrey Blvd
Bangor ME 04401
(207) 947-6721
$139 - $225
SAVE –B&P Discount Available

Pet Policy: Dogs and Cats both welcome, $20 pet fee per stay.

Features: Indoor pool, Fireplace in lobby, Accessible bathroom, Handicapped parking, In-room accessibility, 24-hour business center, Dry cleaning/laundry service, Restaurant(s), Gift shops or newsstand, Number of rooms: 102, Number of floors: 9, Elevator, Conference room(s), Air-conditioned public areas, Breakfast available (additional charge), Parking (free), Free newspapers in lobby, 24-hour front desk, Wireless Internet, Meeting rooms (small groups), Smoke-free property, Bar/lounge, Room service (limited hours), Wedding services, Fitness facilities.

★★★
Holiday Inn Bangor
404 Odlin Rd
Bangor ME 04401
(207) 947-0101
$125 - $174
SAVE –B&P Discount Available

Pet Policy: Pet Friendly Hotel Pets may not be left in guest rooms unattended.

Features: Indoor pool, Restaurant(s), Outdoor pool, Concierge services, Number of rooms: 207, Number of floors: 3, Conference room(s), Coffee in lobby, Parking (free), Free newspapers in lobby, 24-hour front desk, Wireless Internet, Sauna, Handicapped parking, In-room accessibility, Dry cleaning/laundry service, Room service (limited hours), Bar/lounge, Business center, Fitness facilities.

★★
Howard Johnson Inn - Bangor
336 Odlin Rd
Bangor ME 04401
(207) 942-5251
$50 - $99
SAVE –B&P Discount Available

Pet Policy: Dogs only, $10 per dog per night.

Features: Bar/lounge, Restaurant, Room service, Shopping on site, Business services, Arcade/game room, Parking (free), Free newspapers in lobby, Limo or Town Car service available, Wireless Internet, Outdoor pool, Dry cleaning/laundry service.

★★★
Ramada Inn Bangor
357 Odlin Rd
Bangor ME 04401
(800) 997-9629
$159 - $169
SAVE –B&P Discount Available

Pet Policy: Pets accepted, no fee. Please book directly with hotel for pet reservations.

Features: Restaurant(s), Room Arcade/game room, Parking (free), Free newspapers in lobby, Business Center, Indoor pool, Dry cleaning/laundry service, Airport transportation, Bar/lounge, Wireless Internet.

★★
Travelodge Bangor
482 Odlin Road
Bangor ME 04401
(207) 942-6301
$59 - $75
SAVE –B&P Discount Available

Pet Policy: Pets allowed, $10 per pet per night.

Features: Restaurant(s), Shopping on site, Business services, Free breakfast, Health club, Parking (free), Free newspapers in lobby, Dry cleaning/laundry service, Number of floors: 2, Wireless Internet.

Bar Harbor

Also see the following nearby communities that have pet friendly lodging:
Hancock - 8 miles.

Not Rated
Days Inn Bar Harbor
120 Eden Street
Bar Harbor ME US 04609
(207) 288-3321
$135 - $189

Pet Policy: Pets Allowed only in the pet designated rooms at a charge of $10 per stay

Features: Continental breakfast, 24 hour front desk, RV & truck parking, Wireless Internet, Access to nearby swimming, tennis, fitness center and hot tub, In room accessibility.

★★★
Holiday Inn Bar Harbor
123 Eden St
Bar Harbor ME 04609
(207) 288-9723
$142 - $319
SAVE –B&P Discount Available

Pet Policy: Pets under 30 lbs accepted, $30 per pet per night. Must be leashed or crated when in public areas, and may not be left alone in room.

Features: Accessible bathroom, Handicapped parking, Bar/lounge, Restaurant(s), Outdoor pool,

Holiday Inn
Continued from previous page

Concierge services, Gift shop, Number of rooms: 278, Number of suites: 2, Number of floors: 4, Coffee in lobby, Porter/bellhop, Wireless Internet, Meeting rooms (small groups), Laundry facilities, Sauna, Room service, Fitness facilities

★★★

Wonder View Inn & Suites
50 Eden St
Bar Harbor ME 04609
(207) 288-3358
$149 - $209
SAVE –B&P Discount Available

Pet Policy: Pets welcome, $20 per pet per night. Must declare pets both at time of reservation and upon checking in. Your pet may never be left unattended in your room or on the grounds at any time. Pet sitters are available in the area and we can help you arrange for one given enough notice. All pets are to be restrained in public areas. Pets may be walked in any of our 14 plus acres of the property but we ask that you clean up after your pet. Sorry, but your pets are not allowed in the swimming pool or in the dining room. All damages should be reported to the front desk immediately.

Features: Wireless Internet, Bar/lounge, Restaurant(s), Number of rooms: 79, Number of floors: 1, Parking (free), Free newspapers in lobby, Front desk (limited hours), Smoke-free property, Outdoor pool - seasonal, Picnic area, Concierge.

Bath
Also see the following nearby communities that have pet friendly lodging:
Brunswick - 7 miles, Southport - 10 miles, Boothbay Harbor - 11 miles, Freeport - 15 miles.

Not Rated
Galen C Moses House B & B
1009 Washington Street
Bath ME 04530
(207) 442-8771
$179 - $318

Pet Policy: The Carriage Room is pet friendly and we welcome canine pets for a nightly fee of $15 per pet. We hold all pet owners financially responsible for any and all pet stains/damage to the premises/property.

Features: Year built: 1874. Non-smoking rooms, Air conditioning, Wireless Internet, Coffee Maker, Piano, Library, Fireplace in some rooms, Free breakfast.

★★★

Holiday Inn Bath   Brunswick
139 Richardson St.
Bath ME 04530
(207) 443-9741
$127 - $186
SAVE –B&P Discount Available

Pet Policy:. Pets are only allowed in designated pet friendly rooms, mainly located on the 3rd floor. Pets are not allowed in Poolside rooms. Guests must disclose pet info when making reservation and must sign a pet-release form at check-in.
Continued on next page

Holiday Inn Bath
Continued from previous page

Features: Bar/lounge, Restaurant, Gift shop, Number of rooms: 141, Number of floors: 4, Elevator, Secretarial services, Computer rental, Air-conditioned public areas, Fax machine, Parking (free), Free newspapers in lobby, 24-hour front desk, Business center, Concierge desk, Wireless Internet, Sauna, Handicapped parking, In-room accessibility, Outdoor pool, Dry cleaning/laundry service, Room service (limited hours), Beauty services, Fitness facilities, Luggage storage.

Belfast

Also see the following nearby communities that have pet friendly lodging:
Lincolnville - 8 miles.

★★
Admiral's Ocean Inn
222 Sears Port Avenue
Belfast ME 04915
(207) 338-4260
$89 - $179
SAVE –B&P Discount Available

Pet Policy: Pets always allowed with a large field to walk them

Features: Free breakfast, Number of rooms: 20, Number of floors: 1, Air-conditioned public areas, Patio, Coffee in lobby, Parking (free), Room service (24 hours), Accessible bathroom.

Not Rated.
Belfast Harbor Inn
91 Searsport Avenue
Belfast ME 04915
(207) 338-2740
$99 - $179

Pet Policy: Pets are welcomed at the Belfast Harbor Inn. There is a $10 fee per pet per night. Please let us know if you will be bringing your pet as not all rooms are appropriate. Please do not leave pets unattended in your room.

Features: Continental breakfast, laundry facilities, air conditioning, Wireless Internet, Microwaves and fridges available (additional charge $5 per day).

★★★
Colonial Gables Oceanfront
7 Eagle Avenue
Belfast ME 04915
(800) 937-6246
$90 - $114
SAVE –B&P Discount Available

Pet Policy: Dogs and cats accepted, no additional fee, limit 1 per room. Pets must be leashed when in public areas.

Features: Arcade/game room, Garden, Picnic area, Business services, Suitable for children, Parking (free), 24-hour front desk, Patio, Fax machine.

★★☆
Comfort Inn Oceans Edge
159 Searsport Ave
Belfast ME 04915
(207) 338-2090
$179 - $319
SAVE –B&P Discount Available

Pet Policy: Pets welcome, $20 per night. Pets shouldn't be left alone in their room. Pets should be kept on a leash when not in their room (unless, of course, you have a goldfish). When you walk your pet, please do your part to help keep our grounds clean. There is a perfect dog walking area behind the hotel, toward the waterfront. Pet rooms have patio doors which exit to our acres of back lawn.

Features: Wireless Internet, Bar/lounge, Indoor pool, Number of rooms: 83, Number of floors: 3, Business services, Coffee in lobby, Laundry facilities, Video library, Free breakfast, Parking (free), Free newspapers in lobby, Meeting rooms, Sauna.

Not Rated
Gull Motel
196 Searsport Avenue
Belfast ME 04915
(877) 279-9377
Rates from $119

Pet Policy: Pets accepted on case by case basis. $10 per pet per night. Please contact motel directly to get pet approval and reservation.

Features: Wireless Internet, Air conditioning, Coffee & Muffins served every morning.

Bethel

Not Rated
Chapman Inn
2 Church Street
Bethel ME 04217
(877) 359-1498
$109 - $119

Pet Policy: Dogs welcome, $10 per night additional.

Features: Year built: 1865, Air conditioned, Free breakfast, Wireless Internet, No accessibility features for handicapped.

★★★
The Bethel Inn Resort
7 Broad Street
Bethel ME 04217
(207) 824-2175
$150 - $400

Pet Policy: Well behaved dogs are allowed in some accommodations at a charge of $20 per dog, per night. Dogs must be supervised at all times. Please call the Inn directly for reservations. Other pets are not allowed.

Features: Full service health club, Golf course, Fireplace and Jacuzzi bathtubs in some rooms, Air conditioning, Restaurant, Lounge/Bar, , Tennis courts, Outdoor heated pool.

★★☆ 🛏️ ♥

The Victoria Inn B&B
32 Main St
Bethel ME 04217
(207) 824-8060
$113 - $185
SAVE –B&P Discount Available

Pet Policy: Pets accepted, $30 per stay additional.

Features: Number of rooms: 14, Parking (free), Wireless Internet, Smoke-free property, Free breakfast, Suitable for children, Conference room(s), Number of floors 2, Year Built 1895.

Biddeford
Also see the following nearby communities that have pet friendly lodging:
Saco - 5 miles, Old Orchard Beach - 6 miles, Kennebunk - 6 miles, Kennebunkport - 7 miles.

★★

Comfort Suites Biddeford
45 Barra Rd
Exit 4 Business Park
Biddeford ME 04005
(207) 294-6464
$279 - $280
SAVE –B&P Discount Available

Pet Policy: Pet Accommodation: $25 per night. Pet Limit: 3 pets per room, up to 125 lbs.

Features: Indoor pool, Laundry facilities, Free breakfast, Parking (free), Picnic area, Business center, Wireless Internet, Fitness facilities, Number of rooms: 70, Number of floors: 3, Elevator.

Bingham

Not Rated 🎿
Bingham Motor Inn
89 Main Street
Bingham ME 04920
(866) 806-6120
$90 - $150

Pet Policy: Pets allowed. Pet rules apply. Please contact hotel directly for more information.

Features: Car rental desk, Family room, Outdoor pool, Hot tub/Jacuzzi, Sports store, Wireless Internet, Air conditioning, Kitchenettes available.

Boothbay Harbor
Also see the following nearby communities that have pet friendly lodging:
Southport - 1 mile.

Not Rated.
Beachcove Hotel and Resort
48 Lakeview Road
Boothbay Harbor ME 04538
(207) 380-1757
$110 - $135

Pet Policy: Pets accepted, $20 per stay, limit 2 per room. We have only few pet friendly rooms. Call to check for availability of these rooms.

Features: Outdoor heated pool, Private beach, Free

Beachcove Hotel and Resort
Continued from previous page

Not Rated
Flagship Inn
200 Townsend Avenue
Boothbay Harbor ME 04538
(207) 633-5094
$109 - $238

use of canoes and rowboats, Mini fridge, Microwave oven, Continental breakfast.

Pet Policy: Pets accepted,$10 per day plus a credit card imprint. Pets cannot be left unattended in the room for periods longer than 4 hours and we must have a cell phone number to reach you in the event of a problem or emergency. If you need to be gone for more than four hours, there are kennels and daycares in the area. Daily Maid service is required and your pet must vacate the room with its owner or be in a crate. Pets need to be walked on the side of the motel near the garage area. You are responsible for cleaning up after your pet. Please give the Front Desk 15 minutes advance notice prior to checkout so that we may inspect your room. You will be charged for any damages and extra cleaning deemed necessary.

Features: Free parking, RV & truck parking, Jacuzzi, Outdoor pool, Restaurant, 24 hour security, Wireless Internet, Bar/lounge, Smoke-free property.

★★★★½ 🎾
Spruce Point Inn Resort & Spa
88 Grandview Ave
Boothbay Harbor ME 04538
(207) 633-4152
Rates from $329
SAVE –B&P Discount Available

Pet Policy: Dogs and cats welcome.

Features: Full-service health spa, Bar/Lounge, Coffee in lobby, Breakfast, Accessible bathroom, Handicapped parking, Year Built 1894, Tennis on site, Restaurant(s), Supervised child care, Concierge, Gift shop, Number of rooms: 102, Number of suites: 22, Number of floors: 2, Game room, Wireless Internet, Parking, Porter/bellhop, Medical assistance available, Beauty services, Massage - treatment room(s), Meeting rooms, Smoke-free property, Wedding services, Outdoor pool.

Brooklin

Not Rated
Eggemoggin Oceanfront Lodge
Route 175 HCR 64 Box 380
Brooklin ME 04616
(359) 559-5057
$159 - $350

Pet Policy: Pets Allowed At Property That Are Well Trained And Well Behaved. No fee or size limit.
Features: Restaurant, Fireplace in lobby, In-room accessibility.

Brunswick
Also see the following nearby communities that have pet friendly lodging:
Bath - 7 miles, Freeport - 8 miles, Sebasco Estates - 9 miles.

★★

Days Inn - Brunswick Bath Area
224 Bath Rd
Brunswick ME 04011
(207) 725-8883
$79 - $135
SAVE –B&P Discount Available

Pet Policy: Pets up to 50 lbs, $25 per stay. Pets only permitted in smoking rooms. Limit of 2 pets per room.

Features: Free breakfast, Parking (free), 24-hour front desk, Business center, Wireless Internet.

★★

Rodeway Inn & Suites
287 Bath Rd
Brunswick ME 04011
(207) 729-6661
$74 - $139
SAVE –B&P Discount Available

Pet Policy: Rodeway Inns charge a fee of $10 per night per pet plus a $50 refundable damage deposit. Max of 2 pets per room. A veterinarian certificate that the pet is on a flea and parasite program and that they are free from parasites is required. Pets may not be left alone in the room unless in a cage.

Features: Parking (free), Wireless Internet, Number of rooms: 40, Number of floors: 1, 24-hour front desk, Coffee in lobby, Picnic area, Free breakfast.

Camden
Also see the following nearby communities that have pet friendly lodging:
Rockport - 4 miles, Lincolnville - 5 miles.

★★★★

Camden Harbour Inn
83 Bayview Street Knox
Camden ME 04843
(207) 236-4200
$325 - $750
SAVE –B&P Discount Available

Pet Policy: Pets welcome with additional nightly fee. Book directly with property and ask for the Pooch Package which includes dog cookies, pet bowls for food and water, cushioned dog bed or bedspread.

Features: Restaurant, Number of rooms: 18, Number of floors: 3, Air-conditioned public areas, Wireless Internet, Massage - treatment room(s), Fireplace in lobby, Free breakfast, Bar/lounge.

Not Rated

Camden Riverhouse Hotel
11 Tannery Lane
Camden ME 04843
(800 -223-5449
$189 - $269

Pet Policy: Dogs only, $15 per night. Advanced reservation is required to be made directly with hotel for dogs. Dogs may never be left unattended in room and must be leashed when outside.

When you and your dog stay at the Riverhouse, you are greeted by people who truly love dogs and a 2 acre backyard for your dog. We will provide a plush doggie bed, bowls, balls and biscuits. We can steer you to numerous dog activities, as well as to our local veterinarians and dog daycare options.

Features: Wireless Internet, Continental breakfast, 24 hour front desk, Daily newspaper, Laundry facilities, Fitness facility, Indoor pool, Free parking.

Not Rated

Grand Harbor Inn
14 Bay View Landing
Camden ME 04843
(207) 230-7177
$369 - $464

Pet Policy: Dogs only, $35 per dog per night, limit of 2 per room. We love dogs and realize that more and more travelers are taking their beloved pets with them. That is why we are welcoming travelers with dogs with open paws. Our Pampered Pooch Accommodations includes a comfortable and plush fleece dog bed, gourmet dog biscuits, water and food bowl, and an extensive list of local outdoor recreational activities for you and your pet to enjoy, doggy daycare options, and local veterinarians just in case something unexpected occurs.

We have a limit of two well behaved dogs per room (no size restrictions), and require that dogs not be left unattended at any time in your room and be kept on leash in all public areas.

Guests will be asked to sign and adhere to our pet policies and etiquette upon arrival and check-in. Pampered Pooch Accommodations Include: Plush fleece dog bed Gourmet biscuits Food & water bowl Pet welcome packet (list of local pet resources)

Features: Air conditioned, Bathrobes, Coffeemaker, Continental breakfast, Concierge, Elevator, Fireplace in lobby, Free newspapers, Parking, Wireless Internet. Jacuzzi, fridge and microwave available.

Not Rated
Hartstone Inn
41 Elm Street
Camden ME 04843
(207) 236-4259
$145 - $298
SAVE –B&P Discount Available

Pet Policy: Pets up to 25 lbs accepted, $25 per stay. Limit 1 per room.

Features: Restaurant, Free breakfast, Wireless Internet, Parking (free), Library, Gift shop, Smoke free property, coffee makers..

★★★
Lodge At Camden Hills
186 Belfast Road
Camden ME 04843
(207) 236-8478
$99 - $195

Pet Policy: Well-groomed and well-behaved pets are welcome, $20 per night, provided advance notice is given. Pets must be kept quiet at all times. Pets may not be left in the room unattended and must be kept off of the furniture and out of the bathtubs. You are responsible for picking up after your pet.

Features: Efficiency units and Cottages with wood burning fireplace and Jacuzzi, Air conditioning, Number of floors: 2, Self-parking (free).

Not Rated
Lord Camden Inn
24 Main Street
Camden ME 04843
(207) 236-4325
$179 - $369

Pet Policy: Dogs accepted, $25 per night per dog. No size restriction, limit 2 dogs per room.

Features: Year built: 1896, 24 hour security, Business center, Coffee Maker, Concierge, Elevator, Free newspapers, Accessible bathrooms, Wireless Internet, Health Club, Kitchenettes available, Porter/bellhop, Valet Parking (additional charge)

Caribou

Not Rated
Caribou Inn and Convention Ctr
19 Main Street
Caribou ME 04736
(207)498-3733
$109 - $159

Pet Policy: Pets welcome for a nominal fee.

Features: Free parking, Restaurant, Bar/Lounge, Wireless Internet, Indoor heated pool, Gift shop, Wellness center, Coffee maker, Fridge and web bar in rooms, Room service, Dry cleaning and laundry service, Number of room :72, Free morning newspaper, 24 hour front desk.

Not Rated
Crown Park Inn
30 Access Highway
Caribou ME 04736
(888) 493-3311
$74 - $94

Pet Policy: Pets accepted, no additional fee, limit 2 per room.

Features: Number of rooms: 60, Continental breakfast, Game room, Business center, Fitness center, Hot tub, Kitchenettes, Smoking and non-smoking rooms available.

Ellsworth

Also see the following nearby communities that have pet friendly lodging:
Hancock - 9 miles.

★★
Colonial Inn
321 High St
Ellsworth ME 04605
(207) 667-5548
Rates from $125
SAVE –B&P Discount Available

Pet Policy: Small dogs accepted if approved in advance, no fee. Please call hotel directly for pet approval.

Features: Indoor pool, Restaurant, Number of rooms: 67, Business services, 24-hour front desk, Wireless Internet (additional charge).

Not Rated
Homestead Motel and Cottages
143 Bucksport Road
Ellsworth ME 04605
(207) 667-8193
$63 - $86

Pet Policy: Dogs accepted, $10 additional fee.

Features: Continental breakfast, Air conditioned, Restaurant, Wireless Internet, number of floors:2.

★★
Knights Inn Bar Harbor
20 Thorsen Rd
Ellsworth ME 04605
(207) 667-3621
$109 - $129
SAVE –B&P Discount Available

Pet Policy: Pets allowed, $10 per day fee.

Features: Free breakfast, Meeting rooms (small groups), Wireless Internet.

★★★
Ramada Ellsworth
215 High St
Ellsworth ME 04605
(207) 667-9341
$129 - $184
SAVE –B&P Discount Available

Pet Policy: Pets allowed in pet friendly wing only, with maximum of 2 pets per room. $20 fee per day, $10 additional for second pet. Pets may not be left unattended in rooms and must be on a leash at all times. Pet day care is nearby.

Continued on next page

Ramada Ellsworth *Continued from previous page*	**Features:** Restaurant, Concierge , Number of rooms: 102, Number of floors: 2, Conference room(s), Parking (free), Wireless Internet, Smoke-free property, Indoor tennis court, Business center, Laundry facilities, Indoor pool, Room service, Bar/lounge, Sauna, Fitness facilities.

★★
Twilite Motel
147 Bucksport Rd
Ellsworth ME 04605
(207) 667-8165
$104- $144

Pet Policy: Pets under 20 lbs accepted in designated pet-friendly rooms, $10 per night per pet.

Features: Laundry facilities, Children's activities, Continental breakfast, News stand, Parking, Wireless Internet, Coffee makers, Smoke-free property.

Freeport
Also see the following nearby communities that have pet friendly lodging:
Brunswick - 8 miles.

★★
Econo Lodge of Freeport
537 Route 1 South
Freeport ME 04032
(207) 865-3777
$94 - $139
SAVE –B&P Discount Available

Pet Policy: Pet accommodation: $10 per night. Pet Limit: maximum up to 60 pounds. Limited availability of pet friendly rooms.

Features: Free Breakfast, Number of rooms: 108, Number of floors: 2, Coffee in lobby, Parking (free), Free newspapers in lobby, Wireless Internet.

★★★★
Harraseeket Inn
162 Main Street
Freeport ME 04032
(207) 865-9377
$240 - $265

Pet Policy: Dogs welcome, $25 per night additional. You will receive A doggy bed with a freshly laundered cover. A small can of food with a lift off cover. Small plastic bags for cleanup duties. A water and food dish. There are a few house rules that you need to observe. You will be responsible for any damages, so make sure your dog behaves! Dogs must be kept on a leash for safety reasons outside the building, and shouldn't be left alone for more than an hour and a half because even experienced travelers can get lonely and cry in a new place. (Disturbing other guests is a definite no-no.) Housekeepers will only clean the room if the doggies are out of it, and the turndown staff won't come into the room unless you answer the door. Also, unless yours is a service dog, it is not allowed in the main building. The number of pet friendly rooms is limited so book early.

Features: Number of rooms: 84, Fireplaces in many rooms, Indoor pool, 2 Restaurants.

Hebron

Also see the following nearby communities that have pet friendly lodging:
Auburn 10 miles.

Greenwood Mountain Inn
168 Greenwood Mountain Rd.
Hebron ME 04234
(207) 966-2233
$135 - $275

Pet Policy: Pets accepted with advanced approval. Please contact Inn directly for requirements and pet reservations.

Features: Number of rooms: 4, Parlor with fireplace, Gazebo with Hot Tub, Exercise room, Free breakfast.

Kennebunk

Also see the following nearby communities that have pet friendly lodging:
Kennebunkport - 5 miles, Biddeford - 6 miles, Wells - 7 miles.

Econo Lodge Kennebunk
55 York St
Kennebunk ME 04043
(207) 985-6100
$129 - $169
SAVE –B&P Discount Available

Pet Policy: Pets accepted, $20 per pet per night. Limit 2 pets per room.

Features: Wireless Internet, Gift shop, Number of rooms: 46, Number of floors: 2, Parking (free), Free newspapers in lobby, Outdoor pool - seasonal, Free breakfast, Business services.

Not Rated
Kennebunk Gallery Cottages
65 York Street
Kennebunk ME 04043
(207) 967-4691
$94 - $159

Pet Policy: Pets accepted. Please contact property directly for pet approval and reservations.

Features: Free beach parking, Large outdoor pool, Wireless Internet, Smoke-free property, Kitchen units available.

Shorelands Guest Resort
247 Western Avenue
Kennebunk ME 04043
(287) 985-4460
$69 - $99

Pet Policy: Well-behaved pets welcome, $10 per pet per day plus $20 damage deposit. Please observe the following rules: No pets on our beds unless you have your own covering - Extra cleaning for hairs, etc. will be charged $20.00 Our Bath Tubs are not for your Dogs use. Extra Tub Cleaning will be $50.00 Pets on a leash at all times No pets on our lawns or garden areas, Front, Back, or Sides! No walking or accidents on our grounds - All accidents will be charged a $20.00 fee ***Continued on next page***

Shorelands Guest Resort
Continued from previous page

You are responsible for cleanup.

There are several good walking areas within 200 feet of us, Across the street along Route 9 (please do NOT use the fields, they are PRIVATE LANDS); Around the corner along Brown Street; Down the country lane towards the beach. (no pets ON beach in summer) Please ask us for Baggies for your pick up and disposal into our dumpster. Your pet cannot be tied up outside your unit. We would like you to take your pet with you during the day we may not be able to provide you with Housekeeping Service.

Features: Outdoor pool – seasonal, Free breakfast, Coffee in lobby, Laundry facilities, Parking, Fireplace in lobby, Daily newspaper, Smoke-free property.

★★ Shorelands Guest Resort and Cottages
247 Western Ave
Kennebunk ME 04043
(207)985-4460
$78 - $327
SAVE –B&P Discount Available

Well-behaved pets welcome, $10 per pet per day plus $20 damage deposit. Please observe the following rules: No pets on our beds unless you have your own covering - Extra cleaning for hairs, etc. will be charged $20 Our Bath Tubs are not for your Dogs use. Extra Tub Cleaning will be $50 Pets on a leash at all times No pets on our lawns or garden areas, Front, Back, or Sides! No walking or accidents on our grounds - All accidents will be charged a $20 fee You are responsible for cleanup. There are several good walking areas within 200 feet of us, Across the street from us along Route 9 (please do NOT use the fields, they are PRIVATE LANDS); Around the corner along Brown Street; Down the country lane towards the beach. (no pets ON beach in summer) Please ask us for Baggies for your pick up and disposal into our dumpster. Your pet cannot be tied up outside your unit. We would like you to take your pet with you during the day. If you leave your pet in the unit we may not be able to provide you with Housekeeping Service.

Features: Accessible bathroom, Handicapped parking, Number of rooms: 32, Number of floors: 1, Fireplace in lobby, Coffee in lobby, Breakfast available (additional charge), Parking (free), Front desk (limited hours), Wireless Internet, Smoke-free property, Outdoor pool - seasonal, Laundry facilities, Barbecue grill(s).

★★�꜒ 🛏
The Kennebunk Inn
45 Main St
Kennebunk ME 04043
(207) 985-3351
$135 - $215
SAVE –B&P Discount Available

Pet Policy: Both The Kennebunk Inn and beaches are pet friendly, some restrictions do apply, please contact the Inn directly for specific information and to make a pet reservation.

Features: Year Built 1799, Wireless Internet, Bar/Lounge, Coffee in lobby, Library, Restaurant in hotel, Room service, Concierge, Number of rooms: 19, Number of suites: 5, Number of floors: 3, Airport transportation (additional charge), Air-conditioned public areas, Patio, Parking (free), Newspapers in lobby, Meeting rooms, Smoke-free property, Wedding services, Garden, Picnic area, Nearby fitness center (discount), Grocery/convenience store, Media library, Area shuttle), Shopping center shuttle.

★★★�꜒
The Lodge At Kennebunk
95 Alewive Road
Kennebunk ME 04043
(877) 918-3701
$79 - $160

Pet Policy: We do have a limited number of rooms that pets are allowed in. Please be sure to mention at time of booking whether or not a pet friendly room will be needed.

Features: 24 hour front desk, Air conditioning, Restaurant, Wireless Internet, Coffee makers, Continental breakfast, Parking (free), Outdoor pool, Game room.

Kennebunkport

Also see the following nearby communities that have pet friendly lodging:
Kennebunk - 5 miles, Biddeford - 7 miles, Wells - 8 miles.

★★★★ 🛏
English Meadows Inn
141 Port Road
Kennebunkport ME 04043
(207) 967-5766
Rates from $198

Small pets accepted for additional $30 fee. Only the Bungalow can accommodate pets. Pets cannot be left in the Inn unattended. Please respect your fellow guests to quiet enjoyment and keep your pet quiet. Please pickup after your pet, plastic bags will be made available if needed. Inspect your room with the Innkeeper upon checking in and out. Any damage caused during your pets visit will be charged to your credit card. Dogs must be kept on a leash outside the property; there is a Kennebunkport leash law.

Features: Year built: 1860, Free breakfast, Wireless Internet, Restaurant.

★★★☆

Kennebunkport Inn
One Dock Square
Kennebunkport ME 04046
(888) 610-5703
$179 - $439
SAVE –B&P Discount Available

Pet Policy: Pet accepted, $20 per stay.

Features: Bar/Lounge, Conference Room(s), Handicapped parking, Fireplace in lobby, Restaurant, Concierge services, Number of rooms: 49, Number of floors: 3, Business services, Air-conditioned public areas, Patio, Coffee in lobby, Free breakfast, Parking (free), Spa services on site, Front desk (limited hours), Meeting rooms (small groups), Smoke-free property, Outdoor pool - seasonal, Wedding services, Wireless Internet (free).

★★★☆♥⛵

Nonantum Resort
95 Ocean Ave
Kennebunkport ME 04046
(207) 967-4050
$270 - $541
SAVE –B&P Discount Available

Pet Policy: Dogs up to 30 lbs accepted, $30 per dog per night, maximum 2 per room. For pets we offer two of our ground level Portside Lodge, Non-water view rooms. We offer Cuddledown dog beds for the comfort of your four legged friends at $5.00 per-dog, per day. If you would like to make arrangements for your dog(s) to have time away from the family we can offer a list of highly recommended dog-sitters and dog-walkers. Pets are not to be left unattended in guest rooms except during the hours of breakfast service. The Carriage House Inn and common areas (including the courtyard and riverfront areas) do not allow pets. Please keep your pet safe on his or her leash while enjoying Kennebunkport (there is a leash law). Biodegradable doggie pick-up bags, food and water bowls will be provided in your room. We will gladly provide any number of pick-up bags for your use. Please understand that you are responsible for any damages.

Features: Year Built 1883, Bar/lounge, 2 Restaurants, Room service, Concierge, Gift shop, Number of rooms: 111, Number of suites: 13, Number of floors: 4, Fireplace in lobby, Coffee in lobby, Garden, Poolside bar, Free breakfast, Wireless Internet, Parking (free), Free newspapers, Porter/bellhop, Security guard, Marina on site, Smoke-free property, Outdoor pool - seasonal heated, Wedding services, Nearby fitness center (discount), Children's club, Handicapped parking, In-room accessibility, 24-hour business center.

★★★
The Colony Hotel
Ocean Avenue
Kennebunkport ME 04046
(207) 967-3331
$259 - $449

Pet Policy: Dogs welcome, $30 per dog per night. Hosts annual Dog Lovers weekend.

Features: Heated salt water pool, Restaurant, Gardens, Private beach, Room service, Gift shop.

★★
The Lodge at Turbat's Creek
7 Turbat's Creek Road
Kennebunkport ME 04046
(207) 967-8700
$90 - $179
SAVE –B&P Discount Available

Pet Policy: Pet friendly rooms available, $25 per stay additional.

Features: Wireless Internet, Outdoor pool, Free breakfast, Parking (free), Smoke-free property.

★★★★
The Yachtsman Lodge
Ocean Avenue
Kennebunkport ME 04046
(207) 967-2511
$389 - $399

Pet Policy: Dogs accepted $25 per day. Your dog stay must be noted at time of reservation as our dog friendly accommodations are limited and certain restrictions do apply. Please enquire and we will be happy to assist in any way that we can.

Features: Marina, Concierge desk, Wireless Internet, Fitness Center, Room service, Valet parking (additional charge), Restaurant.

Kingfield
Also see the following nearby communities that have pet friendly lodging:
Bingham - 15 miles.

★★
Herbert Grand Hotel
246 Main Street
Route 27
Kingfield ME 04947
(207) 265-2000
$99 - $129

Pet Policy: Dogs only. $25 per stay per dog fee.

Features: Year built: 1918, Wireless Internet. Continental breakfast available (additional charge), Golf package arranged with Sugarloaf Golf Club.

Kittery

Also see the following nearby communities that have pet friendly lodging:
Portsmouth - 3 miles, Durham - 10 miles.

★★★

Coachman Inn
380 US Route 1
Kittery ME 03904
(207) 439-4434
$99 - $219

Pet Policy: Pets accepted, $10 per night per pet additional fee. Please clean up after your pet. Domesticated animals only. (No farm animals)Maximum 2 pets per room. Pets are not allowed on the beds, or chairs. Pet cannot stay in the room unattended. Pets cannot be brought into halls, or non-pet rooms. Pets must always be leashed or crated when outside the room. Guest must have credit card on file.

Features: Continental breakfast, Number of rooms: 43, Restaurant, Free coffee in lobby, Fridge and microwaves, Fireplace, Smoke-free property.

★★

Days Inn Kittery
85 US Route 1 Bypass
Kittery ME 03904
(207) 439-2000
$87 - $179
SAVE –B&P Discount Available

Pet Policy: Pets accepted, $20 per pet per night. Pets allowed only in limited number of smoking rooms.

Features: Outdoor pool, Number of floors: 2, Parking (free), Business services.

Lincolnville

Also see the following nearby communities that have pet friendly lodging:
Camden - 5 miles, Belfast - 8 miles, Rockport- 10 miles.

★★★★

Point Lookout Resort
67 Atlantic Hwy
Lincolnville ME 04849
(207) 789-2000
$209 - $269
SAVE –B&P Discount Available

Pet Policy: Large pets accepted (200 lbs), $15 per night per pet. Limit 2 per room.

Features: Number of rooms: 106, Number of floors: 1, Fitness facilities, 2 Restaurants, Arcade/game room, Health club, Self-parking, Business services, Suitable for children, Coffee in lobby, Wireless Internet, Free newspapers, Security guard, Private beach, Meeting rooms, Smoke-free property, Wedding services, Accessible bathroom, Tennis on site, RV and truck parking, Bar/lounge, Area shuttle (additional charge), Snack bar/deli, Rooftop terrace.

Milford

Also see the following nearby communities that have pet friendly lodging:
Orono - 4 miles.

Not Rated
Milford Motel On The River
174 US Route 2 East
Milford ME 04461
(207) 827-3200
$85 - $125

Pet Policy: Accepts only small dogs, no fee.

Features: Fully equipped kitchens in all units, Wireless Internet, Number of rooms: 10, Non-smoking property, Air conditioning.

Millinocket

★★
Baxter Park Inn
935 Central St
Millinocket ME 04462
(207) 723-9777
$121 - $130
SAVE –B&P Discount Available

Pet Policy: Small pets welcome, $10 per night per pet, limit of 2 per room. Pets require signing of waiver. Policy: Pets MUST be accompanied entire duration of your stay

Features: indoor pool, Fitness facilities, Number of rooms: 48, Number of floors: Suitable for children, Air-conditioned public areas, Coffee in lobby, Arcade/game room, Wireless Internet, Parking (free), Free newspapers in lobby, 24-hour front desk, Business center, Meeting rooms (small groups).

★★★
Katahdin Cabins
181 Medway Rd
Millinocket ME 04462
(207) 723-6305
$80 - $107
SAVE –B&P Discount Available

Pet Policy: Pets welcome, $20 per night per pet, plus $200 refundable security deposit. For all pets, please inquire before making your reservation arrangements. No pets allowed on beds and furniture. Please keep cabins clean after your pet goes swimming, walking, etc. Pet must be on a leash at all times. Please pick up after your pet. Due to barking, damage and summer heat, you may not leave your pet unattended unless in a kennel. If your outdoor or evening experience needs to be pet free, we offer pet sitting, just stop by the office for details.

Features: Fitness center, Free parking, Wireless Internet, BBQ grills, Number of rooms: 6, Fridge and microwave available, Concierge services, Smoke-free property.

★★
Pamola Motor Lodge
973 Central Street
Millinocket ME 04462
(207) 723-9746
Rates from $79
SAVE –B&P Discount Available

Pet Policy: Pet friendly. Please contact Lodge directly for pet reservations.

Features: Restaurant, Parking (free), Arcade/game room, Business services, Fax machine, Breakfast service.

Old Orchard Beach
Also see the following nearby communities that have pet friendly lodging:
Saco - 3 miles, Scarborough - 5 miles, Biddeford - 6 miles, South Portland - 8 miles.

Not Rated
Moby Dick Motel
74 E Grand Avenue
Old Orchard Beach ME 04064
(207) 934-5420
$129 - $219

Pet Policy: Pets allowed, off season only, $10 per night. Please contact motel directly to make sure pet room is available.

Features: Gift shop, Air conditioning, Kitchenettes available, Restaurant.

Not Rated
Waves Motor Inn
87 West Grand Ave
Old Orchard Beach ME 04064
(207) 934-4949
Rates from $129

Pet Policy: Pets are allowed during the spring and fall seasons for $10 per night, plus a $100 deposit.

Features: Full kitchens available in two bedroom suites, Restaurant (seasonal), Fitness center.

Orono
Also see the following nearby communities that have pet friendly lodging:
Brewer - 7 miles, Bangor - 7 miles.

★★★
Black Bear Inn Conference Center & Suites
4 Godfrey Dr
Orono ME 04473
(207) 866-7120
$139 - $158
SAVE –B&P Discount Available

Pet Policy: Pets accepted, $10 per night up to a maximum of $100 per stay.

Features: Sauna, Dry cleaning/laundry service, Fitness facilities, Restaurant(s), Room service, Number of rooms: 68, Number of floors: 3, Conference room(s), Business services, Coffee in lobby, Arcade/game room, Free breakfast, Parking, Newspapers, Wireless Internet, Smoke-free property.

★★

University Inn Academic Suites
5 College Ave
Orono ME 04473
(207) 866-4921
$114 - $124
SAVE –B&P Discount Available

Pet Policy: Small dogs and cats are accepted in designated pet-friendly rooms, no fee.

Features: Free breakfast, Concierge, Small meeting rooms, Outdoor pool - heated, Wedding services, Wireless Internet, Accessible bathroom, Handicapped parking, Area shuttle, Smoke-free property, Business center, Game room, Parking, Room service, Number of rooms: 48, Number of floors: 2, Coffee in lobby, Poolside bar.

Portland

Also see the following nearby communities that have pet friendly lodging:
Westbrook - 3 miles, South Portland - 3 miles, Scarborough - 7 miles.

★★★

Clarion Hotel Portland
1230 Congress St
Portland ME 04102
(207) 774-5611
$129 - $199
SAVE –B&P Discount Available

Pet Policy: Pet Limit: 1 pet per room, 50 lbs or less. No pet fee.

Features: Bar/lounge, Airport transportation (free), Room service (limited hours), Gift shops or newsstand, Number of rooms: 149, Number of floors: 6, Elevator, Conference room(s), Air-conditioned public areas, Coffee in lobby, Parking (free), Free newspapers in lobby, 24-hour front desk, Porter/bellhop, Beauty services, Meeting rooms (small groups), Indoor pool, Business services, Dry cleaning/laundry service, Wireless Internet, Restaurant, Fax machine, Multilingual staff, Fitness facilities.

★★★

Eastland Park Hotel
157 High St
Portland ME 04101
(207) 775-5411
$189 - $274
SAVE –B&P Discount Available

Pet Policy: Pets welcome, $30 per night. At check-in your dog will receive their very own welcome amenity. This amenity includes a copy of The Ultimate Guide to Dog Parks, Beaches and Trails in Maine, a copy of Downeast Dog News, an edible treat, a toy to take home with them and clean up bags. We provide dog walking services which can be arranged with our bellmen by appointment.

Features: Year Built 1927, Parking (valet), Coffee in lobby, Piano, Health club, Nightclub, Room service, Porter/bellhop, Designated smoking areas, Wireless Internet, Pick up service from train station, Accessible bathroom, *Continued on next page*

67

Eastland Park Hotel
Continued from previous page

Security guard, Area shuttle (free), Number of restaurants 2, 24-hour business center, Ferry terminal shuttle (free), Dry cleaning/laundry service, Bar/lounge, Restaurant(s), Gift shop, Number of rooms: 202, Number of floors: 12, Elevator, Conference room(s), Business services, Air-conditioned public areas, Coffee shop, Free newspapers in lobby, 24-hour front desk, Doorman/doorwoman, Massage - treatment room(s), Meeting rooms (small groups), Wedding services, Fitness facilities, Self-parking $16.60/Day w/Stamp.

★★★☆
Embassy Suites Portland
1050 Westbrook St
Portland ME 04102
(207) 775-2200
$167 - $299
SAVE –B&P Discount Available

Pet Policy: Pets up to 75 lbs accepted, $50 for 1, $25 for each additional pet.

Features: Accessible bathroom, Handicapped parking, Dry cleaning/laundry service, Indoor pool, Restaurant, Concierge, Gift shop, Number of rooms: 119, Number of floors: 6, Elevator, Computer rental, Suitable for children, Air-conditioned public areas, Fireplace in lobby, Patio, Free newspapers in lobby, Nearby fitness center (free), 24-hour front desk, Wireless Internet, Meeting rooms), Sauna, Room service (limited hours), Airport transportation (free), Bar/lounge, Business services, Free breakfast, Self-parking (additional charge).

★★★
Fireside Inn & Suites
81 Riverside St
Portland ME 04103
(207) 774-5601
$119 - $189
SAVE –B&P Discount Available

Pet Policy: Pet friendly rooms available, $35 per stay additional fee.

Features: Restaurant(s), Gift shops or newsstand, Number of rooms: 200, Number of floors: 2, Conference room(s), Air-conditioned public areas, Breakfast available (additional charge), Wireless Internet, Parking (free), Front desk (limited hours), Porter/bellhop, Meeting rooms (small groups), Accessible bathroom, Handicapped parking, In-room accessibility, Dry cleaning/laundry service, Sauna, Business center, Indoor pool, Bar/lounge, Room service (limited hours), Outdoor pool, Fitness facilities

★★ 🛏
Fleetwood House B & B
10 Fleetwood Street
Portland ME 04102
(207) 772-9592
$155 - $166
SAVE –B&P Discount Available

Pet Policy: Pets are accepted in a few rooms. Property has several resident cats. Please call property directly for pet approval and reservations.

Features: Smoke-free property, Number of rooms: 4, Barbecue grill(s), Parking (free), Wireless Internet, Suitable for children, Fireplace in lobby, Free breakfast, Year Built 1892.

★★★
Hilton Garden Inn Portland Downtown Waterfront
65 Commercial St
Portland ME 04101
(207) 780-0780
$211 - $359
SAVE –B&P Discount Available

Pet Policy: Pets up to 200 lbs accepted, $50 per stay.

Features: Airport transportation (free), Bar/lounge, Indoor pool, Restaurant, Room service, Number of rooms: 120, Number of floors: 6, Air-conditioned public areas, 24-hour front desk, Business center, Smoke-free property, Valet parking (fee), Fitness facilities, Designated smoking areas, Accessible bathroom, Wireless Internet, Fireplace in lobby, Coffee in lobby, Handicapped parking, Dry cleaning/laundry service, Meeting rooms.

★★★✦
Howard Johnson Plaza
155 Riverside St
Portland ME 04103
(207)774-5861
$84 - $189
SAVE –B&P Discount Available

Pet Policy: Dogs and cats welcome with $50 refundable damage deposit, or credit card imprint. Pets may not be left alone in room at any time.

Features: Bar/lounge, Restaurant(s), Room service, Shopping on site, Conference room(s), Business services, Parking, Newspapers in lobby, Business center, Security guard, Wireless Internet, Accessible bathroom, Handicapped parking, Indoor pool, Dry cleaning/laundry service, Airport transportation (additional charge), Fitness facilities.

★★★✦ 🛏
Inn At St John
939 Congress St
Portland ME 04102
(207) 773-6481
$80 - $109
SAVE –B&P Discount Available

Pet Policy: Allows dogs, $10.75 per dog per day. No other types of animals accepted. Limit 2 per room and may not be left alone in room.

Features: Concierge, Number of rooms: 39, Number of floors: 4, Parking (free), Free newspapers in lobby, 24-hour front desk, Wireless Internet, Coffee in lobby, Free breakfast, Fireplace in lobby, Business services, Handicapped parking, Smoke-free property.

★★★⯪
La Quinta Inn & Suites Portland
340 Park Ave
Portland ME 04102
(207) 871-0611
$114 - $209
SAVE –B&P Discount Available

Pet Policy: Small pets only, no fee.

Features: Accessible bathroom, Handicapped parking, Business services, Dry cleaning/laundry service, Number of rooms: 105, Number of floors: 4, Coffee in lobby, Free breakfast, Parking (free), Free newspapers in lobby, 24-hour front desk, Wireless Internet, Outdoor pool - seasonal, Airport transportation (free), Fitness facilities.

★★★
Residence Inn by Marriott
145 Fore Street
Portland ME 04101
(207) 761-1660
$229 - $339
SAVE –B&P Discount Available

Pet Policy: Pets allowed, $100 per stay cleaning fee.

Features: Bar/lounge, Indoor pool, Free breakfast, Wireless Internet (additional charge), Free reception.

Rockport
Also see the following nearby communities that have pet friendly lodging:
Camden - 4 miles, Lincolnville - 10 miles.

★★★⯪
Glen Cove Suites
866 Commercial Street
Rockport ME 04856
(800) 453-6268
$89 - $139

Pet Policy: Pets accepted with a $10 per day charge added to your room and credit card imprint. Pets cannot be left unattended in the room for periods longer than 4 hours and we must have a cell phone number to reach you if your pet is left unattended. If you need to be gone for more than four hours, we can provide a list of kennels and daycares in the area. Daily Maid service is required and your pet must vacate the room with its owner or be in a crate to ensure that the animal does not escape from the room. Pets need to be walked on the northwest side of the motel near the garage area. You are responsible for cleaning up after your pet. Please give the Front Desk 15 minutes advance notice prior to checkout so that we may inspect your room. You will be responsible for any damages and extra cleaning costs deemed necessary.

Features: Heated pool, Air conditioning, Continental breakfast, Laundry facilities, Wireless Internet, Refrigerators.

Not Rated
The Country Inn
8 Country Inn Way
Rockport ME 04856
(207) 236-2725
$179 - $239

Pet Policy: Pet friendly rooms available, $10 per pet per night additional charge. We provide pet bed and dishes, paw wiping towels and all natural treats. Please leave a cell phone number at the front desk. Please place your pet on a leash or in a carrier when outside the room. Please do not leave pets unattended in rooms. Pet waste bags and a pet waste receptacle are located at the south entrance of the main building.

Features: Wireless Internet, Number of suites: 47, Refrigerators, Whirlpool tubs and fireplaces available in some units, Indoor pool, Hot tub, Sauna, Free breakfast buffet.

Saco

Also see the following nearby communities that have pet friendly lodging:
Old Orchard Beach - 3 miles, Biddeford - 5 miles, Scarborough - 6 miles, South Portland - 9 miles.

Not Rated:
Exit 5 Motel & Cottages
18 Ocean Park Road
Saco ME 04072
(800) 905-4727
$102 - $279

Pet Policy: Pets allowed only in off season, in limited pet-friendly rooms. Please call directly to verify that your pet(s) can be accommodated.

Features: Microwave, Air conditioning, Coffee maker in room, Fridge, Suites have Jacuzzi and Fireplace.

★★★
Hampton Inn Saco Orchard
48 Industrial Park Rd
Saco ME 04072
(207) 282-7222
$160 - $234
SAVE –B&P Discount Available

Pet Policy: Accepts pets up to 100 lbs.

Features: Outdoor pool, Business services, Dry cleaning/laundry service, Airport transportation , Number of rooms: 100, Number of floors: 5, Conference room(s), Coffee in lobby, Free breakfast, Parking, Free newspapers in lobby, Fitness facilities.

★★★
Ramada at Saco Plaza
352 North St
Saco ME 04072
(207)286-9600
$111 - $309
SAVE –B&P Discount Available

Pet Policy: Pets allowed, $25 per stay. May not leave pets alone in room.

Features: Dry cleaning/laundry service, Airport transportation (free), Number of rooms: 88, Number of floors: 4, Conference room(s), Free breakfast, Wireless Internet, Business center, Nearby fitness center (discount), Outdoor pool.

Scarborough

Also see the following nearby communities that have pet friendly lodging:
South Portland - 3 miles, Old Orchard Beach - 5 miles, Saco - 6 miles, Portland - 7 miles, Westbrook - 7 miles.

★★★

Comfort Inn & Suites
A - 329 US Route 1
Scarborough ME 04074
(207) 883-2700
$119- $229
SAVE –B&P Discount Available

Pet Policy: Pet accommodation: $25 per night. Dogs only. Pet deposit: $100 per stay Pet limit: 1 pet per room maximum 30 pounds. Please advise hotel in advance if traveling with pet.

Features: Parking (free), Wireless Internet, Number of rooms: 69, Number of floors: 3, Free breakfast, Children's club, Fitness facilities, Indoor pool.

★★

Extended Stay America
2 Ashley Dr
Scarborough ME 04074
(207) 883-0554
$119 - $129
SAVE –B&P Discount Available

Pet Policy: One pet is allowed in each guest room. A $25 per day non-refundable cleaning fee (not to exceed $150) will be charged the first night of your stay. Weight, size and breed restrictions may apply. Please contact the hotel directly with inquiries.

Features: Laundry facilities, Number of rooms: 92, Number of floors: 3, Elevator, Suitable for children, Barbecue grill(s), Wireless Internet (additional charge), Parking (free), Nearby fitness center (free).

★★★

Homewood Suites by Hilton
200 Southborough Dr
Scarborough ME 04074
(207)-775-2700
$158 - $229
SAVE –B&P Discount Available

Pet Policy: Pets allowed up to 50 lbs. Fee $25.

Features: Airport transportation (free), Indoor pool, Number of suites: 87, Number of floors: 4, Air-conditioned public areas, Parking (free), Business center, Video library, Fitness facilities.

Not Rated.
Pride Motel & Cottages
677 US Route1
Scarborough ME 04074
(207) 883-4816
Rates from $60

Pet Policy: Pets accepted, $15 per pet per day. Please pick up after your pets and to not let them on our furniture or beds. Failure to pick up after your pet is subject to a $20 fee. Pets are not to be left unattended at any time. We have the right to call Animal Control if pets are left unattended.

Features: Number of cottages: 10, Full kitchens, Cottages sleep 2 – 8, Number of rooms: 7. Mini fridge and microwave in motel rooms, heated pool.

★★★
Residence Inn by Marriott Portland Maine
800 Roundwood Dr
Scarborough ME 04074
(207) 883 0400
$169 - $240
SAVE –B&P Discount Available

Pet Policy: Pets allowed, $75 per stay cleaning fee.

Features: Coffee in lobby, Business services, Indoor pool, Dry cleaning/laundry service, Number of rooms: 78, Number of floors: 3, Elevator, Conference room(s), Photocopy machines, Air-conditioned public areas, Barbecue grill(s), Fax machine, Grocery shopping services, Parking (free), Free newspapers in lobby, 24-hour front desk, Wireless Internet.

★★★
TownePlace Suites by Marriott
700 Roundwood Dr
Scarborough ME 04074
(207) 883 6800
$129 - $230
SAVE –B&P Discount Available

Pet Policy: Pets allowed, $75 additional cleaning fee.

Features: Free Breakfast, Handicapped parking, In-room accessibility, Business services, Dry cleaning/laundry service, Smoke-free property, Number of suites: 95, Number of floors: 3, Parking (free), Free newspapers in lobby, Outdoor pool - seasonal, Wireless Internet (additional charge), Fitness facilities.

Sebasco Estates

Also see the following nearby communities that have pet friendly lodging:
Brunswick - 9 miles.

★★★★
Sebasco Harbor Resort
29 Kenyon Rd
Sebasco Estates ME 04565
(207) 389-1161
$179 - $499
SAVE –B&P Discount Available

Pet Policy: Pets up to 70 lbs accepted, $25 per night per pet, limit two per room. Our pet friendly cottages are currently Island View, Captains, Birch Bark, Dogwood, Pine Crest A, B & C and Round Cove and Rocky Crest. All pet guests will receive a special welcome treat; a resort map with designated pet friendly areas; Convenient pick-up bags for cleaning up after your pet.

Features: 2 Restaurants, Security guard, Number of rooms: 133, Elevator, Arcade/game room, Full-service health spa, Marina on site, Wedding services, Wireless Internet, Golf course, Tennis on site, Bar/lounge, Babysitting or child care, Gift shop, Laundry facilities, Parking (free or valet), Newspapers in lobby, Meeting rooms, Smoke-free property, Children's club, Pool table, Handicapped parking, Accessible bathroom, 24-hour business center, Room service, Concierge, Private beach, Outdoor pool - seasonal, Snack bar/deli.

South Portland

Also see the following nearby communities that have pet friendly lodging:.
Scarborough - 3 miles, Portland - 3 miles, Westbrook - 4 miles, Old Orchard Beach - 8 miles, Saco - 9 miles.

★★★
Best Western Merry Manor Inn
700 Main St
South Portland ME 04106
(207) 774-6151
$148 - $309
SAVE –B&P Discount Available

Pet Policy: Well behaved pets allowed. $10 per pet per night. They must be supervised at all times.

Features: Handicapped parking, In-room accessibility, Outdoor pool, Dry cleaning/laundry service, Business services, Conference room(s), Smoke-free property, Wireless Internet, Restaurant, Shopping on site, Number of rooms: 153, Number of floors: 4, Elevator, Air-conditioned public areas, Coffee in lobby, Parking (free), Free newspapers in lobby, Wedding services, Fitness facilities.

★★★
Comfort Inn Airport
90 Maine Mall Rd
South Portland ME 04106
(207) 775-0409
$114 - $129
SAVE –B&P Discount Available

Pet Policy: Pet accommodation: $10.00 per night per pet. Max of 40 pounds, 2 pets per room.

Features: Free Breakfast, Number of rooms: 127, Number of floors: 3, Smoke-free property, Parking (free), Dry cleaning/laundry service, 24-hour front desk, Nearby fitness center (free), Airport transportation (free), Business services, Coffee in lobby, Wireless Internet, Free newspapers in lobby.

★★
Days Inn Airport
461 Maine Mall Rd
South Portland ME 04106
(207) 772-3450
$67 - $229
SAVE –B&P Discount Available

Pet Policy: Pets - dogs only - are allowed and must be 50 pounds or less. Pet fee will be $10 per day plus a $50 refundable deposit. Max 2 dogs per room. Designated pet rooms, smoking and nonsmoking, are available and advance reservation is required. Dogs must be on a leash at all times outside of the room. Dogs are not allowed in common areas - lobby, pool, restaurant, or other guest rooms. Please use your rear entrance only to escort your dog in and out. Please walk your dog on grassy areas and pick up after your dog. Pets are never allowed in an unattended room.

Features: Restaurant, Number of rooms: 149, Number of floors: 2, Coffee in lobby, Free newspapers in lobby, Business center, Wireless Internet, Airport transportation (free), Free breakfast.

★★

Econo Lodge of South Portland
80 John Roberts Rd.
South Portland ME 04106
(207) 772-3838
Rates from $109
SAVE –B&P Discount Available

Pet Policy: Pets up to 40 lbs accepted, $10 per night. Limit 1 pet per room.

Features: Free Breakfast, Number of rooms: 54, Number of floors: 2, Air-conditioned public areas, Coffee in lobby, Parking (free), Free newspapers in lobby, 24-hour front desk, Business services, Wireless Internet.

★★★

Hampton Inn Portland Airport
171 Philbrook Ave
South Portland ME 04106
(207) 773-4400
$135 - $209
SAVE –B&P Discount Available

Pet Policy: Pets up to 45 lbs accepted.

Features: Airport transportation (free), Indoor pool, Number of floors: 4, Elevator, Air-conditioned public areas, Parking (free), Business center, Smoke-free property, Fitness facilities, Free breakfast.

★★★

Holiday Inn Express Hotel & Suites South Portland
303 Sable Oaks Dr
South Portland ME 04106
(207) 775-3900
$144 - $237
SAVE –B&P Discount Available

Pet Policy: All pets accepted, $20 per stay fee.

Features: Handicapped parking, Accessible bathroom, Indoor pool, Business services, Dry cleaning/laundry service, Airport transportation (free), Restaurant, Number of rooms: 130, Number of suites: 130, Number of floors: 6, Elevator, Coffee in lobby, Free breakfast, Parking (free), Free newspapers in lobby, 24-hour front desk, Wireless Internet, Fitness facilities.

★★

Howard Johnson Hotel
675 Main St
South Portland ME 04106
(207) 775-5343
$84 - $209
SAVE –B&P Discount Available

Pet Policy: Pets accepted, $10 per pet per day additional fee.

Features: Handicapped parking, Accessible bathroom, Room service Number of rooms: 120, Conference room(s), Parking, Business center, Wireless Internet, Indoor pool, Dry cleaning/laundry service, Airport transportation, Fitness facilities.

★★★

Marriott Portland at Sable Oaks
200 Sable Oaks Dr
South Portland ME 04106
(207) 871-8000
$179 - $219
SAVE –B&P Discount Available

Pet Policy: Pets allowed. $35 cleaning fee.

Features: Airport transportation (free), Restaurant, Concierge services, Number of rooms: 227, Number of floors: 6, Elevator, Air-conditioned public areas, Wireless Internet, Parking (free), Free newspapers in lobby, *Continued on next page*

Marriott Portland *Continued from previous page*	24-hour front desk, Business center, Porter/bellhop, Meeting rooms (small groups), Sauna, Smoke-free property, Wedding services, Bar/Lounge, Indoor pool, Dry cleaning/laundry service, Coffee in lobby, Room service, Fitness facilities.

★★

Super 8 South Portland
738 Main Street
South Portland ME 04106
(207) 774-5891
$67 - $109
SAVE –B&P Discount Available

Pet Policy: Accepts pets up to 25 lbs, $10 per night per pet, limit 2 per room.

Features: Number of floors: 2, Free breakfast, Self-parking, Business center, Wireless Internet.

★★★

Wyndham Portland Airport
363 Maine Mall Rd
South Portland ME 04106
(207) 775-6161
$143 - $209
SAVE –B&P Discount Available

Pet Policy: Pets up to 80 lbs accepted, no additional fee. Limit 2 per room. Pets not permitted in pool or food areas.

Features: Restaurant, Gift shop, Suitable for children, Air-conditioned, Wireless Internet, Parking (free), Newspapers in lobby, 24-hour front desk, Porter/bellhop, Security guard, Meeting rooms, Accessible bathroom, Handicapped parking,, Dry cleaning/laundry service, Steam room, Sauna, Indoor pool, Bar/lounge, Room service, Concierge, Business services, Elevator, Fitness facilities, Airport transportation (free) available 24 hours.

Southport

Also see the following nearby communities that have pet friendly lodging:
Boothbay Harbor - 1 mile, East Boothbay - 4 miles, Bath - 10 miles.

★★★

Ocean Gate Resort
70 Ocean Gate Rd
Southport ME 04576
(207) 633-3321
$193 - $214
SAVE –B&P Discount Available

Pet Policy: Pets accepted in limited rooms, $25 per stay. Pets are only permitted in the Island View and Overlook Buildings as well as the 2 bedroom Cottage only.

Features: Dry cleaning/laundry service, Outdoor pool, Concierge, Wedding services, Medical assistance available, Free breakfast, Conference room(s), Business services, Tennis on site, Gift shop, Suitable for children, Coffee shop, Parking (free), Free newspapers in lobby, Front desk (limited hours), Meeting rooms (small groups), Outdoor pool - seasonal, Fitness facilities, Self-parking, Wireless Internet, Business center, Rooftop terrace.

Spruce Head

★★✦ 🛏

Craignair Inn
5 3rd St
Spruce Head ME 04859
(207) 594-7644
$150 - $155
SAVE –B&P Discount Available

Pet Policy: Pets accepted, $10 per pet per night. Limit 2 pets (subject to innkeeper's approval.) We prefer our pet-guests to stay in the Vestry Rooms for their comfort, your comfort and the comfort of our other guests. All rooms in the Vestry open directly to the outside, onto a common deck. PLEASE NOTE: Proof of Rabies Vaccination and Flea Prevention purchased from a veterinarian (I.e. Frontline) must be provided at the time of check-in. Pets will not be allowed in the rooms without these documents. Payment of the room deposit indicates that you understand our pet policy: Pets may not be left unattended in your room or on Craignair property. They are not allowed on furniture (including beds), in the dining room or the living room. If extra cleaning is required because of your pet, it will be charged on your credit card.

Features: Year Built 1928, Restaurant, Number of rooms: 20, Suitable for children, Fireplace in lobby, Parking (free), Library, Free breakfast, Wedding services.

The Forks
Also see the following nearby communities that have pet friendly lodging:
West Forks - 6 miles.

Not Rated
Northern Outdoors Adventures
1771 US Route 201
The Forks ME 04985
(800)-765-7238
Please call for various rates

Pet Policy: Pets accepted, $15 per night per pet. Pets are accepted in all of our free standing Cabins and Guest Houses. Pets are not allowed in either Resort Center Lodge nor the following accommodations: Lodge Rooms, Logdominiums, Cabin Tents and Campgrounds. $100 extra cleaning charge will be levied against the credit card left as a security deposit if it is determined by Northern Outdoors staff that the pets have been on the furniture, excessive animal hair found on the carpets, relieved themselves inside the accommodations, etc. Any additional damage and related costs will be charged against the credit card left as a security deposit.
Continued on next page.

Northern Outdoors Adventures
The Forks, ME
Continued from previous page

We expect that pets be crated inside the accommodations if left for more than an hour. No housekeeping make ups will occur UNLESS the pets are crated. All animals must be on a leash and UNDER CONTROL outside. No pets are allowed inside any of the public areas. Please pick up poop and dispose of it in outside trash cans (plastic bags provided). If the pet is disruptive to other guests (excessive barking, intimidating behavior) you will be asked to leave as soon as possible. No refunds will be given under these circumstances. Pet owners are personally liable for any and all injuries or damages caused by their pets and indemnifies Northern Outdoors, its staff, assigns and heirs from any liability caused by their pets while staying at Northern Outdoors and the Eagle Cove Condominiums.

Features: Variety of accommodations ranging from tent cabins to fully furnished cottages and condominium units. Restaurant, Fitness Center, Game room with pool table, hot tub, Outdoor pool, Wireless Internet, Non-smoking property, Fully equipped kitchens available, Jacuzzi rooms available.

Waterville

★
Budget Airport Host Inn
400 Kennedy Memorial Drive
Waterville ME 04901
(207) 873-3366
$58 - $84

Pet Policy: Pets accepted, $10 per night additional fee.

Features: Number of rooms: 43, Wireless Internet, Continental breakfast, Truck & RV parking, Fridge and microwave in some rooms.

★★★
Comfort Inn & Suites Waterville
332 Main St
Waterville ME 04901
(207) 873-2777
$129- $209
SAVE –B&P Discount Available

Pet Policy: Pets accepted, $20 per pet per day.

Features: Wireless Internet, Dry cleaning/laundry service, Indoor pool, Number of rooms: 101, Number of floors: 4, Elevator, Business services, Air-conditioned public areas, Free breakfast, Parking (free), Multilingual staff, Free newspapers in lobby, 24-hour front desk, Fitness facilities.

★★
Econo Lodge Waterville
455 Kennedy Memorial Dr
Waterville ME 04901
(207) 872-5577
$75- $129
SAVE –B&P Discount Available

Pet Policy: Dogs only, $10 per dog per day.

Features: Self-parking, Wireless Internet, Number of rooms: 50, Number of floors: 2, Business services, 24-hour front desk, Outdoor pool - seasonal, Coffee in lobby, Free breakfast.

★★
Fireside Inn & Suites Waterville
356 Main St
Waterville ME 04901
(207) 873-3335
$129 - $159
SAVE –B&P Discount Available

Pet Policy: Pets are welcome, except in kings & suites. There is a one-time $20 (plus tax) pet fee.

Features: Restaurant, Number of rooms: 86, Number of floors: 2, Air-conditioned public areas, Free breakfast, Parking (free), Meeting rooms, Outdoor pool - seasonal, Accessible bathroom, Handicapped parking, Dry cleaning/laundry service, Business services, RV and truck parking, Fitness facilities, Wireless Internet, Coffee in lobby, Free newspapers.

★★★
Waterville Grand Hotel
375 Main St
Waterville ME 04901
(207) 873-0111
$149 - $161
SAVE –B&P Discount Available

Pet Policy: Pets welcome. No Fee.

Features: Wireless Internet, Bar/lounge, Indoor pool, Restaurant, Room service, Number of rooms: 138, Number of floors: 3, Business services, Parking (free), Porter/bellhop, Meeting rooms (small groups), Sauna, Handicapped parking, Accessible bathroom, Dry cleaning/laundry service, Free breakfast, Newspapers in lobby, RV and truck parking, Fitness facilities.

Wells
Also see the following nearby communities that have pet friendly lodging:
Kennebunk - 7 miles, Kennebunkport - 8 miles.

★★★
Majestic Regency
102 Post Road
Wells ME 04090
(207) 646-9601
$109 - $155
SAVE –B&P Discount Available

Pet Policy: Dogs and cats, under 50 lbs accepted, $10 per night per pet additional. Limit 2 pets per room.

Features: Parking (free), Wireless Internet, Number of rooms: 86, Number of floors: 2, Coffee in lobby, Laundry facilities, Free breakfast, Outdoor pool - seasonal, Picnic area, Tennis on site.

★★★
The Coast Village Inn Wells
876 Post Rd
Wells ME 04090
(207) 646-9210
$110 - $164
SAVE –B&P Discount Available

Pet Policy: Small pets allowed with advanced approval, $15 per pet per night, limit 2. You must have permission before arrival so it is advised to book directly with the Inn.

Features: Number of floors: 2, Parking (free), Picnic area, Swimming pool, Smoke-free property.

West Forks

Also see the following nearby communities that have pet friendly lodging:
The Forks - 6 miles

Not Rated
Inn By the River
2777 U S Route 201
West Forks ME 04985
(207)-663-2181
Rates starting at $99

Pet Policy: Pets allowed on first two floors, no fee. Please call Inn directly for pet reservations.

Features: Number of rooms: 10, Whirlpool in some rooms, air conditioned.

Westbrook

Also see the following nearby communities that have pet friendly lodging:
Portland - 3 miles, South Portland - 4 miles, Scarborough - 7 miles.

★★
Super 8 Westbrook Portland
208 Larrabee Rd
Westbrook ME 04092
(207) 854-1881
$84 - $109
SAVE –B&P Discount Available

Pet Policy: Some pets are accepted with a small nightly fee. Please contact hotel directly for pet reservations.

Features: Business services, Free breakfast, Air-conditioned public areas, Indoor pool, Parking (free), 24-hour front desk, Wireless Internet

Not Rated
The Elms B&B
102 Cumberland Street
Westbrook ME 04092
(207) 854-4060
$99 - $150

Pet Policy: Dogs accepted with advanced approval. Please call property directly for approval and pet reservations.

Features: Year built: 1882, Non-smoking property, Number of rooms: 7, Air conditioned, Fireplace available, Wireless Internet, Free breakfast.

Wilton

★★★ 🎿
Comfort Inn And Suites Wilton
1026 Us Route 2 E
Wilton ME 04294
(207) 645 - 5155
Rates from $130
SAVE –B&P Discount Available

Pet Policy: Pets accepted, $35 per night.

Features: Parking (free), Wireless Internet, Number of rooms: 86, Number of floors: 3, Elevator, Fax machine, Picnic area, Indoor pool, Air-conditioned public areas, Laundry facilities, Free breakfast, Meeting rooms (small groups), Fitness facilities.

For best rates, book reservations at BedAndPet.com
Or call:
U.S. & Canada – 1-800-780-5733
Europe - 00-800-11-20-11-40
Please enter Promo Code 102350 when requested by phone

Massachusetts

Amherst
Also see the following nearby communities that have pet friendly lodging:
Hadley - 4 miles, Northampton - 8 miles.

Not Rated
University Lodge
345 North Pleasant Street
Amherst MA 01002
(413) 256-8111
$67- $99

Pet Policy: Small pets accepted in designated pet friendly rooms, $20 per night for first three nights.

Features: Free parking, Free weekend newspapers, Wireless Internet, Morning coffee and juice in lobby, Computer for guest use, Mini fridge and microwaves in each room..

Andover
Also see the following nearby communities that have pet friendly lodging:.
Lawrence - 2 miles, Methuen - 4 miles, Tewksbury - 5 miles, Salem - 7 miles, Lowell - 8 miles, Haverhill - 8 miles.

★★★
Homewood Suites by Hilton
4 Riverside Dr
Andover MA 01810
(978) 475-6000
$92 - $184
SAVE –B&P Discount Available

Pet Policy: Pets up to 40 lbs, $75 per stay.

Features: Number of rooms: 82, Number of floors: 4, Coffee in lobby, Free breakfast, Parking, Meeting rooms, Outdoor pool - seasonal, Wireless Internet, Handicapped parking, In-room accessibility, 24-hour business center, Convenience store, Free reception, Dry cleaning/laundry service, Fitness facilities.

★★★
La Quinta Inn & Suites Andover
131 River Rd
Andover MA 01810
(978) 685-6200
$88 - $99
SAVE –B&P Discount Available

Pet Policy: Cats and dogs up to 50 pounds are accepted in all guest rooms. Housekeeping services for rooms with pets require pet owner be present or pet must be crated. No fees or deposits are required.

Features: Free Breakfast, Indoor pool, Accessible bathroom, Handicapped parking, Bar/lounge, Restaurant, Number of rooms: 181, Coffee in lobby, Meeting rooms, Billiards, Wireless Internet, Parking, Fitness facilities, Business center.

★★★
Residence Inn By Marriott
500 Minuteman Rd
Andover MA 01810
(978) 683 0382
$109 - $119
SAVE –B&P Discount Available

Pet Policy: Pets allowed, $100 cleaning fee per stay.

Features: Free Breakfast, Business services, Dry cleaning/laundry service, Tennis on site, Number of rooms: 120, Number of floors: 3, coffee in lobby, Parking (free), Free newspapers in lobby, Wireless Internet (additional charge), Meeting rooms (small groups), Outdoor pool - seasonal, Fitness facilities.

★★★
Staybridge Suites
4 Technology Dr
Andover MA 01810
(978) 686-2000
$80 - $170
SAVE –B&P Discount Available

Pet Policy: Pets up to 80 lbs accepted, $75 per stay fee for up to 6 nights, $150 per stay fee for longer. Pet agreement must be signed at check in.

Features: Handicapped parking, In-room accessibility, Dry cleaning/laundry service, Business center, Library, Outdoor pool, Number of suites: 133, Number of floors: 3, Free breakfast, Parking (free), Wireless Internet, Fitness facilities.

★★★
Wyndham Boston Andover
123 Old River Rd
Andover MA 01810
(978) 975-3600
$98 - $239
SAVE –B&P Discount Available

Pet Policy: Pets under 20 lbs, $50 per pet per stay.

Features: Restaurant, Number of rooms: 293, Parking (free), Free newspapers in lobby, Wireless Internet, Handicapped parking, Accessible bathroom, Pool table, Conference room(s), Indoor pool, Room service, Business services, Bar/lounge, Dry cleaning/laundry service, Fitness facilities, Smoke-free property.

Arlington

Also see the following nearby communities that have pet friendly lodging:
Somerville - 3 miles, Cambridge - 3 miles, Waltham - 5 miles, Brookline - 5 miles, Newton - 6 miles, Woburn - 6 miles, Revere - 7 miles, Saugus - 8 miles, Wakefield - 8 miles, Boston - 8 miles, Lexington - 8 miles, Needham - 9 miles.

★★★
Homewood Suites by Hilton
1 Massachusetts Ave
Arlington MA 02474
(781) 643-7258
$188 $249
SAVE –B&P Discount Available

Pet Policy: Pets up to 25 lbs, $75 per stay. Walking area for dogs and hotel provides scooper bags and biscuits

Features: Handicapped parking, Accessible bathroom, Dry cleaning/laundry service, Free breakfast, Fitness facilities, Number of suites: 100, Conference room(s), Parking, Newspapers in lobby.

Auburn
Also see the following nearby communities that have pet friendly lodging:
Worcester - 7 miles.

★★
La Quinta Inn
446 Southbridge St
Auburn MA 01501
(508) 832-7000
$82 - $109
SAVE –B&P Discount Available

Pet Policy: Cats and dogs up to 50 pounds are accepted in all guest rooms. Housekeeping services for rooms with pets require pet owner be present or pet must be crated. No fees or deposits are required.

Features: Accessible bathroom, Handicapped parking, Business services, Laundry facilities, Breakfast, Parking, Newspapers, Wireless Internet.

Barnstable
Also see the following nearby communities that have pet friendly lodging:
Hyannis - 3 miles, West Yarmouth - 5 miles, South Yarmouth - 6 miles,
West Dennis - 8 miles, Sandwich - 9 miles.

★★★
Cape Cod's Lamb and Lion Inn
2504 Main St
Rte 6 A
Barnstable MA 02630
(800) 909-6923
$179 - $189
SAVE –B&P Discount Available

Pet Policy: Pets under 25 lbs accepted, $25 per night per pet up to maximum of $100 per stay. Aggressive breeds not accepted. Pets should not be left alone in room, pet sitter service is available. Pets should be leashed when in public areas. Allows only 3 pets in Inn at any one time.

Features: Year built: 1740, Number of rooms: 10, Fireplace in lobby, Parking, Wireless Internet, Smoke-free property, Breakfast, Wedding services, Outdoor pool.

Barre
Also see the following nearby communities that have pet friendly lodging:
Montpelier - 6 miles.

★★★
The Jenkins Inn
7 West Street
Barre MA 01005
(978) 355-6444
$180 - $235

Pet Policy: Dogs are welcome as long as they are quiet, housebroken and not left alone in the guest room. $10 per dog per night. Please let us know in advance that you are bringing your dog(s). Dogs must be on a leash going in and out of the Inn. We can recommend walking areas and have waste bags

The Jenkins Inn
Continued from previous page

SAVE –B&P Discount Available

for guest convenience.

Features: Restaurant, Number of rooms: 4, Fireplace in lobby, Library, Parking (free), Wireless Internet, Free breakfast, Video library

Billerica
Also see the following nearby communities that have pet friendly lodging:
Lexington - 6 miles, Tewksbury - 7 miles, Lowell - 7 miles, Westford - 9 miles, North Chelmsford - 9 miles, Woburn - 9 miles.

★★★
Homewood Suites by Hilton Boston/Billerica
35 Middlesex Tpke
Billerica MA 01821
(978) 670-7111
$89 - $169
SAVE –B&P Discount Available

Pet Policy: Pets up to 100 lbs. Fee required.

Features: Convenience store, Free reception, Dry cleaning/laundry service, Gift shop, Airport transportation (charge), Parking, Business center, Limo or Town Car service, Meeting rooms, Media library, Barbecue grill(s), Elevator, Indoor pool, Free breakfast, Patio, Fitness facilities.

Boston
Also see the following nearby communities that have pet friendly lodging:
Revere - 5 miles, Cambridge - 5 miles, Brookline - 5 miles, Somerville - 6 miles, Arlington - 8 miles, Braintree - 9 miles, Saugus - 9 miles, Newton - 9 miles, Dedham - 10 miles, Needham - 10 miles.

★★★★
Ames, A Morgans Original Hotel
1 Court Street
Boston MA 02108
(617) 979-8100
$305 - $397
SAVE –B&P Discount Available

Pet Policy: Pets accepted, $100 per stay.

Features: Parking (valet), Concierge, Number of rooms: 113, Number of suites: 12, Number of floors: 14, Porter/bellhop, Doorman/doorwoman, Meeting rooms, 24-hour business center, Restaurant, Accessible bathroom, Dry cleaning/laundry service, Wireless Internet (additional charge), Smoke-free property, Fitness facilities.

★★★
Boston Hotel Buckminster
645 Beacon St
Boston MA 02215
(617) 830-1236
$158 - $249
SAVE –B&P Discount Available

Pet Policy: Guests are permitted to have one dog per room. Dogs may not be left in a room unattended at any time. Should you require a pet sitter, our Front Desk would be happy to assist you with advance notice by dialing zero on your room telephone. Dogs must be well behaved and mild mannered while in the hotel. *Continued on next page;*

Boston Hotel Buckminster
Continued from previous page.

We reserve the right to require immediate removal of any dog that displays dangerous or unacceptable behavior, Including but not limited to biting, excessive barking, evidence of disease, or urination or defecation in public areas. You will be responsible for all charges relating to the removal of your pet including transportation and kennel charges. Guests will be responsible for all damages caused to the room by their pets. This includes, but is not limited to scratches, broken furniture, and carpet damage. There will be a $75 deep cleaning charge for your stay that will be posted to your account upon check-in. This fee is nonrefundable. The Boston Hotel Buckminster reserves the right to ask you to change rooms or vacate the hotel should the behavior of your dog cause a disturbance to other guests. We also require that you agree and understand that any compensation, financial or otherwise, issued to another guest who may have been disturbed by your dog during their stay, will be added to your account to be paid in full at check out. We require that you provide us with a contact telephone number so that we may contact you at any time during your stay.

Features: Year Built 1897, Concierge, Number of rooms: 94, Number of suites: 38, Number of floors: 6, Suitable for children, Air-conditioned public areas, Parking (additional charge), Free breakfast, Porter/bellhop, Dry cleaning/laundry service, Meeting rooms (small groups), Smoke-free property, Nearby fitness center (discount), Accessible bathroom, 24-hour business center, Restaurant(s).

★★★★♥
Boston Omni Parker House Hotel
60 School St
Boston MA 02108
(617) 227-8600
$179 - $389
SAVE –B&P Discount Available

Pet Policy: Pets under 25 lbs accepted, $50 cleaning fee per stay.

Features: Year Built 1855, Currency Exchange, Restaurant(s), Gift shop, Number of rooms: 551, Number of floors: 15, , Air-conditioned public areas, Wireless Internet, Porter/bellhop, Meeting rooms (small groups), Smoke-free property, Bar/Lounge, Dry cleaning/laundry service, Concierge, Suitable for children, Breakfast available (additional charge), Free newspapers in lobby, Accessible bathroom, 24-hour business center, Doorman/doorwoman, Room service (24 hours), Security guard, Parking (valet) $39 Per Day, Fitness facilities.

★★
Chandler Inn
26 Chandler St
Boston MA 02116
(617) 482-3450
$179 - $279
SAVE –B&P Discount Available

Pet Policy: Dogs only, up to 25 lbs, accepted.

Features: Bar/Lounge, Number of rooms: 56, Number of floors: 8, Elevator, Air-conditioned public areas, Fax machine, Multilingual staff, Free newspapers in lobby, 24-hour front desk, Wireless Internet, Nearby fitness center (discount), Concierge services, Coffee in lobby.

★★★
Charles Street Inn
94 Charles St
Boston MA 02114
(617) 314-8900
$298 - $385
SAVE –B&P Discount Available

Pet Policy: Small dogs accepted with prior approval, no fee. Please contact hotel directly for reservations.

Features: Number of rooms: 9, Elevator, Smoke-free property, Accessible bathroom, Handicapped parking, Free breakfast, Library, Video library, Laundry facilities, Babysitting or child care, On-site car rental, 24-hour front desk, Parking nearby (additional charge), Luggage storage.

Not Rated
Churchill At Boston View
130 Bowdoin Street
Boston MA 02108
(617) 742-6485
$120 - $140

Pet Policy: Pets accepted. Please contact hotel directly for restrictions and pet reservations.

Features: Extended stay hotel, Car rental desk, Family room.

★★★
Comfort Inn Boston
900 Morrissey Blvd
Boston MA 02122
(617) 287-9200
$137 - $169
SAVE –B&P Discount Available

Pet Policy: Accepts pets up to 70 lbs, $25 per pet per night. Limit of 2 per room.

Features: Handicapped parking, In-room accessibility, Airport transportation (free), Room service, Concierge, Gift shop, Number of rooms: 132, Arcade/game room, Pool table, Parking (free), Free newspapers in lobby, Business center, Dry cleaning/laundry service, Free breakfast, Smoke-free property, Wireless Internet, Fitness facilities.

Not Rated
Copley House
239 West Newton Street
Boston MA 02116
(617) 236-8300
$130 - $215

Pet Policy: Dogs accepted, no fee. Dog park nearby.

Features: Furnished apartments with full kitchens, Wireless Internet.

★★★★
Copley Square Hotel
47 Huntington Ave
Boston MA 02116
(866) 891-2174
$249 - $512
SAVE –B&P Discount Available

Pet Policy: Pets under 30 lbs accepted, $40 per stay fee.

Features: Year Built 1891, Currency Exchange, Restaurant(s), Number of rooms: 143, Number of floors: 7, Elevator, Breakfast available, Nightclub, Shoe shine, Room service, 24-hour front desk, Porter/bellhop, Doorman/doorwoman, Wireless Internet, Concierge desk, Smoke-free property, Business services, Security guard, Dry cleaning/laundry service, Bar/lounge, Coffee in lobby, Fitness facilities, Parking (valet) $42 per day.

★★★★
DoubleTree Suites by Hilton Boston - Cambridge
400 Soldiers Field Rd
Boston MA 02134
(617) 783-0090
$173 - $259
SAVE –B&P Discount Available

Pet Policy: Pets up to 75 lbs accepted, doggie bed and bowls provided. With pre-approval, there are a limited number of suites that allow pets. It is advised to book directly with the hotel. We do request that guests with pets avoid public areas by using our service entrance and elevators for hotel access.

Features: Restaurant(s), Room service, Concierge services, Number of rooms: 308, Wireless Internet (additional charge), Health club, Free newspapers in lobby, 24-hour front desk, Security guard, Smoke-free property, Indoor pool, Business center, Parking (additional), Bar/lounge, Dry cleaning/laundry service, On-site car rental, Shopping on site.

★★★★♥⛵
Fairmont Battery Wharf Boston
Three Battery Wharf
Boston MA 02109-1006
(617) 994-9000
$288 - $559
SAVE –B&P Discount Available

Pet Policy: Pets up to 25 lbs welcome, $25 per day. Pets must be leashed when in public areas, and may not be left alone in room.

Features: Wireless Internet, Health club, Parking nearby, Spa services on site, Beauty services, Full-service health spa, Massage - spa treatment room(s), Steam room, Sauna, Dry cleaning/laundry service, Breakfast available (additional charge), Room service (24 hours), Shoe shine, Free newspapers in lobby, Security guard, Music library, Media library, Accessible bathroom, Handicapped parking, In-room accessibility, 24-hour business center, Bar/lounge, Restaurant(s), Concierge services, Number of rooms: 150, Number of floors: 5, Elevator, Computer rental, Suitable for children, Fireplace in lobby, Babysitting or child care, Multilingual staff, 24-hour front desk, Porter/bellhop,

Fairmont Battery Wharf Boston
Continued from previous page

Doorman/doorwoman, Limo or Town Car service available, Meeting rooms, Smoke-free property, Parking - $40 for 24 hours, Patio, Marina on site, Wedding services, Air-conditioned public areas, Shopping on site, On-site car rental, Currency exchange, Area shuttle (additional charge), Rooftop terrace, Luggage storage.

★★★★✦♥
Fifteen Beacon
15 Beacon St
Boston MA 02108
(877) 982-3226
$375 - $1,425
SAVE –B&P Discount Available

Pet Policy: For those who are traveling with their furry friends, well behaved dogs are always welcome. Pamper your pup with homemade healthy dog biscuits, a plush bed and turn down water. Dog sitting and walking can be arranged prior to arrival. 100% of your optional $25 pet donation goes to the MSPCA Angell Memorial hospital.

Features: Accessible bathroom, Handicapped parking, Dry cleaning/laundry service, Wireless Internet, Babysitting or child care, Parking (valet – additional charge), Airport transportation (additional charge), Air-conditioned public areas, Multilingual staff, Porter/bellhop, Doorman/doorwoman, Limo or Town Car service available, Concierge desk, Meeting rooms (small groups), Smoke-free property, Fitness facilities, Bar/lounge, Restaurant(s), On-site car rental, Shopping on site, Shoe shine, Room service, 24-hour front desk, Luggage storage.

★★★★★♥
Four Seasons Boston
200 Boylston St
Boston MA 02116
(617) 338-4400
$475 - $2,235
SAVE –B&P Discount Available

Pet Policy: Small pets welcome, no fee. Limit 2 per room. Special pet menu available.

Features: Valet parking (additional), Bar/lounge, Babysitting or child care, Full-service health spa, Indoor pool, Restaurant(s), Number of rooms: 273, Number of suites: 77, Conference room(s), Business services, Room service (24 hours), Concierge, Meeting rooms, Steam room, Sauna, Smoke-free property, Wireless Internet (additional charge), Beauty services, Massage - treatment room(s).

★★★✦
Hilton Boston Back Bay
40 Dalton St
Boston MA 02115
(617) 236-1100
$189 - $389
SAVE –B&P Discount Available

Pet Policy: Pets up to 75 lbs, $50 per stay. Limited beds/bowls provided.

Features: Fitness facilities, Babysitting or child care, Bar/lounge, Indoor pool, Restaurant(s), Number of rooms: 390, Cell phone/mobile rental, Secretarial services, ***Continued on next page***

Hilton Boston Back Bay
Continued from previous page

Translation services, Wireless Internet (additional charge), Coffee shop, Multilingual staff, 24-hour front desk, Business center, Porter/bellhop, Security guard, Smoke-free property, Room service, Air-conditioned public areas, Self-parking (additional charge), On-site car rental, Concierge services, Shopping on site, Currency exchange, Dry cleaning/laundry service, Luggage storage.

★★★★
Hilton Boston Financial District
89 Broad St
Boston MA 02110
(617) 556-0006
$203- $459
SAVE –B&P Discount Available

Pet Policy: Pets up to 75 lbs, $75 per stay. Limited beds/bowls provided.

Features: Sauna, Conference Room(s), Bar/Lounge, Babysitting or child care, Dry cleaning/laundry service, Restaurant(s), Parking (valet – additional charge), Concierge, Number of rooms: 362, Translation services, Computer rental, Air-conditioned public areas, Wireless Internet (additional charge), Free newspapers in lobby, 24-hour front desk, Business center, Porter/bellhop, Medical assistance available, Nearby fitness center (discount), Library, Security guard, Shoe shine, Doorman/doorwoman, Room service (limited hours), Shopping on site, Room service, Luggage storage.

★★★★
Hilton Boston Logan Airport
One Hotel Drive
Boston MA 02128
(617) 568-6700
$179 - $359
SAVE –B&P Discount Available

Pet Policy: Pets up to 75 lbs. Pet fee: $25.

Features: Indoor pool, Business center, Dry cleaning/laundry service, Bar/lounge, Room service, Airport transportation (free), 3 Restaurants, Parking (valet – additional charge), Concierge, Number of rooms: 599, Conference room(s), Secretarial services, Computer rental, Air-conditioned public areas, Wireless Internet (additional charge), Currency exchange, Health club, Free newspapers in lobby, Porter/bellhop, Doorman/doorwoman, Security guard, Limo or Town Car service available, Smoke-free property, Airport transportation (free) available 24 hours, Shopping on site.

★★★★
Hotel Commonwealth
500 Commonwealth Ave
Boston MA 02215
(617) 933-5000
$239 - $459
SAVE –B&P Discount Available

Pet Policy: Guests are permitted to have one dog per guest room. A $125 deep cleaning charge for your stay will be posted to your account upon check in. Hotel Commonwealth reserves the right to ask you to change rooms or vacate the hotel should the behavior of your dog cause a disturbance to other guests. *Continued on next page*

Hotel Commonwealth
Continued from previous page

We also require that you agree to and understand that any compensation, financial or otherwise, issued to another guest who may have been disturbed by your dog during their stay, will be added to your account. You must provide us with a contact telephone number so that we may contact you at any time during your stay.

Please call Reservations directly to book a room for you and your pet.

Dog amenities are available upon request.

Dogs may not be left in a guest room unattended at any time. Should you require a pet sitter our Concierge would be happy to assist you with advance notice by dialing our Concierge at 617.532.5001.

Dogs must be well behaved and mild mannered while in the hotel. We reserve the right to require immediate removal of any dog that displays dangerous or unacceptable behavior, including but not limited to biting, excessive barking, evidence of disease, or urination or defecation in public areas.

Guests will be responsible for any damage caused to the room by their pets. This includes, but is not limited to scratches, broken furniture, and carpet damage.

Features: Shoe Shine, Bar/Lounge, Concierge, Dry cleaning/laundry service, Suitable for children, Health club, Smoke-free property, Wireless Internet, 24-hour business center, Shopping on site, Accessible bathroom, Room service (24 hours), Wedding services, Coffee in lobby, Video library, Valet parking (additional charge), Restaurant(s), Number of rooms: 150, Number of floors: 5, Porter/bellhop, Doorman/doorwoman, Security guard, Meeting rooms (small groups), Library, Rooftop terrace, Luggage storage.

★★
Howard Johnson Inn Fenway
1271 Boylston St
Boston MA 02215
(617) 267-8300
$119 - $199
SAVE –B&P Discount Available

Pet Policy: Pet friendly.

Features: Restaurant, Room service (limited hours), Business services, Parking (additional charge), Free newspapers in lobby, Outdoor pool - seasonal, Bar/lounge, Designated smoking areas.

★★★★
Hyatt Regency Boston
1 Avenue De Lafayette
Boston MA 02111
(617) 912-1234
$174- $474
SAVE –B&P Discount Available

Pet Policy: Pets welcome. Special pet packages available, call hotel directly for details and reservations. With Boston Common just steps from the front door, your pet can play with a new, Larry the Lobstah dog toy. Review the Dog Lover's Companion to Boston book for walking paths, pet friendly restaurants and much more.

Features: Currency Exchange, Sauna, Business Center, Bar/Lounge, Accessible bathroom, Handicapped parking, In-room accessibility, Restaurant(s), Room service (limited hours), Number of rooms: 500, Number of floors: 22, Breakfast available (additional charge), Wireless Internet, Multilingual staff, 24-hour front desk, Porter/bellhop, Doorman/doorwoman, Meeting rooms (small groups), Security guard, Indoor pool, Dry cleaning/laundry service, Steam room, Designated smoking areas, Wedding services, Concierge desk, Health club, Parking ($32 Daily).

★★★★✦
InterContinental Boston
510 Atlantic Ave
Boston MA 02210
(617) 747-1000
$217 - $664
SAVE –B&P Discount Available

Pet Policy: Pets up to 25 lbs accepted, $150 per night additional. Limit 1 pet per room.

Features: Poolside bar, Dry cleaning/laundry service, Accessible bathroom, Handicapped parking, In-room accessibility, Restaurant(s), Gift shop, Number of rooms: 424, Number of suites: 38, Number of floors: 12, Elevator, Conference room(s), Cell phone/mobile rental, Business services, Air-conditioned public areas, Multilingual staff, Free newspapers in lobby, Room service, Porter/bellhop, Concierge desk, Wireless Internet (additional charge), Smoke-free property, Concierge services, Indoor pool, Business center, Babysitting or child care, Health club, Currency exchange, Bar/lounge, Parking (valet) $39 Per Day, On-site car rental, Shopping on site, Garden, Shoe shine, 24-hour front desk, Sauna.

★★★★★
Mandarin Oriental Boston
776 Boylston St
Boston MA 02199
(617) 535-8888
$495 - $1,219
SAVE –B&P Discount Available

Pet Policy: Dogs and cats accepted, no fee.

Features: Dry cleaning/laundry service, Bar/lounge, Restaurant(s), Number of rooms: 148, Number of floors: 8, Elevator, Floor butler, Translation services, Fireplace in lobby, Coffee in lobby, Room service (24 hours), Spa services on site, Accessible bathroom,

Mandarin Oriental Boston
Continued from previous page

In-room accessibility, Wireless Internet (additional charge), Gift shop, Airport transportation (additional charge), Multilingual staff, Porter/bellhop, Limo or Town Car service available, Massage - treatment room(s), Meeting rooms (small groups), Smoke-free property, On-site medical assistance available, Valet parking (additional charge), Doorman/doorwoman, Fitness facilities, Babysitting or child care, Steam room, Supervised child care/activities, Conference room(s), Air-conditioned public areas, Wedding services, Currency exchange, Business center, Concierge desk, Full-service health spa, Hair salon, On-site car rental, Shopping on site, Shoe shine, Room service, 24-hour front desk, Sauna.

★★★★
Nine Zero Hotel - a Kimpton Hotel
90 Tremont St
Boston MA 02108
(617) 772-5800
$238- $399
SAVE –B&P Discount Available

Pet Policy: Pets welcome. No size restriction. No Fees. Special pet amenities include treats, bowls, tags with hotel info, and even pet packages with special food, dog walking, and toys

Features: Bar/Lounge, Accessible bathroom, Handicapped parking, Spa services on site, 24-hour business center, Free reception, Dry cleaning/laundry service, Wireless Internet, Shoe shine, Smoke-free property (fines apply), Room service (24 hours), Conference room(s), Valet parking (additional charge), Fitness facilities, Restaurant(s), Number of rooms: 190, Number of floors: 19, 24-hour front desk, Porter/bellhop, Meeting rooms (small groups), Babysitting or child care.

Not Rated
Oakwood Boston
One India Street
Boston MA 02109
(800) 724-9660
$180 - $236

Pet Policy: Pets accepted, $10 per day to a maximum of $300.

Features: Extended stay fully furnished apartments, fully equipped kitchens, Washer & Dryer in Suites. May require 30 day minimum stay.

★★★★
Onyx Hotel - a Kimpton Hotel
155 Portland St
Boston MA 02114
(617) 557-9955
$239 - $340
SAVE –B&P Discount Available

Pet Policy: Pets welcome. No size restriction. No Fees. Special pet amenities include treats, bowls, tags with hotel info, and even pet packages with special food, dog walking, and toys

Continued on next page

Onyx Hotel - a Kimpton Hotel
Continued from previous page

Features: Shoe Shine, Currency Exchange, Restaurant(s), Parking (valet), Number of rooms: 112, Number of floors: 11, Elevator, Conference room(s), Air-conditioned public areas, Breakfast available (additional charge), Multilingual staff, Free newspapers in lobby, 24-hour front desk, Porter/bellhop, Meeting rooms (small groups), Smoke-free property, Wedding services, Bar/Lounge, Concierge desk, Spa services on site, 24-hour business center, Free reception, Dry cleaning/laundry service, Wireless Internet, Room service (24 hours), Parking (valet) $40/day, Fitness facilities.

★★½

Ramada Inn Boston
800 Morrissey Blvd
Boston MA 02122
(617) 287-9100
$119 - $159
SAVE –B&P Discount Available

Pet Policy: Pets accepted, no additional fee.

Features: Elevator, Restaurant(s), Airport transportation (additional charge), Conference room(s), Wireless Internet (additional charge), Pool table, Free breakfast, Currency exchange, Outdoor pool - seasonal, Parking (additional charge), RV and truck parking, Outdoor pool, Arcade/game room, Business center, Dry cleaning/laundry service, Airport transportation, Area shuttle (free), 24-hour front desk, Luggage storage

★★★

Residence Inn by Marriott Boston Harbor on Tudor
34-44 Charles River Ave
Boston MA 02129
(617) 242 9000
$248 - $339
SAVE –B&P Discount Available

Pet Policy: Pets allowed, $100 cleaning fee per stay.

Features: Free Breakfast, Business Center, Indoor pool, Dry cleaning/laundry service, Valet parking (additional charge), Fitness facilities, Restaurant(s), Room service, Parking (valet), Number of rooms: 168, Number of floors: 8, Elevator, Conference room(s), Business services, Air-conditioned public areas, Coffee in lobby, Grocery, Free newspapers in lobby, 24-hour front desk, Wireless Internet, Meeting rooms (small groups), Babysitting or child care, Concierge services, Barbecue grill(s), Airport transportation, Area shuttle (additional charge).

★★★★

Seaport Boston Hotel
1 Seaport Lane
Boston MA 02210
(617) 385-4000
$218 - $339
SAVE –B&P Discount Available

Pet Policy: Accepts dogs under 50 lbs. No additional fee. May not leave alone in room. Everyone is welcome to join us for Yappy Hour, held each Wednesday at TAMO Terrace! Bring your four-legged friend and mix & mingle with other dog owners!

Seaport Boston Hotel
Continued from previous page

Features: Number of rooms: 428, Bar/lounge, Indoor pool, Concierge, Dry cleaning/laundry service, Wireless Internet, Health club, Steam room, Security guard, Restaurant(s), On-site car rental, Gift shop, Number of rooms: 426, Number of floors: 18, Air-conditioned public areas, Currency exchange, Coffee shop, Shoe shine, Multilingual staff, Free newspapers in lobby, Room service, 24-hour front desk, Porter/bellhop, Doorman/doorwoman, Beauty services, Full-service health spa, Massage - treatment room(s), Meeting rooms, 24-hour business center.

★★★★
Sheraton Boston Hotel
39 Dalton St
Boston MA 02199
(617) 236-2000
$229 - $479
SAVE –B&P Discount Available

Pet Policy: Pets are allowed without additional fee. Pets must be accompanied by owner at all times on leash or in a crate. Waiver must be signed at check-in. Guest will be responsible for costs if excess damage or deep cleaning is required. If damage is discovered after checkout, credit card on record will be charged.

Features: Restaurant(s), Concierge services, Number of rooms: 1,215, Conference room(s), Computer rental, Coffee shop, Health club, 24-hour front desk, Porter/bellhop, Limo or Town Car service available, Wireless Internet, Currency Exchange, Business Center, Bar/Lounge, Indoor pool, Dry cleaning/laundry service, Air-conditioned public areas, Room service, Security guard, Shopping on site, Sauna, Shoe shine, Parking - $38/day, Outdoor pool, Room service, Luggage storage.

★★★★✦
Taj Boston
15 Arlington St
Boston MA 02116
(617) 536-5700
$298 - $450
SAVE –B&P Discount Available

Pet Policy: Small pets up to 20 lbs accepted, $150 per stay fee.

Features: Year Built 1927, Accessible bathroom, Restaurant(s), Number of rooms: 273, Airport transportation (additional charge), Computer rental, Air-conditioned public areas, Wireless Internet, 24-hour front desk, Doorman/doorwoman, Limo or Town Car service available, Medical assistance available, Massage - treatment room(s), Meeting rooms, Dry cleaning/laundry service, Bar/lounge, Wedding services, Babysitting or child care, Room service (24 hours), Currency exchange, Concierge, Translation services, Business center, Valet parking (additional charge), Shopping on site, Shoe shine, Security guard, Fitness facilities, Luggage storage.

★★★☆
**The Boston Park Plaza Hotel &
Towers**
50 Park Plaza at Arlington
Street
Boston MA 02116-3912
(617) 426-2000
$99 - $449
SAVE –B&P Discount Available

Pet Policy: Pets welcome without size restrictions.
$50 additional cleaning fee per stay. Inquire with our
concierge about dog sitting or walking services by
calling 617.654.1912. There are plenty of walking
options for your pet-just outside the hotel entry there
are a host of options available within 2 - 5 blocks of
the hotel

Features: Year Built 1927, Currency Exchange, Shoe
Shine, Concierge, Bar/lounge, Dry cleaning/laundry
service, Restaurant(s), Shopping on site, Number of
rooms: 941, Number of floors: 15, Air-conditioned
public areas, Wireless Internet (additional),
Doorman/doorwoman, Security guard, Meeting
rooms, Business center, Room service (24 hours),
Porter/bellhop, Designated smoking areas, Valet
parking (additional charge), Beauty services, Health
club.

★★★☆
The Bulfinch Hotel
107 Merrimac St
Boston MA 02114
(617) 624-0202
$177 - $699
SAVE –B&P Discount Available

Pet Policy: Pets up to 50 lbs accepted with a nightly
fee.

Features; Bar/Lounge, Restaurant(s), Number of
rooms: 80, Number of floors: 9, Free newspapers in
lobby, Doorman/doorwoman, Smoke-free property,
Dry cleaning/laundry service, Room service,
Concierge, Parking $25/day, Fitness facilities,
Business center, Area shuttle (additional charge).

★★★★
The Colonnade Hotel Back Bay
120 Huntington Avenue
Boston MA 02116
(617) 424-7000
$199 - $1,109
SAVE –B&P Discount Available

Pet Policy: Dogs and cats welcome. We are pleased
to offer free use of one of our fluffy pet beds and
food bowl. Please contact our housekeeping
department at extension 3236 for delivery. We offer
three brands of dry dog and cat food in case your pet
had a larger appetite than you planned for. We offer
Purina One, Iams and Pedigree dog food brands for
your convenience. Please dial our Concierge at
extension 3228. The Colonnade Hotel is happy to
provide pet walking services through our Concierge.

A service fee of $15 per walk will be added to your
bill. This fee is in lieu of a gratuity, and will be paid to
the staff member that cares for your pet.

Our Concierge staff is happy to assist you in

The Colonnade Hotel Back Bay
Continued from previous page

arranging for veterinarian services, pet sitting services, dog grooming and spa services for our welcome guest. As a small favor, we would be extremely grateful if you signed our Pet Register at the Front Desk. This way, we can add you to our list of pet members and you will be entitled to special benefits and offers for future visits.

Features: Accessible bathroom, Handicapped parking, Bar/lounge, Dry cleaning/laundry service, 2 Restaurants, Supervised child care/activities, Number of rooms: 285, Number of floors: 11, Cell phone/mobile rental, Computer rental, Free newspapers in lobby, Concierge, Porter/bellhop, Doorman/doorwoman, Limo or Town Car service available, Medical assistance available, Outdoor pool - seasonal, Shoe shine, Concierge, Currency exchange, Room service (24 hours), Translation services, Wedding services, Security guard, Parking (valet) $36 Per Day, Wireless Internet, Smoke-free property, Poolside bar, Health club, Meeting rooms (small groups), 24-hour business center.

★★★★♥
The Eliot Hotel
370 Commonwealth Ave
Boston MA 02215
(888) 379-6794
$255 - $545
SAVE –B&P Discount Available

Pet Policy: Pets welcome, no fee or size limits. Pet sitting service offered through the concierge.

Features: Year Built 1925, Bar/lounge, Business center, Accessible bathroom, Handicapped parking, In-room accessibility, Babysitting or child care, Dry cleaning/laundry service, 2 Restaurants, Concierge, Number of suites: 95, Number of floors: 9, Secretarial services, Translation services, Computer rental, Air-conditioned public areas, Room service (24 hours), Shoe shine, Free newspapers in lobby, Nearby fitness center (free), 24-hour front desk, Porter/bellhop, Doorman/doorwoman, Limo or Town Car service available, Meeting rooms (small groups), Parking (valet) $34.00/day, Smoke-free property, Wireless Internet (additional charge).

★★★★♪♥
The Fairmont Copley Plaza
138 Saint James Ave
Boston MA 02116
(617) 267-5300
$268 - $459
SAVE –B&P Discount Available

Pet Policy: Pets any size are welcome, $25 per night additional. Pets must be leashed in public areas and never left alone in room.

Features: Year Built 1912, Currency Exchange, Restaurant(s), Concierge services, Gift shop, Number of rooms: 383, Elevator, Conference room(s), Translation services, ***Continued on next page***

The Fairmont Copley Plaza
Continued from previous page

Computer rental, Wireless Internet (additional charge), Ski storage, Room service (24 hours), Shoe shine, Multilingual staff, Free newspapers in lobby, Room service, 24-hour front desk, Doorman/doorwoman, Security guard, Limo or Town Car service available, Porter/bellhop, Handicapped parking, In-room accessibility, Secretarial services, Babysitting or child care, Dry cleaning/laundry service, Bar/lounge, Designated smoking areas, Valet parking (additional charge), Fitness facilities, Shopping on site.

★★★★✦♥
The Langham, Boston
250 Franklin St
Boston MA 02110
(617) 451-1900
$244 - $595
SAVE –B&P Discount Available

Pet Policy: Pets under 50 lbs accepted, $100 per stay fee.

Features: Year Built 1922, Sauna, Currency Exchange, Handicapped parking, In-room accessibility, 2 Restaurants, Number of rooms: 318, Number of floors: 9, Elevator, Secretarial services, Air-conditioned public areas, Wireless Internet (additional charge), Shoe shine, Multilingual staff, Free newspapers in lobby, 24-hour front desk, Doorman/doorwoman, Security guard, Massage - treatment room(s), Meeting rooms (small groups), Smoke-free property, Concierge desk, Indoor pool, Dry cleaning/laundry service, Bar/lounge, Room service (24 hours), Health club, Gift shop, Coffee in lobby, Wedding services, Conference room(s), Business center, Spa services on site, Valet parking (additional charge), Babysitting or child care, Shopping on site, Luggage storage.

★★★★♥
The Lenox Hotel Boston
61 Exeter Street
Boston MA 02116
(800) 653-9734
$175 - $526
SAVE –B&P Discount Available

Pet Policy: Small pets accepted, $125 per stay fee.

Features: Year Built 1900, Currency Exchange, Restaurant(s), Number of rooms: 212, Number of floors: 11, Breakfast available, Wireless Internet, Multilingual staff, 24-hour front desk, Porter/bellhop, Meeting rooms, Doorman/doorwoman, Smoke-free, Dry cleaning/laundry service, Air-conditioned public areas, Fireplace in lobby, Bar/lounge, Concierge Room service, Designated smoking areas, Security guard, Shoe shine, Wedding services, Valet parking (additional charge), Fitness facilities, Accessible bathroom, Coffee in lobby, 24-hour business center.

★★★★✦♥
The Liberty Hotel
215 Charles St
Boston MA 02114
(617) 224-4000
$248. - $358
SAVE –B&P Discount Available

Pet Policy: Small pets accepted, $100 per stay cleaning fee.

Features: Year Built 1851, Wireless Internet, Shoe shine, Porter/bellhop, Security guard, Limo or Town Car service, Meeting rooms, Dry cleaning/laundry service Smoke-free property, Wedding services, Restaurant(s), Number of rooms: 300, Concierge, Business center, Bar/lounge, Parking (valet) $42 Per Night, Fitness facilities, Room service (24 hours), Doorman/doorwoman,.

★★✦
The Midtown Hotel
220 Huntington Ave
Boston MA 02115
(617) 262-1000
$149 - $259
SAVE –B&P Discount Available

Pet Policy: We are pleased to be able to welcome your gentle, well socialized dog to join you at The Midtown Hotel, $30 per stay pet fee. We will have dishes for food and water, pickup bags, and treats waiting for your canine friend in your room. Dogs must be kept on leash when in any public or common space. Dogs may not be brought into the pool area. We ask that you crate your dog if it is to be left unattended in your room at any time.

Features: Hair salon, Concierge, Gift shop, Number of rooms: 159, Conference room(s), Limo or Town Car service, Smoke-free property, Outdoor pool - seasonal, Dry cleaning/laundry service, Security guard, Wireless Internet (fee), Parking limited (fee).

★★★★★
The Ritz-Carlton, Boston Common
10 Avery St
Boston MA 02111
(617) 574-7100
$395 - $665
SAVE –B&P Discount Available

Pet Policy: Accepts pets under 60 lbs, $30 fee. Homemade dog biscuits and other treats are prepared by the pastry chef. The concierge can arrange for walks and pet sitters.

Features: Dry cleaning/laundry service, Computer rental, Babysitting or child care, Room service (24 hours), Concierge, Wedding services, Shopping on site, Hair salon, Conference room(s), Parking (valet – additional charge), Security guard, Currency exchange, Secretarial services, Translation services, Cell phone/mobile rental, Bar/lounge, Wireless Internet (additional charge), Restaurant(s), Number of rooms: 193, Number of floors: 7, Shoe shine, Free newspapers, Porter/bellhop, Business center, Limo or Town Car service, Medical assistance available, Indoor pool, Health club, Doorman/doorwoman,.

★★★★
The Westin Boston Waterfront
425 Summer St
Boston MA 02210
(617) 532-4600
$179 - $524
SAVE –B&P Discount Available

Pet Policy: Accepts dogs up to 75 lbs. No additional fee but responsible for any damages.

Features: Handicapped parking, In-room accessibility, Number of restaurants 4, Dry cleaning/laundry service, Gift shop, Number of rooms: 793, Number of floors: 16, Computer rental, Suitable for children, Air-conditioned public areas, Breakfast available, Wireless Internet, Health club, Multilingual staff, 24-hour front desk, Porter/bellhop, Doorman/doorwoman, Concierge desk, Meeting rooms (small groups), Smoke-free property, Children's club, Business center, Indoor pool, Room service (24 hours), Bar/lounge, Currency exchange, Security guard, Conference room(s), Wedding services, Parking $32 Daily, Fitness facilities.

★★★★
The Westin Copley Place
10 Huntington Ave
Boston MA 02116
(617) 262-9600
$258 - $449
SAVE –B&P Discount Available

Pet Policy: Dogs up to 40 pounds are allowed without additional fee. Acceptance of any other pet is at the hotel's discretion and must be discussed with the General Manager. Guests are required to sign a waiver form at check-in.

Features: Year Built 1877, Indoor pool, Dry cleaning/laundry service, Bar/lounge, Spa services Airport transportation (additional charge), Shoe shine, Business center, Concierge desk, Room service (24 hours), Babysitting or child care, On-site car rental, Wireless Internet (additional charge), Parking limited (additional), Restaurant(s), Shopping on site, Number of rooms: 800, Fireplace in lobby, Breakfast available, Doorman/doorwoman, Health club, Multilingual staff, 24-hour front desk, Porter/bellhop, Security guard, Limo or Town Car service available, Beauty services, Meeting rooms (small groups).

★★★★
W Boston
100 Stuart Street
Boston MA 02116
(617) 261-8700
$229 - $499
SAVE –B&P Discount Available

Pet Policy: We welcome cats and dogs 40 pounds or less. Guests must sign a waiver upon check-in and there is a one-time, non-refundable $50 cleaning fee regardless of length of stay.

Features: Handicapped parking, In-room accessibility, Dry cleaning/laundry service, Wireless Internet, 3 Restaurants, Bar/lounge, Full-service

W Boston
Continued from previous page

health spa, Concierge services, Shopping on site, Number of rooms: 235, Number of suites: 24, Number of floors: 15, Porter/bellhop, Limo or Town Car service available, Meeting rooms (small groups), Smoke-free property, Wedding services, Valet parking (additional charge), Babysitting or child care, Currency exchange, Health club, Room service, 24-hour front desk, Business center, Luggage storage.

Boxborough

Also see the following nearby communities that have pet friendly lodging:
Westford - 9 miles, Marlborough - 9 miles.

★★★
Holiday Inn Boxborough
242 Adams Pl
Boxborough MA 01719
(978) 263-8701
$119 - $253
SAVE –B&P Discount Available

Pet Policy: Pets welcome, $25 per stay fee plus $100 refundable damage deposit. Pets may not be left in room unattended.

Features: Area shuttle (free), Handicapped parking, In-room accessibility, Restaurant(s), Number of rooms: 143, Number of floors: 3, Business services, Parking (free), 24-hour front desk, Wireless Internet, Meeting rooms (small groups), Indoor pool, Dry cleaning/laundry service, Bar/lounge, Room service (limited hours), Fitness facilities.

Braintree

Also see the following nearby communities that have pet friendly lodging:
Boston - 9 miles, Brockton - 9 miles.

★★ 🏊
Candlewood Suites
235 Wood Rd
Braintree MA 02184
(781) 849-7450
$115 - $140
SAVE –B&P Discount Available

Pet Policy: Pets allowed with a nonrefundable fee of $15 for the first night and $10 for each additional night up to a maximum of $150. Size limit is 80 lbs. A record of complete and up-to-date vaccinations may be required.

Features: Accessible bathroom, Handicapped parking, Dry cleaning/laundry service, Number of suites: 133, Number of floors: 4, Elevator, Parking (free), Video library, Fitness facilities, Shopping on site, 24-hour front desk, Business center.

★★ 🐾
Extended Stay America
20 Rockdale St
Braintree MA 02184
(781) 356-8333
$116 - $144
SAVE – B&P Discount Available

Pet Policy: One pet is allowed in each guest room. A $25 per day non-refundable cleaning fee (not to exceed $150) will be charged the first night of your stay. Weight, size and breed restrictions may apply. Please contact the hotel directly with inquiries.

Features: Laundry facilities, Number of rooms: 103, Number of floors: 3, Elevator, Suitable for children, Parking, Wireless Internet, Nearby fitness center (discount).

★★⌐ 🐾
Hampton Inn Boston/Braintree
215 Wood Rd
Braintree MA 02184
(781) 380-3300
$126 - $209
SAVE – B&P Discount Available

Pet Policy: Pet Friendly

Features: Free Breakfast, indoor pool, Area shuttle (free), Dry cleaning/laundry service, Number of rooms: 103, Number of floors: 4, Elevator, Conference room(s), Air-conditioned public areas, Coffee in lobby, Library, Parking (free), Free newspapers in lobby, 24-hour front desk, Wireless Internet, Fitness facilities, Business center.

Brockton
Also see the following nearby communities that have pet friendly lodging:
Norwood - 8 miles, Braintree - 9 miles, Mansfield - 10 miles.

★★
Quality Inn Brockton
1005 Belmont St
Brockton MA 02301
(508) 588-3333
$109 - $119
SAVE – B&P Discount Available

Pet Policy: Pets accepted, $10 per night per pet. Pets must be kenneled when unattended.

Features: Wireless Internet, Coffee in lobby, Pool table, Business services, Bar/lounge, Number of rooms: 64, Number of floors: 2, Air-conditioned public areas, Free breakfast, Parking (free), 24-hour front desk, Meeting rooms (small groups), Outdoor pool – seasonal.

★★★
Residence Inn By Marriott
124 Liberty St
Brockton MA 02301
(508) 583-3600
$119 - $179
SAVE – B&P Discount Available

Pet Policy: Pets allowed, $100 cleaning fee per stay.

Features: Business services, Indoor pool, Dry cleaning/laundry service, Free breakfast, Tennis on site, Fitness facilities, Number of rooms: 88, Number of floors: 4, Barbecue grill(s), Parking, Multilingual staff, Free newspapers in lobby, Meeting rooms.

Brookline
Also see the following nearby communities that have pet friendly lodging:
Cambridge - 3 miles, Newton - 4 miles, Somerville - 4 miles, Arlington - 5 miles, Boston - 5 miles, Needham - 5 miles, Waltham - 6 miles, Dedham - 6 miles, Revere - 8 miles.

★★★
Holiday Inn Boston-Brookline
1200 Beacon St
Brookline MA 02446
(617) 277-1200
$174 - $299
SAVE –B&P Discount Available

Pet Policy: Pet Friendly. $15 per night.

Features: Restaurant(s), Number of rooms: 225, Elevator, Parking (additional charge), Wireless Internet, Accessible bathroom, Handicapped parking, Business services, Dry cleaning/laundry service, Conference room(s), Bar/lounge, Concierge, Room service, Fitness facilities, Indoor pool.

Burlington
Also see the following nearby communities that have pet friendly lodging:
Billerica - 5 miles, Woburn - 5 miles, Lexington - 6 miles, Arlington - 6 miles, Wakefield - 7 miles, Somerville - 8 miles, Waltham - 9 miles, Cambridge - 9 miles, Saugus - 10 miles.

★★
Candlewood Suites
130 Middlesex Tpke
Burlington MA 01803
(781) 229-4300
$70 - $125
SAVE –B&P Discount Available

Pet Policy: Pets under 80 lbs allowed with nonrefundable fee Up to $75 for 1-6 nights and up to $150 for 7+ nights. Pet agreement must be signed at check-in. Record of complete and up-to-date vaccinations required. No more than 2 pets.

Features: 24-hour front desk, Area shuttle (free), Business services, Parking (free), Handicapped parking, In-room accessibility, Dry cleaning/laundry service, Number of rooms: 149, Number of floors: 4, Video library, Grocery, Concierge, Fitness facilities.

★★
Homestead Boston Burlington
40 South Ave
Burlington MA 01803
(781) 359-9099
$94 - $109
SAVE –B&P Discount Available

Pet Policy: One pet is accepted per guest room, any size. The general manager has the discretion to allow additional pets per room. A pet fee of $25 per day, up to a maximum of $150, is charged. The guest room carpet is cleaned, all bedding is washed, and a professional exterminator treats the room after a guest with a pet checks out. Guest rooms are similarly cleaned monthly in the event of a long-term stay. ***Continued on next page***

Homestead Boston Burlington
Continued from previous page

Features: Dry cleaning/laundry service, Wireless Internet (additional charge), Accessible bathroom, Handicapped parking, Parking, Number of rooms: 140, Number of floors: 3, Elevator.

★★★
Hyatt Summerfield Suites
2 Van De Graaff Dr
Burlington MA 01803
(800) 323-7249
$206 - $259
SAVE –B&P Discount Available

Pet Policy: Small pets accepted, Limit 2 per room. $5 per pet per day plus $150 per stay cleaning fee.

Features: Dry cleaning/laundry service, Fitness facilities, Number of suites: 150, Number of floors: 3, Elevator, Coffee in lobby, Video library, Free breakfast, Parking (free), Free newspapers in lobby, 24-hour front desk, Business center, Security guard, Meeting rooms (small groups), Smoke-free property, Outdoor pool - seasonal.

★★★
Staybridge Suites
11 Old Concord Rd
Burlington MA 01803
(781) 221-2233
$84 - $150
SAVE –B&P Discount Available

Pet Policy: Pets up to 80 lbs accepted, $15 for first night, $10 each additional to a maximum of $150. Also a $150 refundable damage deposit. A record of complete and up-to-date vaccinations required. Guests must sign pet agreement upon check in.

Features: Accessible bathroom, Handicapped parking, Dry cleaning/laundry service, Barbecue grill(s), Outdoor pool, Business center, Gift shop, Number of rooms: 141, Number of floors: 4, Elevator, Air-conditioned public areas, Free breakfast, Grocery, Parking (free), Front desk (limited hours), Wireless Internet, Fitness facilities.

Cambridge
Also see the following nearby communities that have pet friendly lodging:
Somerville - 2 miles, Brookline - 3 miles, Arlington - 3 miles, Boston - 5 miles, Revere - 5 miles, Newton - 6 miles, Waltham - 6 miles, Saugus - 8 miles, Needham - 8 miles, Woburn - 8 miles, Dedham - 9 miles, Wakefield - 9 miles.

★★★
Best Western Plus Hotel
220 Alewife Brook Pkwy
Cambridge MA 02138
(617) 491-8000
$152 - $229
SAVE –B&P Discount Available

Pet Policy: Pets allowed based on the availability of pet friendly rooms. Up to 2 dogs per room with an 80 pound weight limit. Additional pet types (cats, birds, etc.) may be accepted at the hotel's discretion. Pet rate is $20.00 per day with a $100 per week maximum.

Features: Number of rooms: 121, Number of floors: 4, Coffee in lobby, Free breakfast, Accessible

Best Western Plus Hotel
Continued from previous page

bathroom, Handicapped parking, In-room accessibility, Elevator, Area shuttle (free), Bar/lounge, Parking (additional charge), Dry cleaning/laundry service, 24-hour business center, Gift shop, Conference room(s), Suitable for children, Patio, Health club, On-site medical assistance available, RV and truck parking, Restaurant, Room service (limited hours), Concierge services, Pool table, Pick up service from train station, Air-conditioned public areas, Multilingual staff, Free newspapers in lobby, 24-hour front desk, Wireless Internet, Meeting rooms, Fitness facilities.

★★★★
Hotel Marlowe - a Kimpton Hotel
25 Edwin H. Land Blvd
Cambridge MA 02141
(617) 868-8000
$179 - $534
SAVE –B&P Discount Available

Pet Policy: Pets welcome. No size restriction. No Fees. Special pet amenities include treats, bowls, tags with hotel info, and even pet packages with special food, dog walking, and toys

Features: Concierge desk, 24-hour business center, Free reception, Dry cleaning/laundry service, Wireless Internet, Bar/lounge, Room service (24 hours), Conference room(s), Coffee in lobby, Spa services on site, Nearby fitness center (free), Shoe shine, Wedding services, Number of floors 8, Handicapped parking, Parking (valet) $30 Per Day, Restaurant(s), Supervised child care/activities, Number of rooms: 236, Elevator, Air-conditioned public areas, Multilingual staff, 24-hour front desk, Doorman/doorwoman, Medical assistance available, Meeting rooms (small groups), Smoke-free property.

★★★★♥
Hyatt Regency Cambridge
575 Memorial Dr
Cambridge MA 02139
(617) 492-1234
$161 - $370
SAVE –B&P Discount Available

Pet Policy: Pets up to 50 lbs, $50 per stay additional cleaning fee. Limit 1 pet per room.

Features: Piano, Restaurant(s), Concierge services, Gift shop, Number of rooms: 469, Elevator, Air-conditioned public areas, Patio, Currency exchange, Free newspapers in lobby, 24-hour front desk, Porter/bellhop, Doorman/doorwoman, Limo or Town Car service available, Meeting rooms (small groups), Wedding services, Wireless Internet (additional charge), Area shuttle (free), Suitable for children, Shopping center shuttle (free), 24-hour business center, Accessible bathroom, Handicapped parking, Steam room, Sauna, Indoor pool, Health club, Conference room(s), Dry cleaning/laundry service, Bar/lounge, Room service (limited hours), Valet parking (additional charge).

★★★★
Le Meridien Cambridge-MIT
20 Sidney Street
Cambridge MA 02139
(617) 577-0200
$143 - $454
SAVE –B&P Discount Available

Pet Policy: Pets accepted, $150 per stay.

Features: Bar/Lounge, Area shuttle (free), Security guard, Concierge, Dry cleaning/laundry service, Restaurant(s), Room service, Number of rooms: 210, Elevator, Shoe shine, Doorman/doorwoman, Meeting rooms (small groups), Wedding services, Wireless Internet, Porter/bellhop, 24-hour business center, Currency exchange, Valet parking (additional charge), Fitness facilities.

★★★
Residence Inn By Marriott Boston Cambridge Center
6 Cambridge Ctr
Cambridge MA 02142
(617) 349 0700
$269 - $321
SAVE –B&P Discount Available

Pet Policy: Pets allowed, $150 cleaning fee per stay.

Features: Indoor pool, Business services, Dry cleaning/laundry service, Free breakfast, Number of suites: 221, Number of floors: 16, Fireplace in lobby, Coffee in lobby, Wireless Internet (additional charge), Video library, Newspapers in lobby, Meeting rooms (small groups), Fitness facilities.

★★★★
Sheraton Commander Hotel
16 Garden Street
Cambridge MA 02138
(617) 547-4800
$169 - $484

Pet Policy: Pets under 80 lbs accepted, no additional fee. Sheraton Sweet Sleeper Dog Bed Available

Features: Year built: 1927, Number of rooms: 175, Wireless Internet, Fitness Center, Restaurants, Shopping on site.

★★★★
The Charles Hotel
1 Bennett St
Cambridge MA 02138
(617) 864.1200
$198- $4,500
SAVE –B&P Discount Available

Pet Policy: Pets accepted, $50 per stay fee. Pets must be accompanied by owner at all times.

Features: Currency Exchange, Shoe Shine, Meeting rooms (small groups), 4 Restaurants, Wireless Internet, Beauty services, Massage - treatment room(s), Accessible bathroom, Steam room, Smoke-free property, 24-hour business center, Full-service health spa, Bar/lounge, Indoor pool, Babysitting or child care, Dry cleaning/laundry service, Valet parking (additional charge), On-site car rental, Concierge, Gift shop, Number of rooms: 294, Number of floors: 10, Cell phone/mobile rental, Secretarial services, Translation services, Computer rental, Ski storage, Video library, Nightclub, Room service (24 hours), Doorman/doorwoman, Newspapers, Porter/bellhop, Security guard, Limo or Town Car service, Medical assistance available.

★★★ 🛏️
Whitman House
17 Worcester Street
Cambridge MA 02139
(617) 945-5350
Rates from $185
SAVE –B&P Discount Available

Pet Policy: Pets accepted in off season, $25 per pet per night. Please call for pet reservations and current policy.

Features: Fireplace in lobby, Laundry facilities, Media library, Wireless Internet, Self-parking (free), Free breakfast, Library.

Chicopee
Also see the following nearby communities that have pet friendly lodging:
Springfield - 3 miles, West Springfield - 4 miles, Holyoke - 5 miles, Westfield - 8 miles.

★★
Days Inn Chicopee
450 Memorial Dr
Chicopee MA 01020
(413) 739-7311
$67 - $107
SAVE –B&P Discount Available

Pet Policy: Pets accepted, $35 per stay.

Features: Free Breakfast, Elevator, Conference room(s), Business services, Coffee in lobby, Laundry facilities, Health club, Parking (free), Free newspapers in lobby, 24-hour front desk, Wireless Internet, Concierge desk.

★↗
Econo Lodge Chicopee
357 Burnett Rd
Chicopee MA 01020
(413) 592-9101
$70 - $75
SAVE –B&P Discount Available

Pet Policy: Pet accommodation: $10 per night, per pet, Pet friendly designated rooms only.

Features: Number of rooms: 115, Number of floors: 2, Air-conditioned public areas, Parking (free), 24-hour front desk, Free breakfast, Bar/lounge.

★★
Quality Inn
Chicopee/Springfield
463 Memorial Dr
Chicopee MA 01020
(413) 592-6171
$79 - $89
SAVE –B&P Discount Available

Pet Policy: Quality Inns charge a fee of $10 per night per pet and may require a $50 damage deposit, which is refunded if the room is in order at check out. Quality Inns accept any well-behaved pets with a maximum of 3 per room, but dogs are limited to 50 pounds. They do not currently require a veterinarian certificate. Pets may not be left alone in the room unless in a cage.

Features: Business services, Free breakfast, Outdoor pool, Parking (free), Wireless Internet, Fitness facilities, Number of rooms: 100, Number of floors: 2.

Concord

Also see the following nearby communities that have pet friendly lodging:
Lexington - 3 miles, Sudbury - 7 miles, Billerica - 8 miles, Boxborough - 8 miles, Waltham - 9 miles, Framingham - 9 miles, Westford - 10 miles.

★★★

Best Western Plus at Historic Concord
740 Elm St
Concord MA 01742
(978) 369-6100
$129- $149
SAVE –B&P Discount Available

Pet Policy: Pets allowed based on the availability of pet friendly rooms. Up to 2 dogs per room with an 80 pound weight limit. Additional pet types (cats, birds, etc.) may be accepted at the hotel's discretion. Pet rate is $15 per day with a $100 per week maximum.

Features: Wireless Internet, Dry cleaning/laundry service, Fitness facilities, Bar/lounge, Restaurant, Number of rooms: 106, Number of floors: 2, Elevator, Business services, Free breakfast, Parking (free), Newspapers in lobby, Business center, Smoke-free property, Outdoor pool – seasonal.

Danvers

Also see the following nearby communities that have pet friendly lodging:
Peabody - 4 miles, Wakefield - 7 miles, Saugus - 8 miles, Woburn - 9 miles.

★★★

CoCo Key Hotel and Water Resort - Boston
50 Ferncroft Rd
Danvers MA 01923
(978) 777-2500
$129 - $159
SAVE –B&P Discount Available

Pet Policy: Dogs up to 75 lbs accepted. Limit 1 per room.

Features: Accessible bathroom, Indoor pool, Poolside bar, Wireless Internet, Bar/lounge, Restaurant(s), Arcade/game room, Health club, Parking, Swimming pool - children's, Meeting rooms, Waterslide, Private beach, Children's club, Area shuttle (free), 24-hour business center, Snack bar/deli, Computer station.

★★★

Comfort Inn North Shore
50 Dayton St
Danvers MA 01923
(978) 777-1700
$114 - $134
SAVE –B&P Discount Available

Pet Policy: Pet Charge:$25 One-time cleaning fee Plus $10 Per night. Limit: 2 pets per room 40 lbs or under.

Features: Breakfast, Handicapped parking, In-room accessibility, Wireless Internet, Dry cleaning/laundry service, Indoor pool, Number of rooms: 140, Number of floors: 5, Conference room(s), Coffee in lobby, Parking, Newspapers, Outdoor pool - seasonal, Tennis on site, Fitness facilities, Business center.

★★★ 🎾🏃
Danvers Residence Inn by Marriott
51 Newbury St./Route 1
Danvers MA 01923
(978) 777-7171
Rates from $159
SAVE –B&P Discount Available

Pet Policy: Pets accepted, $100 cleaning fee.

Free Breakfast, Handicapped parking, In-room accessibility, Number of rooms: 96, Number of floors: 2, Business services, Barbecue grill(s), Coffee in lobby, Parking (free), Free newspapers in lobby, Picnic area, 24-hour front desk, Wireless Internet, Outdoor pool - seasonal, Dry cleaning/laundry service, Tennis on site, Fitness facilities.

★★★
Danvers TownePlace Suites by Marriott
238 Andover St
Danvers MA 01923
(978) 777-6222
$89 - $169
SAVE –B&P Discount Available

Pet Policy: Pets accepted, $75 additional cleaning fee.

Features: Dry cleaning/laundry service, Number of rooms: 127, Number of floors: 4, Business services, Air-conditioned public areas, Barbecue grill(s), Coffee in lobby, Free breakfast, Parking (free), Picnic area, 24-hour front desk, Wireless Internet, Outdoor pool - seasonal, Fitness facilities.

★★
Extended Stay America
102 Newbury St
Danvers MA 01923
(978) 762-7414
$70- $124
SAVE –B&P Discount Available

Pet Policy: One pet is allowed in each guest room. A $25 per day non-refundable cleaning fee (not to exceed $150) will be charged the first night of your stay. Weight, size and breed restrictions may apply. Please contact the hotel directly with inquiries.

Features: Bar/lounge, Number of rooms: 104, Number of floors: 3, Wireless Internet (additional charge), Parking (free), 24-hour front desk.

Dedham

Also see the following nearby communities that have pet friendly lodging:
Needham - 2 miles, Newton - 5 miles, Brookline - 6 miles, Waltham - 7 miles, Norwood - 8 miles, Cambridge - 9 miles, Boston - 10 miles.

★★★★ 🎾🏃🏃
Hilton Boston/Dedham
25 Allied Dr
Dedham MA 02026
(781) 329-7900
$129 - $139
SAVE –B&P Discount Available

Pet Policy: Pets up to 35 lbs, $75 per stay.

Features: Business Center, Bar/lounge, Restaurant(s), Room service (limited hours), Number of rooms: 256, Elevator, Conference room(s), Secretarial services, Air-conditioned public areas, *Continued on next page*

Hilton Boston/Dedham
Continued from previous page

Patio, Barbecue grill(s), Wireless Internet (fee), Arcade/game room, Coffee shop, Health club, Parking (free), Free newspapers in lobby, 24-hour front desk, Porter/bellhop, Security guard, Limo or Town Car service, Massage - treatment room(s), Meeting rooms (small groups), Sauna, Wedding services, Indoor pool, Dry cleaning/laundry service, Tennis on site, Shopping on site, Luggage storage.

★★★ Residence Inn Dedham
259 Elm St
Dedham MA 02026
(781) 407-0999
$127 - $309
SAVE –B&P Discount Available

Pet Policy: Pets allowed, $100 per stay cleaning fee.

Features: Indoor pool, Gift shop, Number of rooms: 81, Number of floors: 3, Elevator, Barbecue grill(s), Free breakfast, Parking (free), Free newspapers in lobby, Wireless Internet, Patio, Smoke-free property, Free reception, Smoke-free property (fines apply), Computer station, Dry cleaning/laundry service, Grocery/convenience store, Outdoor tennis court, Coffee in lobby, Business center, Fitness facilities, On-site car rental, 24-hour front desk.

Eastham
Also see the following nearby communities that have pet friendly lodging:
Orleans - 5 miles.

★★ Captains Quarters Motel & Conference Center
5000 State Highway/Route 6
Eastham MA 02651
(508) 255-5686
$129- $159
SAVE –B&P Discount Available

Pet Policy: Pet fee is $15 per night/per pet. We are located on six and half acres of land so there is plenty of room for playing, exploring and walking for your pets.
1. Standard rooms are pet friendly and prior arrangement MUST be made, so that you can reserve this type of room where pets are allowed. Not all rooms are pet friendly. Please contact hotel directly for reservations.

2. We try to limit two pets per room.

3. Pets must be leashed when out of the guest room.

4. Pets should not be left unattended for more than 2 hours and never unattended at night. Please leave a cell phone number with us when your dog is left unattended.

5. Pets must be clean and on flea medication prior to arrival.

**Captains Quarters Motel &
Conference Center**
Continued from previous page

6. Pet owner agrees to the hotel pet policies, to be responsible for any damage or injury caused by the pet.

7. You can walk your pet to the side of the hotel, front or the back lawn.

8. Please clean up after your pets.

Features: Handicapped parking, Parking (free), Outdoor pool - seasonal, Barbecue grill(s), Accessible bathroom, Tennis on site, Number of rooms: 75, Wireless Internet, Conference room(s), Outdoor pool, Coffee in lobby, 24-hour front desk, Free breakfast, Suitable for children, Library, Business center.

Not Rated
Ocean Park Inn
3900 Route 6
Eastham MA 02642
(508)-255-1132
$119 - $164

Pet Policy: Pets accepted, $20 per room per night pet fee. Housekeeping attendants will not enter your room with your pet in the room. We ask that you walk your pet while housekeeping cleans your room. You may call the front desk to arrange a convenient time for cleaning service available until 2:00PM. Daily housekeeping in pet rooms is required. PLEASE!!! If you leave your pet in the room, put the DO NOT DISTURB sign on the door. We are not responsible if your DO NOT DISTURB sign is not on your door and your pet gets out. We provide doggie bags to make cleanup of any messes easy.

Please leave your cell phone number at the front desk if you are leaving the pet in your room. We will need to reach you if your pet is barking and disturbing other guests. You will be responsible for any room damages incurred by your pet. These charges will appear on your statement and is in addition to the pet fee.

If for any reason, at any time during your stay, your pet is being disruptive or destructive, we will ask you to remove the pet. In this instance, there is a wonderful kennel very close by. I personally use this kennel and they offer day care services at reasonable rates ($13/day) so if you want to go to the beach for the day (where pets are not allowed), you may want to consider bringing your pet to the kennel where they will have fun and be well cared for. The phone number for Nauset Kennel is 508-255-0081. *Continued on next page*

Ocean Park Inn – Eastham
Continued from previous page

We appreciate your business and thank you for cooperating with our policies! We would love to add a photo of your pet at our Inn on our Facebook Fan page if you would like to email the picture to opi@cape.com and tell us when you stayed with us.

Features: Outdoor pool, Laundry facilities, Picnic area, Number of rooms: 54, Smoke-free property, Wireless Internet, mini fridge in rooms.

★★★ 🛏️

The Inn at the Oaks
3085 Rte 6
Eastham MA 02642
(508) 255-1886
$175 - $195
SAVE –B&P Discount Available

Pet Policy: Dogs welcome in one of 3 pet-friendly rooms. When it comes to the Inn At the Oaks, the term pet friendly is really an understatement. We adore our pets, and often travel with them just as you do. You can also arrange daycare for your dog when you are out and about and even grooming at the nearby Nauset kennels. As you probably know, the Outer Cape is great for dog lovers, where they are allowed on most beaches and in many of the stores. Provincetown, just 20 to 30 minutes away, was voted the Most Dog Friendly Town in the U.S., and boasts a great dog park where your best friend can run around and meet some playful friends.

Features: Number of rooms: 11, Parking (free), Wireless Internet, Free breakfast, Wedding services, Fireplace in lobby, Suitable for children.

Fairhaven

Also see the following nearby communities that have pet friendly lodging:
New Bedford - 1 mile, North Dartmouth 2 miles, Westport - 9 miles.

★★★ 🛏️ ⛵

Seaport Inn & Marina
110 Middle St
Fairhaven MA 02719
(508) 997-1281
$119 - $134
SAVE –B&P Discount Available

Pet Policy: Pets welcome, $25 per stay per pet.

Features: Parking (free), Wireless Internet, Dry cleaning/laundry service, Number of rooms: 88, Number of suites: 2, Number of floors: 2, Conference room(s), Business services, Air-conditioned public areas, Free breakfast, Multilingual staff, Free newspapers in lobby, 24-hour front desk, Fitness facilities, Marina.

Falmouth

Not Rated
Capewind Waterfront Resort
34 Maravista Avenue Extension
Falmouth MA 02540
(508) 548-3400
$222 - $282

Pet Policy: Well behaved small to medium size dogs are permitted with advanced approval, fee charged is $10 per night per pet. You must contact the hotel directly for approval

Pets are not allowed in or on our beds or furniture. Pet owners are expected to bring crates or pet bedding and pet dishes. A large fine will be charged to the pet owner if our policy is ignored.

The town of Falmouth requires that pets must be leashed; therefore, we must enforce that pets are leashed at all times outside of the room.

Pets are not allowed on the front lawn by the ocean inlet, in the pool area, or in the ice/soda room at any time. Pets are to be walked on a leash on the grassy area behind the parking lot at rooms 24-41. Owners are expected to pick up after their pets and dispose of waste properly in a plastic bag and placed in the dumpster behind the soda and ice room in the parking lot.

Pets may not be left unattended for more than 3 hours and never unattended at night. If you plan to leave your pet unattended, please leave a phone number with the Front Desk.

Pets must be washed and on flea medication prior to arrival.

Please do not allow wet, salty, and/or sandy pets in the room. Please clean and dry your pet before arrival or entering the room.

Housekeeping is not allowed to enter a guest room with a pet. If you would like your room cleaned, please arrange a time with the Front Desk to service your room between 10 AM and 2 PM when your pet is out of the room.

Features: Boat dock, Free use of row boats, 30 foot boat and captain available for charter, Front desk closes at 7:30 PM.

Not Rated
Green Harbor Waterfront Lodging
134 Acapesket Rd
Falmouth MA 02536
(508) 548-4747
$141 - $274

Pet Policy: Pets welcome, $10 per stay, limit 2 per room. When booking a room either online or by telephone you MUST let us know if you are bringing a pet. All pets must have current vaccinations for rabies, distemper and bordetella. If documentation is not available at check-in, owners must sign a guarantee that all shots are current and be able to provide documentation supporting that fact upon request. Pets may not be left alone in rooms, and must be leashed when outside. Pets are not allowed in the pool area. Pet owner is liable for any damage caused.

Features: Coffee makers in room, Wireless Internet.

★★★
The Beach Rose Inn
17 Chase Road
Falmouth MA 02540
(508) 540-5706
$175 - $176
SAVE –B&P Discount Available

Pet Policy. Pets are welcome in specified rooms for an additional fee of $20 a night. Call the Inn at 800-498-5706 for more information.

Features: Year Built 1863, Wireless Internet, Number of rooms: 8, Massage - treatment room(s), Free breakfast.

Fitchburg

Also see the following nearby communities that have pet friendly lodging:
Leominster - 4 miles, Westminster - 5 miles, Gardner - 9 miles.

★★★
Courtyard by Marriott Fitchburg
150 Royal Plaza Dr
Fitchburg MA 01420
(978)342 7100
$119 - $219
SAVE –B&P Discount Available

Pet Policy: Pets allowed, $75 cleaning fee.

Features: Bar/Lounge, Indoor pool, Dry cleaning/laundry service, Room service (limited hours), On-site car rental, Concierge services, Gift shops or newsstand, Number of rooms: 233, Conference room(s), Business services, Computer rental, Air-conditioned public areas, Patio, Fax machine, Arcade/game room, Pool table, Wireless Internet, Parking (free), Free newspapers in lobby, 24-hour front desk, Porter/bellhop, Breakfast available (additional charge), Fitness facilities

Foxborough
Also see the following nearby communities that have pet friendly lodging:
Mansfield - 3 miles, Norwood - 7 miles, Franklin - 8 miles, Norton - 9 miles.

★★★
Residence Inn by Marriott
250 Foxborough Blvd
Foxborough MA 02035
(508) 698-2800
$99 - $209
SAVE –B&P Discount Available

Pet Policy: Pets allowed, $100 additional cleaning fee per stay.

Features: Grocery, Accessible bathroom, Handicapped parking, Number of rooms: 108, Number of floors: 3, Conference room(s), Parking, Free newspapers, Wireless Internet, Outdoor pool - seasonal, Dry cleaning/laundry service, Fitness facilities, Business center, Tennis on site, Snack bar/deli.

Framingham
Also see the following nearby communities that have pet friendly lodging:
Southborough - 7 miles, Marlborough - 8 miles,
Waltham - 10 miles, Newton - 10 miles, Needham - 10 miles.

★★★
Best Western Framingham
130 Worcester Rd
Framingham MA 01702
(508) 872-8811
$103 - $165
SAVE –B&P Discount Available

Pet Policy: Pets allowed based on the availability of pet friendly rooms. Up to 2 dogs per room with an 80 pound weight limit. Additional pet types (cats, birds, etc.) may be accepted at the hotel's discretion. No fee.

Features: Sauna, Business Center, Restaurant, Bar/Lounge, Accessible bathroom, Handicapped parking, Indoor pool, Dry cleaning/laundry service, Wireless Internet, Number of rooms: 184, Number of floors: 6, Coffee in lobby, Parking, Newspapers in lobby, Meeting rooms, Free breakfast, Doorman/doorwoman, Designated smoking areas, Porter/bellhop.

★★
Monticello Inn Framingham
90 Worcester Rd
Framingham MA 01702
(508) 875-1394
$59 - $79
SAVE –B&P Discount Available

Pet Policy: Dogs & cats, up to 50 lbs are allowed at the hotel in designated rooms only. Guests must indicate they have a pet and sign our Pet Policy at check in. Failure to do so will result in a $250 fine and immediate eviction. Max 2 pets per reservation. There is a $10 Pet Fee per night per pet.

Features: Wireless Internet, Number of rooms: 63, Number of floors: 1, Parking (free), Free breakfast.

★★
**Red Roof Inn Boston -
Framingham**
650 Cochituate Rd
Framingham MA 01701
(508) 872-4499
$75 - $103
SAVE –B&P Discount Available

Pet Policy: Red Roof's Pet Policy: One well-behaved family pet is permitted unless prohibited by state law or ordinance. Service animals are always welcome. Pets must be declared during guest registration. In consideration of all Red Roof guests, pets must never be left unattended in the guestroom.

Features: Wireless Internet, Business services, Parking (free), 24-hour front desk, Accessible bathroom, Handicapped parking, In-room accessibility, Number of rooms: 170, Number of floors: 2, Coffee in lobby, Free newspapers in lobby.

★★★
**Residence Inn by Marriott
Boston Framingham**
400 Staples Dr
Framingham MA 01702
(508) 370-0001
$98 - $229
SAVE –B&P Discount Available

Pet Policy: Pets allowed, $100 cleaning fee per stay.

Features: Indoor pool, Elevator, Business services, Dry cleaning/laundry service, Air-conditioned public areas, Patio, Barbecue grill(s), Coffee in lobby, Parking (free), Free newspapers in lobby, Picnic area, 24-hour front desk, Wireless Internet, Meeting rooms (small groups), Fitness facilities.

★★★★
**Sheraton Framingham Hotel &
Conference Center**
1657 Worcester Rd
Exit 12 To Route 9 West
Framingham MA 01701
(508) 879-7200
$145 - $275
SAVE –B&P Discount Available

Pet Policy: Pets up to 50 lbs welcome, no fee, limit 2 per room. Sheraton Sweet Sleeper Dog Bed Available.

Features: Bar/lounge, Restaurant, Concierge services, Gift shop, Number of rooms: 380, Number of suites: 22, Elevator, Number of floors: 6, Airport transportation (additional charge), Conference room(s), Breakfast available (additional charge), Wireless Internet, Health club, Multilingual staff, Free newspapers in lobby, 24-hour front desk, Security guard, Limo or Town Car service available, Meeting rooms (small groups), Steam room, Smoke-free property, Outdoor pool - seasonal, Wedding services, Sauna, Air-conditioned public areas, Room service (limited hours), Parking (free), Indoor pool, Fireplace in lobby, Pool table, Area shuttle (free), 24-hour business center, Dry cleaning/laundry service.

Franklin
Also see the following nearby communities that have pet friendly lodging:
Foxborough - 6 miles.

★★✦
Hawthorn Suites by Wyndham
835 Upper Union Street
Franklin MA 02038
(508) 553-3500
$139 - $219
SAVE –B&P Discount Available

Pet Policy: Pets welcome, $100 per stay fee.

Features: Indoor pool, Dry cleaning/laundry service, Number of rooms: 100, Elevator, Conference room(s), Business services, Air-conditioned public areas, Patio, Barbecue grill(s), Coffee in lobby, Arcade/game room, Pool table on site, Free breakfast, Grocery, Parking (free), Multilingual staff, Free newspapers in lobby, 24-hour front desk, Wireless Internet, Meeting rooms (small groups), Fitness facilities, Airport transportation (free).

★★★
Residence Inn by Marriott
4 Forge Pkwy
Franklin MA 02038
(508) 541 8188
$98 - $170
SAVE –B&P Discount Available

Pet Policy: Pets allowed, $100 per stay cleaning fee.

Features: Accessible bathroom, Handicapped parking, Dry cleaning/laundry service, Coffee in lobby, Indoor pool, Tennis on site, Fitness facilities, Number of rooms: 108, Number of floors: 3, Elevator, Conference room(s), Business services, Computer rental, Suitable for children, Air-conditioned public areas, Patio, Barbecue grill(s), Grocery, Parking (free), Free newspapers in lobby, Picnic area, 24-hour front desk, Wireless Internet, Meeting rooms (small groups).

Gardner

Also see the following nearby communities that have pet friendly lodging:
Westminster - 6 miles, Fitchburg - 9 miles.

★★
Super 8 Gardner Ma
22 North Pearson Blvd
Gardner MA 01440
(978) 630-2888
$75 - $90
SAVE –B&P Discount Available

Pet Policy: Cats and Dogs accepted, $15 per pet per night. Limit of 2 pets per room.

Features: Business services, Number of rooms: 48, Number of floors: 2, Air-conditioned public areas, Coffee in lobby, Free breakfast, Parking (free), 24-hour front desk, Wireless Internet.

★★★
The Colonial Hotel
625 Betty Spring Road
Gardner MA 01440
(978) 630-2500
$119 - $126

Pet Policy: Pets allowed, $15 per night per pet.

Features: Restaurant, Bar/Lounge, Wedding services, Meeting rooms, Indoor heated pool, 24 hour front desk, Wireless Internet.

Great Barrington
Also see the following nearby communities that have pet friendly lodging:
Stockbridge - 6 miles, West Stockbridge - 8 miles, Lee - 8 miles.

Not Rated
Monument Mountain Hotel
247 Stockbridge Rd
Great Barrington MA 01230
(413) 528-3272
$80 - $120

Pet Policy: Pets accepted, please contact directly for pet reservations.

Features: Number of rooms: 18, Number of floors: 1, Coffee makers in room, Air conditioning, Outdoor pool, Tennis, Free parking, Free newspapers.

Not Rated
Thornewood Inn
452 Stockbridge Road
Great Barrington MA 01230
(413) 528-3828
$115 - $295

Pet Policy: 2 pet friendly rooms, no fee. Please book directly with the Inn.

Features: Year built: 1920, Restaurant, Free breakfast, Wedding services, Number of rooms: 15, Wireless Internet, Fireplace in some rooms.

Greenfield
Also see the following nearby communities that have pet friendly lodging:
Hadley - 15 miles.

★★
Days Inn Greenfield
21 Colrain Rd
Greenfield MA 01301
(413) 774-5578
$92 - $145
SAVE –B&P Discount Available

Pet Policy: Pets accepted, $20 per night per pet.

Features: Free newspapers in lobby, Coffee in lobby, Fitness facilities, Business Center, Parking (free), Dry cleaning/laundry service, In-room accessibility, Free breakfast.

★★
Quality Inn Greenfield
125 Mohawk Trl
Greenfield MA 01301
(413) 774-2211
$89 - $119
SAVE –B&P Discount Available

Pet Policy: Pet accommodation: $20 per night per pet. Limit of 2pets per room. Pets must not be left unattended. Guest is responsible for any damage.

Features: Dry cleaning/laundry service, Wireless Internet, Restaurant, Number of rooms: 100, Number of floors: 2, Business services, Coffee in lobby, Free breakfast, Parking (free), Meeting rooms (small groups), Outdoor pool – seasonal.

Hadley

Also see the following nearby communities that have pet friendly lodging:
Amherst - 4 miles, Northampton - 4 miles, Holyoke - 9 miles.

★★
Comfort Inn Hadley
237 Russell St
Hadley MA 01035
(413) 584-9816
$79 - $175
Continued from previous page

Pet Policy: Pet accommodation: $25/night for one pet in room. $35 charge for two pets for 1st night and $25 for each additional night. Pet limit: 2 pets per room

Features: Number of rooms: 70, Number of floors: 2, Coffee in lobby, Free breakfast, Parking (free), Free newspapers in lobby, 24-hour front desk, Meeting rooms (small groups), Indoor pool, Laundry facilities, Arcade/game room, Fitness facilities.

★★
Howard Johnson
401 Russell St
Hadley MA 01035
(413) 586-0115
$116 - $159
SAVE –B&P Discount Available

Pet Policy: Pets welcome, $20 additional fee. Must book in advance.

Features: Shopping on site, Conference room(s), Coffee in lobby, Wireless Internet (additional charge), Free breakfast, Parking (free), Free newspapers in lobby, 24-hour front desk, Business center, Limo or Town Car service available, Outdoor pool - seasonal, Dry cleaning/laundry service.

★★★★
Ivory Creek Bed and Breakfast
31 Chimera Rd
Hadley MA 01035
(413) 587-3115
$160 - $259
SAVE –B&P Discount Available

Pet Policy: Pets accepted in 2 of the rooms, no fee. Please contact property directly for pet reservations.

Features: Wireless Internet, Suitable for children, Number of rooms: 6, Number of floors: 3, Business services, Fax machine, Arcade/game room, Free breakfast, Free newspapers in lobby, Porter/bellhop.

★★
Knights Inn Hadley
208 Russell St
Hadley MA 01035
(413) 585-1552
$68 - $79
SAVE –B&P Discount Available

Pet Policy: Pets accepted, $10 per night.

Features: Free breakfast, Wireless Internet, Outdoor pool.

Hancock
Also see the following nearby communities that have pet friendly lodging:.
Bar Harbor - 8 miles, Ellsworth - 9 miles.

★★★ 🐾
Vacation Village in the Berkshires
276 Brodie Mountain Rd
Hancock MA 01237
(413)738.2000
$81 - $250
SAVE –B&P Discount Available

Pet Policy: Pets accepted but must be approved in advance. Please call directly.

Features: Fitness facilities, Indoor pool, Outdoor pool, Number of floors 2, Health club, Parking (free), 24-hour front desk, Laundry facilities, Arcade/game room, Accessible bathroom, Concierge, Fireplace in lobby, Pool table, Business center, Luggage storage.

Haverhill
Also see the following nearby communities that have pet friendly lodging:
Methuen - 6 miles, Lawrence - 6 miles, Salem - 7 miles, Andover - 8 miles.

★★★ 🐾
Best Western Plus Merrimack Valley
401 Lowell Ave
Haverhill MA 01832
(978) 373-1511
$94 - $139
SAVE –B&P Discount Available

Pet Policy: Pets allowed based on the availability of pet friendly rooms. Up to 2 dogs per room with an 80 pound weight limit. Additional pet types (cats, birds, etc.) may be accepted at the hotel's discretion. Pet rate is $20 per day with a $100 per week maximum.

Features: Business center, Accessible bathroom, Handicapped parking, In-room accessibility, Indoor pool, Free breakfast, Dry cleaning/laundry service, Wireless Internet, Number of rooms: 127, Conference room(s), Parking (free), Multilingual staff, Free newspapers in lobby, 24-hour front desk, Smoke-free property, Fitness facilities.

★★ 🐾
Comfort Suites
106 Bank Rd
Haverhill MA 01832
(978) 374-7755
$74 - $139
SAVE –B&P Discount Available

Pet Policy: Pets welcome, $35 first night, $10 each additional night.

Features: Number of suites: 131, Elevator, Conference room(s), Business services, Ski storage, Free breakfast, Currency exchange, Parking (free), Free newspapers in lobby, 24-hour front desk, Meeting rooms (small groups), Dry cleaning/laundry service, Wireless Internet, RV and truck parking, Fitness facilities.

Holyoke
Also see the following nearby communities that have pet friendly lodging:
Chicopee - 5 miles, Northampton - 6 miles, West Springfield - 7 miles, Springfield - 9 miles, Westfield - 9 miles, Hadley - 9 miles.

★★★
Homewood Suites by Hilton
375 Whitney Ave
Holyoke MA 01040
(413) 532-3100
$130 - $334
SAVE –B&P Discount Available

Pet Policy: Pets up to 100 lbs. $100 fee.

Features: Dry cleaning/laundry service, Indoor pool, Number of rooms: 114, Number of floors:5, Suitable for children, Fireplace in lobby, Barbecue grill(s), Coffee in lobby, Free breakfast, Parking (free), Free newspapers in lobby, 24-hour front desk, Business center, Wireless Internet, Meeting rooms (small groups), Area shuttle (free), Fitness facilities, In-room accessibility, Handicapped parking.

Hyannis
Also see the following nearby communities that have pet friendly lodging:
Barnstable - 3 miles, West Yarmouth - 3 miles, South Yarmouth - 6 miles, West Dennis - 7 miles, Sandwich - 10 miles.

★★
Comfort Inn Cape Cod
1470 Iyannough Rd. Rte 132
Hyannis MA 02601
(508) 771-4804
$149 - $184
SAVE –B&P Discount Available

Pet Policy: Pet accommodation:$25/night. Pets are not to be left unattended. Pets allowed only in designated/Pet Allowed/ rooms. Maximum: 3 pets, per room.

Features: Wireless Internet, Sauna, Business services, Indoor pool, Number of rooms: 104, Number of floors: 3, Coffee in lobby, Free breakfast, Parking (free), Free newspapers in lobby, Meeting rooms (small groups), Fitness facilities, Dry cleaning/laundry service, Rooftop terrace.

★★
Econo Lodge Hyannis
59 E Main St
Hyannis MA 02601
(508) 771-0699
$89 - $149
SAVE –B&P Discount Available

Pet Policy: Pets up to 50 lbs, $10 per night per pet plus $50 refundable deposit. Limit 2 per room.

Features: Arcade/game room, Indoor pool, Gift shop, Number of rooms: 48, Number of floors: 2, Laundry facilities, Free breakfast, Parking (free), Room service, Business center, Designated smoking areas.

★★★

Heritage House Hotel
259 Main Street
Hyannis MA 02601
(508) 775-7000
$109 - $279
SAVE –B&P Discount Available

Pet Policy: Small pets accepted, $10 per day, in designated pet rooms. Pets are not permitted in common areas of the Inn. Pets must be kept quiet at all times. Pets that continue to disrupt the operation of the Inn cannot remain as guests. Please keep pets off all bedding and furniture. Pets should be crated when left alone. Owners are responsible for the cost of repairs, and/or replacement. Please walk your dog on public property and pick up after them.

Features: Sauna, Bar/Lounge, Outdoor pool, Indoor pool, Handicapped parking, Restaurant(s), Number of rooms: 143, Number of floors: 4, Wireless Internet, Parking (free), 24-hour front desk, Meeting rooms (small groups), Wedding services, Nearby fitness center (discount), Airport transportation.

Kingston
Also see the following nearby communities that have pet friendly lodging:
Plymouth - 6 miles

Not Rated
Plymouth Bay Inn & Suites
Route 3 at North Plymouth
Kingston MA 02364
(781) 585-3831
$92 - $139

Pet Policy: Pets welcome but cannot be left alone at any time.

Features: Number of rooms: 108, Microwaves, Refrigerators, Wireless Internet, Fully equipped kitchens in 2 bedroom suites, Continental breakfast, Indoor pool, Whirlpool spa, Fitness center, Restaurant, Bar/lounge.

Lawrence
Also see the following nearby communities that have pet friendly lodging:
Andover - 2 miles, Methuen - 3 miles, Salem - 6 miles, Haverhill - 6 miles, Tewksbury - 7 miles, Lowell - 9 miles.

★★★ 🦮

Holiday Inn Express Lawrence
224 Winthrop Ave
Lawrence MA 01843
(978) 975-4050
$75 - $104
SAVE –B&P Discount Available

Pet Policy: Pets welcome, $25 per night. Free pet treats available at front desk.

Features: Accessible bathroom, Handicapped parking, Number of rooms: 126, Number of floors: 5, Free breakfast, Parking (free), Wireless Internet, Dry cleaning/laundry service, Business center, Fitness facilities.

Lee
Also see the following nearby communities that have pet friendly lodging:
Stockbridge - 3 miles, Lenox - 4 miles, West Stockbridge - 5 miles, Great Barrington - 8 miles, Pittsfield - 10 miles.

Not Rated
1800 Devonfield Inn
85 Stockbridge Road
Lee MA 01238
(413) 243-3298
$250 - $325

Pet Policy: Pets accepted, $100 per stay. Limit 3 per room.

Features: Fireplaces, Whirlpool baths, Fridge and microwaves available, Number of rooms: 6, Number of suites: 3, Free full breakfast.

Americas Best Value Inn
980 Pleasant Street Route 102
Lee MA 01238
(413) 43-0501
$67 - $175

Pet Policy: Pets under 20 lbs accepted, $20 per pet additional fee.

Features: Number of rooms: 26, Jacuzzi rooms available, Continental breakfast, Wireless Internet, Microwave, Mini fridge.

Rodeway Inn Lee
200 Laurel St
Lee MA 01238
(413) 243-0813
$73 - $199
SAVE –B&P Discount Available

Pet Policy: Rodeway Inns charge a fee of $10 per night per pet plus a $50 refundable damage deposit. Max of 2 pets per room. A veterinarian certificate that the pet is on a flea and parasite program and that they are free from parasites is required. Pets may not be left alone in the room unless in a cage.

Features: Free breakfast, Outdoor pool - seasonal, Parking, Wireless Internet, Number of rooms: 23.

Lenox
Also see the following nearby communities that have pet friendly lodging:
Lee - 4 miles, West Stockbridge - 5 miles, Pittsfield - 6 miles, Stockbridge - 6 miles.

Blantyre
16 Blantyre
Lenox MA 01240
(413) 637-3556
$550 - $1,950

Pet Policy: 1 pet friendly cottage, $75 per night pet fee. Please contact property directly to reserve.

Features: Year built: 1902, Restaurant, Full treatment spa, Tennis, Fireplaces in many rooms, 4 separate cottages, Rated #1 small hotel in US by Conde Nast.

★★★★ 🐾
Cranwell Resort Spa & Golf
55 Lee Road
Lenox MA 01240
(413) 881-1636
$355 - $545

Pet Policy: Dogs only, up to 35 lbs. Only 1 suite is pet friendly so advised to book directly with the resort.

Features: Full service spa, 18 hole golf course, Restaurants, Cross country skiing center, Large inside heated pool, Whirlpool, Saunas, Steam rooms, Shopping on site.

★♪ 🐾
Knights Inn Lenox
474 Pittsfield Rd
Lenox MA 01240
(413) 443-4468
$65 - $185
SAVE –B&P Discount Available

Pet Policy: Small Pets are permitted. We have some specific pet friendly rooms and there is an additional $15 fee for each pet per room, per night - maximum 2 pets per room.

Features: Free parking, Continental breakfast, Wireless Internet, Microwaves and mini fridges available on request, Truck & RV parking.

Leominster
Also see the following nearby communities that have pet friendly lodging:
Fitchburg - 4 miles, Westminster - 7 miles.

★★ 🐾
Super 8 Leominster Fitchburg
482 N Main St
Leominster MA 01453
(978) 537-2800
$68 - $159
SAVE –B&P Discount Available

Pet Policy: Pets accepted with refundable deposit.

Features: Free breakfast, Business center, Elevator, Parking (free), Barbecue grill(s), Coffee in lobby, Free newspapers in lobby, 24-hour front desk, Security guard, Wireless Internet.

Lexington
Also see the following nearby communities that have pet friendly lodging:.
Billerica - 6 miles, Waltham - 6 miles, Arlington - 8 miles, Newton - 9 miles.

★★★♪
Aloft Lexington
727 Marrett Road - A
Lexington MA 02421
(781) 761-1700
$103 - $239
SAVE –B&P Discount Available

Pet Policy: Animals are family, too! That's why Aloft Lexington welcomes dogs up to 40 pounds. Our pet-friendly arf(SM) program offers a special bed, bowl, and a doggie bag of woof-alicious treats and toys, all free to use during your stay. Please make sure they're on their best behavior, we don't want to charge you extra for housekeeping! Please also note

Aloft Lexington
Continued from previous page

that pets must be attended at all times while staying with us - both in the rooms and the public space. If your dog weighs more than 40 pounds, please contact the hotel directly to discuss.

Features: Number of rooms: 136, Number of floors: 4, Fireplace in lobby, Coffee in lobby, Breakfast available, Laundry facilities, Pool table, Health club, Parking, Free newspapers, Business center, Wireless Internet, Meeting rooms (small groups), Smoke-free property, Children's club, Indoor pool, Bar/lounge.

★★★✦
Element Lexington
727 Marret RD B
Lexington MA 02421
(781) 761-1750
$109 - $274
SAVE –B&P Discount Available

Pet Policy: We welcome dogs weighing up to 40 pounds, no additional fee. Other pets may be allowed at the discretion of the hotel manager. Please contact the hotel to discuss your needs. Pet owners must sign a waiver at check-in agreeing to our pet regulations, and we reserve the right to charge for damage caused by the pet or any additional cleaning needed.

Features: Parking (free), Dry cleaning/laundry service, Number of rooms: 123, Number of floors: 4, Elevator, Air-conditioned public areas, Free breakfast, Free newspapers in lobby, 24-hour front desk, Wireless Internet, Meeting rooms (small groups), Smoke-free property, Children's club, Indoor pool, Security guard, Suitable for children, Business center, Barbecue grill(s), Fitness facilities.

★★
Quality Inn & Suites Lexington
440 Bedford St
Lexington MA 02420
(781) 861-0850
$83 - $104
SAVE –B&P Discount Available

Pet Policy: Quality Inns charge a fee of $10 per night per pet plus a $50 refundable damage deposit. Quality Inns accept any well-behaved pets, up to 50 lbs, with a maximum of 3 per room. Pets may not be left alone in the room unless in a cage.

Features: Free Breakfast, Meeting rooms (small groups), Outdoor pool - seasonal, Wireless Internet, Laundry facilities, Nearby fitness center, Number of rooms: 204, Number of floors: 2, Conference room(s), Parking, Free newspapers, Coffee in lobby, Restaurant, 24-hour business center.

Lowell

Also see the following nearby communities that have pet friendly lodging:
North Chelmsford - 3 miles, Tewksbury - 4 miles, Westford - 7 miles, Billerica - 7 miles, Andover - 8 miles, Methuen - 9 miles, Lawrence - 9 miles, Salem - 10 miles.

★★★

UMass Lowell Inn and Conference Center
50 Warren Street
Lowell MA 01852
(978) 934-6920
$70- $264
SAVE –B&P Discount Available

Pet Policy: Pet accepted, $25 per stay plus $100 refundable deposit.

Features: Wireless Internet, Bar/Lounge, Smoke-free property, Suitable for children, 24-hour business center, Smoke-free property, Conference center, Restaurant, Number of rooms: 252, Number of suites: 1, Number of floors: 9, Parking (free).

Mansfield

Also see the following nearby communities that have pet friendly lodging:.
Foxborough - 5 miles, Norton - 6 miles, Norwood - 9 miles, Brockton - 10 miles.

★★★

Holiday Inn
31 Hampshire St
Mansfield MA 02048
(800) 345-8082
$115 - $202
SAVE –B&P Discount Available

Pet Policy: Pets under 30 lbs accepted, $15 per night per pet additional fee.

Features: Sauna, Business Center, Handicapped parking, In-room accessibility, Indoor pool, Dry cleaning/laundry service, Restaurant, Room service, Number of rooms: 202, Number of suites: 16, Number of floors: 3, Parking, Free newspapers, Room service, Porter/bellhop, Wireless Internet, Meeting rooms, Bar/lounge, Fitness facilities, Shopping on site.

★★

Red Roof Inn
60 Forbes Blvd
I-95 At Exit #7-a, Mansfield
Mansfield MA 02048
(508) 339-2323
$74 - $119
SAVE –B&P Discount Available

Pet Policy: Red Roof's Pet Policy: One well-behaved family pet is permitted unless prohibited by state law or ordinance. Service animals are always welcome. Pets must be declared during guest registration. Pets must never be left unattended in the guestroom.

Features: Business services, Wireless Internet, Outdoor pool, Number of rooms: 134, Number of floors: 5, Coffee in lobby, Parking (free), Free newspapers in lobby, Meeting rooms (small groups).

Marlborough
Also see the following nearby communities that have pet friendly lodging:
Southborough - 4 miles, Northborough - 4 miles, Westborough - 5 miles,
Framingham - 8 miles, Boxborough - 9 miles.

★★★ 🐾
Best Western Royal Plaza Hotel
181 Boston Post Rd W
Marlborough MA 01752
(508)460-0700
$77 - $154
SAVE –B&P Discount Available

Pet Policy: Pets may be accepted. Please contact the hotel directly for full details.

Features: Bar/Lounge, Business services, Indoor pool, Dry cleaning/laundry service, Wireless Internet, Fitness facilities, Restaurant(s), Room service, Concierge, Gift shop, Number of rooms: 441, Number of floors: 6, Game room, Pool table, Parking, Newspapers in lobby, Security guard, Limo or Town Car service, Meeting rooms, Wedding services.

★★★ 🐾
Courtyard by Marriott
75 Felton St
Marlborough MA 01752
(508) 480 0015
$99 - $159
SAVE –B&P Discount Available

Pet Policy: Pets allowed, $75 per stay.

Features: Indoor pool, Bar/lounge, Restaurant(s), Room service, Number of rooms: 196, Number of suites: 6, Number of floors: 5, Coffee in lobby, Currency exchange, Health club, Parking, Free newspapers, 24-hour front desk, Business center, Wireless Internet, Meeting rooms, Fitness facilities.

★★★✦ 🐾
Embassy Suites
123 Boston Post Rd W
Marlborough MA 01752
(508) 485-5900
$129 - $149
SAVE –B&P Discount Available

Pet Policy: Pets up to 50 lbs. $25 per day.

Features: Business Center, Bar/Lounge, Indoor pool, Dry cleaning/laundry service, Restaurant(s), Room service, Gift shop, Number of suites: 229, Conference room(s), Wireless Internet (fee), Game room, Breakfast, Parking, Fitness facilities.

★★ 🐾
Homestead
19 Northboro Rd
Marlborough MA 01752
(508) 490-9911
$89 - $114
SAVE –B&P Discount Available

Pet Policy: One pet is accepted per guest room, any size. The general manager has the authority to allow additional pets per room, based on his or her own discretion. Guests with a pet will be charged upon check-in a fee of $25 per day, up to a maximum of $150. The guest room carpet is cleaned, all bedding is washed, and a professional exterminator treats the room after a guest with a pet checks out.
Continued on next page

Homestead
Continued from previous page

Occupied guest rooms with pets are similarly cleaned monthly in the event of a long-term stay.

Features: Bar/lounge, Laundry facilities, Number of rooms: 135, Number of floors: 3, Airport transportation (additional charge), Barbecue grill(s), Wireless Internet (additional charge), Parking (free), Free newspapers in lobby, Nearby fitness center (free), Picnic area, 24-hour front desk.

Residence Inn by Marriott
112 Donald Lynch Blvd
Marlborough MA 01752
(508) 481-1500
$119 - $199
SAVE –B&P Discount Available

Pet Policy: Pets allowed, $75 cleaning fee per stay.

Features: Accessible bathroom, Handicapped parking, Indoor pool, Patio, Parking (free), Free newspapers in lobby, Wireless Internet, Meeting rooms (small groups), Grocery/convenience store, Barbecue grill(s), Free breakfast, Tennis on site.

Methuen

Also see the following nearby communities that have pet friendly lodging:
Lawrence - 3 miles, Salem - 3 miles, Andover - 4 miles, Haverhill - 6 miles, Tewksbury - 8 miles, Lowell - 9 miles.

Days Hotel Conference Center
159 Pelham Street Essex
Methuen MA 01844
(978) 686-2971
$63 - $119
SAVE –B&P Discount Available

Pet Policy: Pets accepted with nightly fee.

Features: Restaurant(s), Number of rooms: 118, Number of floors: 6, Coffee in lobby, Free breakfast, Parking, Newspapers in lobby, Room service, Wireless Internet, Meeting rooms , Business center, Laundry facilities, Indoor pool, Fitness facilities.

Middleboro

Also see the following nearby communities that have pet friendly lodging:
Raynham - 6 miles.

Days Inn
30 E Clark St
Middleboro MA 02346
(508) 946-4400
$79 - $87
SAVE –B&P Discount Available

Pet Policy: Small pets, $15 per pet, limit of 2 per room Pet walking area nearby.

Features: Number of rooms: 113, Number of floors: 2, Suitable for children, Free breakfast, Parking, Free newspapers, Security guard, Wireless Internet, Meeting rooms, Coffee in lobby, Laundry facilities, Business services, Outdoor pool, Fitness facilities.

Milford

Also see the following nearby communities that have pet friendly lodging:
Franklin - 8 miles.

★★★

Holiday Inn Express
50 Fortune Blvd
Milford MA 01757
(800) 345-8082
$90 - $154
SAVE –B&P Discount Available

Pet Policy: Dogs only, $35 per pet per stay. All dogs must be registered at check in and are restricted to rooms on the first floor.

Features: Indoor pool, Accessible bathroom, Handicapped parking, Dry cleaning/laundry service, Business center, Gift shop, Number of rooms: 117, Number of floors: 4, Conference room(s), Coffee in lobby, Free breakfast, Parking, Free newspapers, Wireless Internet, Fitness facilities.

★★★

La Quinta Inn Milford
24 Beaver St
Milford MA 01757
(508) 478-8243
$89 - $100
SAVE –B&P Discount Available

Pet Policy: Cats and dogs up to 50 pounds are accepted in all guest rooms. Housekeeping services for rooms with pets require pet owner be present or pet must be crated. No fees or deposits are required.

Features: Free Breakfast, Accessible bathroom, Handicapped parking, Number of rooms: 93, Number of floors: 6, Elevator, Conference room(s), Business services, Air-conditioned public areas, Coffee in lobby, Wireless Internet, Laundry facilities, Parking (free), Multilingual staff, 24-hour front desk, Meeting rooms (small groups), Children's club.

Nantucket

★★

The Beachside At Nantucket
30 N Beach Street
Nantucket MA 02554
(508) 228-2241
$290 - $480

Pet Policy: Pet friendly rooms are available on both first- and second-floor, from the pool and courtyard area, surrounded by additional parking area and conservation land.

Features: Non-smoking property, Free breakfast, Air conditioning, Fitness center, Wireless Internet, Laundry facilities, Business center, Outdoor heated pool, Concierge services, Free parking.

★★☆ 🛏
The Brass Lantern Inn
11 N Water St
Nantucket MA 02554
(800) 377-6609
$255 - $366
SAVE –B&P Discount Available

Pet Policy: Pets accepted, $20 per day. Must crate pets when leaving in room alone.

Features: Year Built 1850, number of rooms: 15, Smoke-free property, Free breakfast.

Needham
Also see the following nearby communities that have pet friendly lodging:
Dedham - 2 miles, Newton - 3 miles, Brookline - 5 miles, Waltham - 6 miles, Cambridge - 8 miles, Arlington - 9 miles, Norwood - 9 miles, Somerville - 9 miles, Framingham - 10 miles, Boston - 10 miles.

★★★☆ 🐾
Sheraton Needham Hotel
100 Cabot St
Needham MA 02494
(781) 444-1110
$128 - $264
SAVE –B&P Discount Available

Pet Policy: Dogs accepted up to 80 lbs without a fee. Limit 1 per room. The weight of the dog must be noted in the reservation and the guest must sign a waiver at check-in. Dogs must not be left unattended in a guest room. No other pets are permitted.

Features: Restaurant(s), Concierge services, Gift shop, Number of rooms: 247, Number of floors: 5, Conference room(s), Air-conditioned public areas, Patio, Parking (additional charge), Free newspapers in lobby, 24-hour front desk, Porter/bellhop, Security guard, Wireless Internet, Meeting rooms, Wedding services, Business Center, Bar/Lounge, Indoor pool, Dry cleaning/laundry service, Room service (limited hours), Fitness facilities, Smoke-free property.

New Ashford
Also see the following nearby communities that have pet friendly lodging:
Hancock - 7 miles, Pittsfield - 9 miles, North Adams - 10 miles, Lenox - 15 miles.

★★ 🐾
Econo Lodge The Springs
94 Route 7
New Ashford MA 01237
(518) 487-2000
$59 - $100
SAVE –B&P Discount Available

Pet Policy: Pets accepted, No Fee. Limit 2 per room.

Features: Self-parking (free) Number of rooms: 40, Free breakfast, Outdoor pool - seasonal, Wireless Internet.

New Bedford

Also see the following nearby communities that have pet friendly lodging:
Fairhaven - 1 mile, North Dartmouth- 3 miles, Westport - 9 miles.

★★
Days Inn New Bedford
500 Hathaway Rd
New Bedford MA 02740
(508) 997-1231
$79 - $139
SAVE –B&P Discount Available

Pet Policy: Pets welcome, $10 per pet per day.

Features: Indoor pool, Number of rooms: 153, Number of floors: 3, Conference room(s), Business services, Coffee in lobby, Parking, Free newspapers Wireless Internet, Free breakfast, Laundry facilities, Designated smoking areas.

Newton

Also see the following nearby communities that have pet friendly lodging:
Waltham - 2 miles, Needham - 3 miles, Brookline - 4 miles, Dedham - 5 miles, Cambridge - 6 miles, Arlington - 6 miles, Somerville - 7 miles, Lexington - 9 miles, Boston - 9 miles, Framingham - 10 miles.

★★★★
Crowne Plaza Newton
320 Washington Street
Newton MA 02458
(617) 969-3010
$122 - $309
SAVE –B&P Discount Available

Pet Policy: Pets up to 30 lbs. Fee $25 plus $25 deposit.

Features: Bar/Lounge, Handicapped parking, In-room accessibility, Indoor pool, Dry cleaning/laundry service, Wireless Internet (additional charge), Self-parking (fee), Fitness facilities, Smoke-free property, Restaurant(s), Room service, Concierge services, Number of rooms: 270, Number of floors: 12, Free newspapers, Business center, Porter/bellhop, Security guard, Meeting rooms, Wedding services.

★★★★♥
Hotel Indigo
399 Grove St
Newton MA 02162
(877) 270 1392
$114 - $419
SAVE –B&P Discount Available

Pet Policy: Pets up to 65 lbs accepted, $75 per stay. All designated pet-friendly rooms are on the second floor. Pets must be crated if left alone in room, and must be on leash when outside in public areas.

Features: Business Center, Handicapped parking, In-room accessibility, Dry cleaning/laundry service, Restaurant, Number of rooms: 191, Number of floors: 7, Porter/bellhop, Wireless Internet, Smoke-free property, Outdoor pool - seasonal, Room service, Bar/lounge, Parking (fee), Fitness facilities, Concierge.

North Adams

Also see the following nearby communities that have pet friendly lodging:
Adams - 6 miles, New Ashford - 10 miles.

★★♪

Redwood Motel
915/919 State Road
North Adams MA 01247
(413) 664-4351
Rates from $130
SAVE –B&P Discount Available

Pet Policy: Pets accepted, $20 per day additional.

Features: Number of rooms: 18, Number of floors: 1, Parking (free), 24-hour front desk, Smoke-free property, Air-conditioned public areas, Suitable for children.

Not Rated ♥

The Porches Inn At Mass Moca
231 River Street
North Adams MA 01247
(413) 664-0400
$245 - $430

Pet Policy: Well-behaved pets are permitted in a limited number of designated rooms based on availability. A $40 charge per reservation will apply.

Features: Number of rooms: 47, Continental breakfast, Wireless Internet, Outdoor heated pool.

North Chelmsford

Also see the following nearby communities that have pet friendly lodging:
Lowell - 3 miles, Westford - 5 miles, Tewksbury - 7 miles, Billerica - 9 miles, Nashua - 9 miles.

★★♪ 🐾

Hawthorn Suites by Wyndham
25 Research Place
North Chelmsford MA 01863
(978) 256-5151
$93 - $129
SAVE –B&P Discount Available

Pet Policy: Pets welcome, $75 per stay fee.

Features: Free Breakfast, Dry cleaning/laundry service, Gift shop, Number of rooms: 105, Number of floors: 3, Coffee in lobby, Video library, Parking (free), Free newspapers, Business center, Wireless Internet, Meeting rooms, Fitness facilities.

North Dartmouth

Also see the following nearby communities that have pet friendly lodging:
Fairhaven - 2 miles, New Bedford - 3 miles, Westport - 6 miles.

★★

Comfort Inn
171 Faunce Corner Rd
North Dartmouth MA 02747
(508) 996-0800
$109 - $119

Pet Policy: Pets accepted without size limits, $50 per stay.

Features: Outdoor pool, Continental breakfast, Parking, Gift shop, Number of rooms: 84, Mini fridge and microwave available, Non-smoking property.

★★★
Residence Inn by Marriott
181 Faunce Corner Rd
North Dartmouth MA 02747
(508) 984-5858
$189 - $199
SAVE –B&P Discount Available

Pet Policy: Pets allowed, $100 per stay cleaning fee.

Features: Handicapped parking, In-room accessibility, Dry cleaning/laundry service, Fitness facilities, Indoor pool, Concierge, Gift shop, Number of rooms: 96, Number of floors: 3, Elevator, Suitable for children, Coffee in lobby, Free breakfast, Parking, Free newspapers, Nearby fitness center (free), Business center, Wireless Internet, Meeting rooms.

Northampton
Also see the following nearby communities that have pet friendly lodging:
Hadley - 4 miles, Holyoke - 6 miles, Amherst - 8 miles.

★★★
Clarion Hotel & Conference Center
1 Atwood Dr
Northampton MA 01060
(413) 586-1211
$119 - $209
SAVE –B&P Discount Available

Pet Policy: Hotel states it is pet friendly but there have been reports of pets being turned away, so please be sure to call directly for pet reservations.

Features: Wireless Internet, Dry cleaning/laundry service, Room service, Business center, RV and truck parking, Bar/lounge, Indoor pool, Restaurant(s), Concierge, Number of rooms: 122, Number of floors: 2, Elevator, Arcade/game room, Poolside bar, Parking (free), Free newspapers in lobby, Porter/bellhop, Security guard, Meeting rooms, Outdoor pool - seasonal, Smoke-free property, Wedding services, Conference center, Number of outdoor tennis courts: 2, Computer station.

Northborough
Also see the following nearby communities that have pet friendly lodging:
Westborough - 3 miles, Marlborough - 4 miles, Southborough - 5 miles, Worcester - 10 miles.

★★
Econo Lodge Inn and Suites Northborough
380 SW Cutoff
Northborough MA 01532
(508) 842-8941
Rates from $74
SAVE –B&P Discount Available

Pet Policy: Pets up to 100 lbs accepted, $10 per pet per night. Limit 2 per room.

Features: Free breakfast, Bar/lounge, Restaurant(s), Number of rooms: 78, Number of floors: 2, Air-conditioned public areas, Laundry facilities, Pool table, Parking (free), 24-hour front desk.

Norton

Also see the following nearby communities that have pet friendly lodging:
Mansfield - 6 miles, Raynham - 7 miles, Foxborough - 9 miles.

★★
Extended Stay America
271 S Washington St
Norton MA 02766
(508) 285-7800
$94 - $104
SAVE –B&P Discount Available

Pet Policy: One pet is allowed in each guest room. A $25 per day non-refundable cleaning fee (not to exceed $150) will be charged the first night of your stay. Weight, size and breed restrictions may apply. Please contact the hotel directly with inquiries.

Features: Rooms: 101, Number of floors: 3, Elevator, Parking (free), Free newspapers in lobby, 24-hour front desk, Wireless Internet, Nearby fitness center (discount), Laundry facilities.

Norwood

Also see the following nearby communities that have pet friendly lodging:
Foxborough - 7 miles, Dedham - 8 miles, Brockton - 8 miles, Mansfield - 9 miles, Needham - 9 miles.

★★★
Hampton Inn
434 Providence Hwy
Norwood MA 02062
(781) 769-7000
$107- $199
SAVE –B&P Discount Available

Pet Policy: Pets up to 25 lbs. $25 cleaning fee.

Features: Business center, Bar/lounge, Restaurant, Number of rooms: 150, Elevator, Conference room(s), Laundry facilities, Parking (free), Smoke-free property, Wireless Internet, In-room accessibility, Indoor pool, Free breakfast, Fitness facilities, Shopping on site, Pool table, Room service.

★★★
Residence Inn by Marriott
275 Norwood Park S
Norwood MA 02062
(781) 278-9595
$119 - $179
SAVE –B&P Discount Available

Pet Policy: Pets allowed, $100 per stay cleaning fee.

Features: Dry cleaning/laundry service, Concierge services, Number of rooms: 96, Number of floors: 4, Elevator, Fireplace in lobby, Patio, Coffee in lobby, Library, Grocery, Parking (free), Free newspapers in lobby, 24-hour front desk, Wireless Internet, Meeting rooms (small groups), Indoor pool, Business center, Fitness facilities, Shopping on site, Barbecue grill(s), Tennis on site.

Oak Bluffs

Not Rated
M V Surfside Motel
7 Oak Bluffs Avenue
Oak Bluffs MA 02557
(800) 537-3007
$220 - $221

Pet Policy: Pets welcome, all breeds and sizes, $15 per pet per night. We do ask our guests to provide the Front Desk with a cell phone number when their dog is left alone in a room, as we need to be able to reach guests in case of excessive barking. Dogs must be kept under control and on a leash at all times.

Features: Number of rooms: 31, Number of suites: 4, In-room accessibility, Mini fridge and microwave, In-room coffee maker, Air conditioning, Wireless Internet.

Orleans

Also see the following nearby communities that have pet friendly lodging:
Eastham - 5 miles.

★★
Rodeway Inn Orleans
48 Cranberry Hwy
Orleans MA 02653
(508) 255-1514
$145 - $249
SAVE –B&P Discount Available

Pet Policy: Rodeway Inns charge a fee of $10 per night per pet plus a $50 refundable damage deposit. Max of 2 pets per room. A veterinarian certificate that the pet is on a flea and parasite program and that they are free from parasites is required. Pets may not be left alone in the room unless in a cage.

Features: Wireless Internet, Floors: 2, Business services, Parking (free), 24-hour front desk, Outdoor pool - seasonal, Laundry facilities, Free breakfast, Number of rooms: 43, Restaurant(s).

Not Rated:
Skaket Beach Motel
203 Cranberry Highway
Orleans MA 02653
(508) 255-1020
$78 - $228

Pet Policy: Pets allowed only during off season (essentially September through mid-June), $12 per pet per night.

Features: Outdoor heated pool, Air conditioning, Coffee maker and mini fridge in room, laundry facilities.

Not Rated:
The Governor Prence Inn
66 Route 6A
Orleans MA 02653
(508) 255-1216
$144 - $184

Pet Policy: Pet rooms available, $20 per night pet fee.

Features: Mini fridge and microwave, Outside pool, Gardens, Picnic area, Air conditioning.

Peabody
Also see the following nearby communities that have pet friendly lodging:
Danvers - 4 miles, Saugus - 5 miles, Wakefield - 5 miles, Woburn - 7 miles, Revere - 9 miles.

★★★
Holiday Inn Hotel & Suites
1 Newbury St
Peabody MA 01960
(978) 535-4600
$108 - $197
SAVE –B&P Discount Available

Pet Policy: Pets Allowed.

Features: Bar/lounge, Restaurant(s), Hair salon, Gift shop, Number of rooms: 183, Number of suites: 23, Number of floors: 4, Business services, Air-conditioned public areas, Parking (free) Free newspapers in lobby, Room service, 24-hour front desk, Wireless Internet, Accessible bathroom, Handicapped parking, In-room accessibility, Indoor pool, Business center, Fitness facilities.

★★
Homestead
200 Jubilee Dr
Peabody MA 01960
(978) 531-6632
$104 - $119
SAVE –B&P Discount Available

Pet Policy: We gladly welcome one pet per guest room. A $25 per day non-refundable cleaning fee (not to exceed $150) will be charged the first night of your stay. There are size and breed restrictions. Please contact hotel directly for pet approval.

Features: Indoor pool, Dry cleaning/laundry service, Number of suites: 95, Elevator, Business services, Coffee in lobby, Wireless Internet (additional charge), Free breakfast, Parking (free), Fitness facilities.

★★★
Homewood Suites
57 Newbury St
Peabody MA 01960
(978) 536-5050
Rates from $149
SAVE –B&P Discount Available

Pet Policy: Pets up to 75 lbs, $75 per stay.

Features: Dry cleaning/laundry service, Free breakfast, Indoor pool, Business center, Elevator, Air-conditioned public areas, Self-parking, 24-hour front desk, Porter/bellhop, Wireless Internet, Meeting rooms (small groups), Fitness facilities.

Pittsfield
Also see the following nearby communities that have pet friendly lodging:
Lenox - 6 miles, New Ashford - 9 miles, Lee - 10 miles.

★★★★ 🏃
Crowne Plaza Berkshires
1 West St
Pittsfield MA 01201
(413) 499-2000
$152- $289
SAVE –B&P Discount Available

Pet Policy: Well-behaved small sized pets with $50 per stay fee. Owner-accepting full responsibility for cost of any additional cleaning or damages. Guest agrees not to leave their pet alone in room.

Features: Accessible bathroom, Handicapped parking, Babysitting or child care, Restaurant(s), Hair salon, Number of suites: 2, Number of floors: 14, Conference room(s), Coffee in lobby, Free newspapers, Room service, Porter/bellhop, Wireless Internet, Room service, Indoor pool, Sauna, Bar/lounge, Business center, Shopping on site, Garden, Pool table, Health club, Dry cleaning/laundry service, Parking limited (additional charge), Rooftop terrace.

★★ 🏃
Pittsfield Travelodge
16 Cheshire Rd
Pittsfield MA 01201
(413) 443-5661
$57 - $219
SAVE –B&P Discount Available

Pet Policy: Pets allowed with advanced permission. Please contact hotel directly.

Features: Parking (free), Business services, Free newspapers in lobby.

Not Rated **🏃**
The Yankee Suites Extended Stay
20 West Housatonic Street
Pittsfield MA 01201
(413) 629-2141
$89 - $99

Pet Policy: Pets accepted, $25 per week additional.

Features: Number of Suites: 26, Non-smoking property, Laundry facilities, Fully equipped kitchens, Wireless Internet.

Plymouth
Also see the following nearby communities that have pet friendly lodging:
Kingston - 6 miles.

★★
Bradford Inn and Suites
98 Water St
Plymouth MA 02360
(800) 332-1620
$141 - $160
SAVE –B&P Discount Available

Pet Policy: Pets accepted with nightly fee. Please contact property directly for updated details and reservations.

Features: Fitness facilities, Restaurant(s), Number of floors 3, Laundry facilities, Free breakfast, Parking (free), Swimming pool, Wireless Internet.

Not Rated,
Comfort Inn
155 SAMOSET ST US 44
Plymouth MA 02360
(508) 746-2800
$159 - $169

Pet Policy: Pets accepted, $10 per pet per night. Please contact hotel directly for additional information and to make pet reservations.

Features: Free breakfast, Coffee in Lobby, Wireless Internet, Free daily newspaper, Indoor pool

★★☆
Hampton Inn Suites Plymouth
10 Plaza Way
Plymouth MA 02360
(508) 747-5000
$139 - $159
SAVE –B&P Discount Available

Pet Policy: Pets accepted, $35 per day additional fee.

Features: Coffee in lobby, Dry cleaning/laundry service, Meeting rooms, Fitness facilities, Area shuttle, Free newspapers, Shopping center shuttle (free), Wireless Internet, Indoor pool, Shopping on site, Number of suites: 32, Number of floors: 4, Coffee shop, Parking (free), Business center, Smoke-free property, Free breakfast.

Provincetown

Not Rated
Cape Inn Resort
698-716 Commercial Street
Provincetown MA 02657
(508) 487-1711
$169 - $219

Pet Policy: Dogs welcome in one of 20 designated pet-friendly room, no fee. For your pet's protection and the enjoyment of all, we ask that you follow few simple guidelines when vacationing with your pet here. Your pet doesn't want to miss you or be left out of all the fun, so please don't leave him unattended in your guestroom. When out and about keep your pet leashed for safety's sake. If you do need to slip away without Fido for a short period of time, tell the front desk and leave a cell phone number where you may reached. The comfort of all our guests and the local health code dictates that all common areas, including the lobby, breakfast room, lounge, fire pit and pool, remain quadruped-free. Even the best behaved pet may have an off day. In the unlikely event yours should cause damage with some rock star worthy bad boy behavior we'll ask you to do the right thing and take responsibility.

Features: Bar/lounge, Number of rooms - 10, Number of floors - 2, Air-conditioned, Coffee in lobby, Pool table, Poolside bar, Free breakfast, Parking (free), Outdoor pool - seasonal, Restaurants: 2.

Not Rated
Four Gables Cottages & Suites
15 Race Road
Provincetown MA 02657
(508) 487-2427
$202 - $296

Pet Policy: Pet friendly, $20 per night per pet, ($90 per week on weekly rentals), limit 2 per room. By Town ordinance pets must be kept on a leash in public and droppings must be removed and properly disposed. Pet charges are due and payable on arrival. Guests are advised to please bring proper materials to accommodate these regulations.

Features: Fireplaces in some units, Full kitchens available.

★★★
Gabriel's at The Ashbrooke Inn
102 Bradford Street
Provincetown MA 02657
(508) 487-3232
$160 - $235
SAVE –B&P Discount Available

Pet Policy: Well-behaved, quiet dogs are welcome, $20 per night per dog, limit 2 per room. If your pet likes to sit on furniture, please cover with blankets – we'll provide them if needed.

Features; Smoke-free property, Parking (free), Wireless Internet, Patio, In-room accessibility, Barbecue grill(s), Accessible bathroom, Restaurant(s), Air-conditioned public areas.

★★✦
Moffett House Inn
296A Commercial Street
Provincetown MA 02657
(508) 487-6615
$214- $292
SAVE –B&P Discount Available

Pet Policy: Quiet pets accepted, $15 per night additional.

Features: Coffee in lobby, Number of rooms: 9, Number of floors: 2, Parking (additional charge), Wireless Internet, Barbecue grill(s), Front desk (limited hours)

★★★✦
Prince Albert Guest House
164-166 Commercial Street
Provincetown MA 02657
(508) 487-1850
Rates from $155
SAVE –B&P Discount Available

Pet Policy: Pets accepted with advanced approval, $25 per day pet fee. Damage in excess of that amount is your full responsibility. Our Atlantic St. house has a separate pet fee of $300 per stay Pets MUST be kept quiet at all times. If the pet cannot be left alone in the room without making noise, they must be taken with you. Pets that continue to disrupt the operation of the Inn cannot remain as guests (including complaints from other guests on same). You may be asked to leave without a refund. If you know your pet is a barker or occasionally whines we suggest considering to board your pet professionally INSTEAD OF BRINGING PET to avoid an issue as described herein. *Continued on next page*

Prince Albert Guest House
Provincetown
Continued from previous page

You will be required to board your pet with a local vet or sitter of your choosing if your pet is barking, whining, sick or doing damage. Refunds will not be issued if you opt to check out early due to an issue with your pet.

Please keep pets off all bedding and furniture. Pets that chew must be crated when left alone. If damage occurs, please report it prior to checkout. Owner is responsible for the cost of repairs and/or replacement. If you take your pet to the beach or swimming YOU MUST hose them off at the front door of 164 Commercial. We are glad to provide you with an area & supplies to shampoo; pet towels for drying will be kept inside the front door (& on request if needed).

Please do not use bathroom facilities or guest towels for this; just ask us!! Please walk your pet on public property and you MUST pick up after them every time pet defecates (please bring your own pet waste bags available at Petsmart, Petco, etc.); Provincetown's Residents are VERY particular about your pet being on a leash at all times and about picking up their poop (they can ticket you for not doing so). If your pet does get sick, or begins feeling ill, let us know and we'll secure some pet pads or wee-wee pads to assist you!

Features: Parking (additional charge), Number of rooms: 17, Number of floors: 2, Front desk (limited hours), Wireless Internet, Free breakfast, Barbecue grill(s), Air-conditioned public areas, Patio, Computer rental, Spa Tub.

Raynham
Also see the following nearby communities that have pet friendly lodging:.
Middleboro - 6 miles, Norton - 7 miles.

★★★⫞

Quality Inn Raynham
164 New State Hwy
Raynham MA 02767
(508) 824-8647
$94 - $109.
SAVE –B&P Discount Available

Pet Policy: Quality Inns charge a fee of $10 per night per pet and may require a $50 refundable damage deposit. Quality Inns accept any well-behaved pets with a maximum of 3 per room, but dogs are limited to 50 pounds. They do not currently require a veterinarian certificate. Pets may not be left alone in the room unless in a cage.

Features: Free breakfast, Restaurant, Shopping on site, Coffee in lobby, Parking (free), Free newspapers

Quality Inn Raynham
Continued from previous page

in lobby, 24-hour front desk, Concierge desk, Wireless Internet, Outdoor pool - seasonal, Business center, Number of rooms: 67, Number of floors: 2, Laundry facilities.

Revere

Also see the following nearby communities that have pet friendly lodging:
Saugus - 4 miles, Somerville - 5 miles, Boston - 5 miles, Cambridge - 5 miles, Arlington - 7 miles, Wakefield - 7 miles, Brookline - 8 miles, Woburn - 8 miles, Peabody - 9 miles.

★★★
Comfort Inn & Suites Boston/Airport
85 American Legion Hwy
Revere MA 02151
(781) 485-3600
$159 - $219
SAVE –B&P Discount Available

Pet Policy: Pet accommodation: $25 per night /per pet. Pet Limit: 2 per room under 60 pounds.

Features: Free Breakfast, Indoor pool, Business center, Wireless Internet, Restaurant, Number of rooms: 208, Number of floors: 8, Bar/lounge, Parking (free), Free newspapers in lobby, Coffee in lobby, Smoke-free property, Fitness facilities, Airport transportation (free) available 24 hours.

★★★
Hampton Inn Logan Airport
230 Lee Burbank Hwy
Revere MA 02151
(781) 286-5665
$143 - $219
SAVE –B&P Discount Available

Pet Policy: Pets allowed.

Features: Free Breakfast, Indoor pool, Dry cleaning/laundry service, Parking (free), Bar/lounge, Gift shop, Coffee in lobby, Wireless Internet, Smoke-free property, Fitness facilities, Number of rooms: 227, Number of floors: 7, Conference room(s), Free newspapers in lobby, 24-hour front desk, Business center, Airport transportation (free) available 24 hours.

★★
Rodeway Inn Logan Airport
309 American Legion Hwy.,
Route 60 West
Revere MA 02151
(781) 284-3663
$99 - $136
SAVE –B&P Discount Available

Pet Policy: Rodeway Inns charge a fee of $10 per night per pet and require a $50 refundable damage deposit. Max of 2 pets per room. A veterinarian certificate that the pet is on a flea and parasite program and that they are free from parasites is required. Pets may not be left alone in the room unless in a cage.

Features: Wireless Internet, In-room accessibility, Coffee in lobby, Area shuttle, Airport transportation (free), Number of rooms: 34, Number of floors: 3, Parking, Free newspapers, Smoke-free property.

Salem
Also see the following nearby communities that have pet friendly lodging:
Peabody - 4 miles, Danvers - 5 miles, Saugus - 8 miles, Wakefield - 9 miles.

★★★
Hawthorne Hotel
18 Washington Square West
Salem MA 01970
(978) 744-4080
$130 - $234

Pet Policy: Pets up to 100 lbs accepted, $10 per night plus $100 refundable damage deposit. Pets should not be left alone in room and should be leashed or created when outside room in public areas. Do not give pet a bath in the room!

Features: Year built: 1925, Number of rooms: 74, Number of Suites: 6, Non-smoking property, Air conditioning, Bathrobes, Free morning newspaper, Wireless Internet.

Sandwich
Also see the following nearby communities that have pet friendly lodging:
Barnstable - 9 miles, Hyannis - 10 miles.

★★
Sandwich Lodge & Resort
54 Route 6A
Sandwich MA 02563
(508) 888-2275
$129 - $259
SAVE –B&P Discount Available

Pet Policy: Dogs welcome except in summer months. $15 per dog per night, limit 2 per room. Must not leave alone in room, must keep leashed outside of room, and dogs must have evidence of receiving flea treatment before coming. Pets must be approved in advance so please call directly for reservations.

Features: Number of rooms: 67, Number of floors: 2, Laundry facilities, Parking, Newspapers in lobby, Meeting rooms, Indoor pool, Smoke-free property, Outdoor pool - seasonal, Pool table, Wireless Internet, Handicapped parking, 24-hour business center, Coffee in lobby, Free breakfast, Spa Tub.

Saugus
Also see the following nearby communities that have pet friendly lodging:
Wakefield - 4 miles, Revere - 4 miles, Woburn - 5 miles, Peabody - 5 miles, Somerville - 6 miles, Arlington - 8 miles, Cambridge - 8 miles, Danvers - 8 miles, Boston - 9 miles.

★★
Red Roof Inn Boston - Logan
920 Broadway I-93 North
Saugus MA 01906
(781) 941-1400
$99 - $124
SAVE –B&P Discount Available

Pet Policy: Red Roof's Pet Policy: One well-behaved family pet is permitted unless they are prohibited by state law or ordinance. Service animals are always welcome. Pets must be declared during guest registration. Pets must never be left unattended in the guestroom.

Red Roof Inn – Boston - Logan	**Features:** Business services, Wireless Internet, Handicapped parking, In-room accessibility, RV and truck parking, Parking, Number of rooms: 117, Number of floors: 3, Coffee in lobby, Free newspapers.

Seekonk
Also see the following nearby communities that have pet friendly lodging:
East Providence - 3 miles, Providence - 6 miles, Cranston - 6 miles.

★★★

Comfort Inn Seekonk
341 Highland Ave
Seekonk MA 02771
(508) 336-7900
$89 - $129
SAVE –B&P Discount Available

Pet Policy: Pets up to 50 lbs accepted, $15 per night per pet. Limit 2 pets per room

Features: Wireless Internet, Free breakfast, Laundry facilities, Number of rooms: 90, Number of floors: 2, Parking (free), Free newspapers in lobby, Outdoor pool, Business services, Business center

★★

Ramada Inn
940 Fall River Ave
Seekonk MA 02771
(508) 336-7300
$71 - $159
SAVE –B&P Discount Available

Pet Policy: Pets accepted, $10 per night additional.

Features: Restaurant(s), Conference room(s), Accessible bathroom, Handicapped parking, Indoor pool, Free breakfast, Parking (free), Dry cleaning/laundry service, Wireless Internet, 24-hour business center, RV and truck parking.

Somerset
Also see the following nearby communities that have pet friendly lodging:
Westport - 7 miles.

★★

Quality Inn Somerset
1878 Wilbur Ave
Somerset MA 02725
(508) 678-4545
$84 - $129
SAVE –B&P Discount Available

Pet Policy: Quality Inns charge a fee of $10 per night per pet and may require a $50 refundable damage deposit Quality Inns accept any well-behaved pets with a maximum of 3 per room, but dogs are limited to 50 pounds. They do not currently require a veterinarian certificate. Pets may not be left alone in the room unless in a cage.

Features: Indoor pool, Conference room(s), Number of rooms: 106, Fitness facilities, Restaurant, Laundry facilities, Bar/lounge, Free breakfast, Newspapers in lobby, Coffee in lobby, Parking, Wireless Internet.

★★
Super 8 Motel
537 Riverside Ave
Somerset MA 02725
(508) 678-7665
$55 - $72
SAVE –B&P Discount Available

Pet Policy: Pets accepted with advanced approval and a small nightly fee. Please contact hotel directly for restrictions and reservations.

Features: Business center, Air-conditioned public areas, Coffee in lobby, Free breakfast, Parking (free), 24-hour front desk, Outdoor pool – seasonal.

Somerville
Also see the following nearby communities that have pet friendly lodging::
Cambridge - 2 miles, Arlington - 3 miles, Brookline - 4 miles, Revere - 5 miles, Boston - 6 miles, Saugus - 6 miles, Woburn - 7 miles, Waltham - 7 miles, Newton - 7 miles, Wakefield - 7 miles, Needham - 9 miles.

★★↲
La Quinta Inn & Suites
23 Cummings St
Somerville MA 02145
(617) 625-5300
$134 - $199
SAVE –B&P Discount Available

Pet Policy: Cats and dogs up to 50 pounds are accepted in all guest rooms. Housekeeping services for rooms with pets require pet owner be present or pet must be crated. No fees or deposits are required.

Features: Accessible bathroom, Handicapped parking, Dry cleaning/laundry service, Wireless Internet, Airport transportation (free), Number of rooms: 147, Elevator, Air-conditioned public areas, Free breakfast, Parking (free), Free newspapers in lobby, 24-hour front desk, Business center, Meeting rooms (small groups), Fitness facilities.

South Yarmouth
Also see the following nearby communities that have pet friendly lodging::
West Dennis - 2 miles, West Yarmouth - 3 miles,
Hyannis - 6 miles, Barnstable - 6 miles.

★★
Ambassador Inn & Suites
1314 Route 28
South Yarmouth MA 02664
(508) 394-4000
$124 - $159
SAVE –B&P Discount Available

Pet Policy: Pets up to 100 lbs accepted, $15 per day.

Features: Free Breakfast, Coffee in lobby, Number of rooms: 85, Number of floors: 2, Elevator, Air-conditioned public areas, Parking (free), Free newspapers in lobby, 24-hour front desk, Meeting rooms (small groups), Sauna, Accessible bathroom, Handicapped parking, Arcade/game room, Indoor pool, Multilingual staff, Wireless Internet, 24-hour business center, Outdoor pool - seasonal.

★★
Brentwood Motor Inn
961 Route 28
South Yarmouth MA 02664
(508) 398-8812
$85 - $160
SAVE –B&P Discount Available

Pet Policy: Pets accepted, $10 per pet per day.

Features: Handicapped parking, Wireless Internet (additional charge), Indoor pool, Number of rooms: 32, Number of suites: 10, Number of floors: 1, Multilingual staff, Picnic area, Concierge desk, Parking (free), 24-hour front desk, Sauna.

Southborough

Also see the following nearby communities that have pet friendly lodging:
Westborough - 3 miles, Marlborough - 4 miles, Northborough - 5 miles, Framingham - 7 miles.

★★ 🏃
Red Roof Inn Boston -
Southborough
367 Turnpike Rd
Southborough MA 01772
(508) 481-3904
$65- $85
SAVE –B&P Discount Available

Pet Policy: Red Roof's Pet Policy: One well-behaved family pet is permitted unless they are prohibited by state law or ordinance. Service animals are always welcome. Pets must be declared during guest registration. In consideration of all Red Roof guests, pets must never be left unattended in the guestroom.

Features: Wireless Internet, Parking (free), 24-hour front desk, Accessible bathroom, Handicapped parking, Number of rooms: 108, Number of floors: 2, Coffee in lobby, Free newspapers in lobby.

Springfield

Also see the following nearby communities that have pet friendly lodging:
Chicopee - 3 miles, West Springfield - 4 miles, Holyoke - 9 miles, Enfield - 9 miles, Westfield - 10 miles.

★★★
City Place Inn & Suites
711 Dwight St
Springfield MA 01104
(413) 781-0900
$88 - $149
SAVE –B&P Discount Available

Pet Policy: Dogs and cats, up to 35 lbs accepted, $30 per stay additional. Limited pet-friendly rooms, advised to book directly with hotel.

Features: Number of rooms: 242, Number of suites: 11, Number of floors: 12, Suitable for children, Parking (free), Free newspaper, Indoor pool, Dry cleaning/laundry service, Free breakfast, Security guard, Wireless Internet, Handicapped parking, 24-hour business center, RV and truck parking, Arcade/game room, Fitness facilities, Coffee in lobby.

★★★ 🛏

Lathrop House B&B
188 Sumner Ave
Springfield MA 01108
(413) 736-6414
$150 - $175
SAVE –B&P Discount Available

Pet Policy: Dogs and Cats allowed, $25 additional fee per pet. Cat owners: please bring your own food, litter and water pans and supplies. Dog owners: no dogs left alone in rooms at any time, except if in a crate and does not bark; must be on leash when going through the house; pick up after your dog in the yard and neighborhood.

Features: Year Built 1899, Gift shop, Number of rooms: 3, Business services, Patio, Laundry facilities, Library, Parking (free), Wireless Internet, Smoke-free property, Wedding services, Conference room(s), Barbecue grill(s), Video library, Free breakfast.

★★★ 🛏

Naomi's Inn
20 Springfield St
Springfield MA 01107
(413) 433-6019
Rates from $175
SAVE –B&P Discount Available

Pet Policy: All non-aggressive breed pets accepted, $10 per pet per day. We place people traveling with their pet in our ground floor rooms (each with exits close by. I do not detail rooms while pets are inside. Pet owners will be responsible for their companions and for any excessive damage they may cause. You will be required to sign a pet waiver upon check in.

Features: Wireless Internet, Massage - treatment room(s), Number of rooms: 6, Meeting rooms (small groups), Air-conditioned public areas, Concierge.

★★★★

Sheraton Springfield Hotel
1 Monarch Pl
Springfield MA 01144
(413) 781-1010
$119 - $169
SAVE –B&P Discount Available

Pet Policy: Up to 2 dogs per room, no size limit. $50 per stay.

Features: Bar/lounge, Restaurant, Room service, Gift shop, Number of rooms: 325, Number of floors: 12, Arcade/game room, Wireless Internet, Spa services on site, Free newspapers in lobby, Sauna, Business Center, Health Club, Conference Room(s), Indoor pool, Dry cleaning/laundry service (M-F), Parking (valet) $9.95 Daily.

Stockbridge

Also see the following nearby communities that have pet friendly lodging:
Lee - 3 miles, West Stockbridge - 3 miles, Great Barrington - 6 miles, Lenox - 6 miles.

★★★
The Red Lion Inn
30 Main Street
Stockbridge MA 01262
(413) 298-5545
$135 - $395

Pet Policy: Well-trained and quiet pets are welcome at The Red Lion Inn in selected guestrooms and suites. Dogs and cats will receive a welcome treat upon arrival. Prior reservations are necessary and a $40 fee (per pet, per night) is applicable. Pets must be created if left in room alone, but may not be left alone all day. Pets must be on leash in public areas.

Features: Year built: 1773, Number of rooms: 108. Bathrobes, Wireless Internet, Fireplaces available, Restaurant, Bar/Lounge, Massage on site, Shopping, Continental breakfast.

Sturbridge

★★
Americas Best Value Inn
408 Main Street
Sturbridge MA 01566
(508) 347-7327
$55 - $121

Pet Policy: Pets welcome, $10 fee.

Features: Number of rooms: 50, Mini fridge and coffee makers in all rooms, Continental breakfast.

★★
Comfort Inn & Suites Colonial
215 Charlton Rd US Route 20
Sturbridge MA 01566
(508) 347-3306
$120 - $199

Pet Policy: Limited Pet Accommodations which are in a different building with exterior corridors. Limit 2 pets per room up to 100 pounds. No additional fee.

Features: Wireless Internet, Continental breakfast, Indoor heated pool and whirlpool, Outdoor pool, Fitness center, Bar/lounge, Fireplace suites with whirlpools available.

★★
Publick House Inn And Lodge
277 Main Street
Route 131
Sturbridge MA 01566
(508) 347-3313
$59 - $199
SAVE –B&P Discount Available

Pet Policy: Pets up to 100 lbs are permitted to stay in the Motor Lodge only. Pet fee of $15 per stay.

Features: Bar/Lounge, Restaurant, Number of rooms: 119, Business services, Parking, Swimming pool - children's, Newspapers, Porter/bellhop, Meeting rooms, Outdoor pool - seasonal, Wedding services, Nearby fitness center (discount).

★
Scottish Inns Sturbridge
142 Main Street
Sturbridge MA 01566
(508) 347-9514
$60 - $72

Pet Policy: Small pets allowed.

Features: Wireless Internet, Continental breakfast, Mini fridge and microwave in each room.

★★
Sturbridge Days Inn
66-68 Haynes St
Sturbridge MA 01566
(508) 347-3391
$63 - $79
SAVE –B&P Discount Available

Pet Policy: Pets accepted, $10 per night per pet.

Features: Business services, Air-conditioned public areas, Coffee in lobby, Wireless Internet (additional charge), Free breakfast, Parking, Free newspapers in lobby, Concierge, Outdoor pool – seasonal.

★★★
Sturbridge Host Resort
366 Main St
Sturbridge MA 01566
(508) 347-7393
$114 - $189
SAVE –B&P Discount Available

Pet Policy: Pets accepted, $25 per night additional fee.

Features: Bar/lounge, Gift shop, Number of rooms: 233, Number of floors: 2, Elevator, Business services, Fireplace in lobby, Patio, Wireless Internet, Parking, Free newspapers, Private beach, Meeting rooms, Indoor pool, Arcade/game room, Accessible bathroom, Handicapped parking, Number of restaurants 2.

★★
Super 8 Sturbridge
358 Main St
Sturbridge MA 01566
(508) 347-9000
$89 - $214
SAVE –B&P Discount Available

Pet Policy: Pets accepted, $20 per stay. Limit 2 per room.

Features: Handicapped parking, In-room accessibility, Wireless Internet, Swimming pool - children's, Outdoor pool, Free breakfast, Parking (free), Meeting rooms (small groups).

★★
Travelodge Sturbridge
400 Route 15
Sturbridge MA 01566
(508) 347-1978
$63 - $159
SAVE –B&P Discount Available

Pet Policy: Pets accepted, $10 per night.

Features: Swimming pool - children's, Number of rooms: 83, Number of suites: 22, Number of floors: 3, Elevator, Coffee in lobby, Free breakfast, Free newspapers in lobby, Business center, Wireless Internet, Outdoor pool - seasonal, Parking (free).

Tewksbury

Also see the following nearby communities that have pet friendly lodging:
Lowell - 4 miles, Andover - 5 miles, Billerica - 7 miles, Lawrence - 7 miles, North Chelmsford - 7 miles, Methuen - 8 miles, Salem - 9 miles.

★★

Extended Stay America Boston
1910 Andover St
Tewksbury MA 01876
(978) 863-9888
$84 - $109
SAVE –B&P Discount Available

Pet Policy: One pet is allowed in each guest room. A $25 per day non-refundable cleaning fee (not to exceed $150) will be charged the first night of your stay. Weight, size and breed restrictions may apply. Please contact the hotel directly with inquiries.

Features: Dry cleaning/laundry service, Number of rooms: 92, Number of floors: 3, Business services, Parking, Limo or Town Car service, Wireless Internet.

★★★

Holiday Inn Tewksbury Andover
4 Highwood Drive
Tewksbury MA 01876
(978) 640-9000
$83 - $210
SAVE –B&P Discount Available

Pet Policy: All pets must be registered at check-in. A $50 nonrefundable cleaning fee will be collected at check-in. Pets are not to be left unattended in hotel rooms. Pets are not allowed in first floor rooms. Pet Fee: $50 per night

Features: Restaurant(s), Concierge, Number of rooms: 227, Number of suites: 21, Number of floors: 5, Wireless Internet, Parking (free), Handicapped parking, In-room accessibility, Dry cleaning/laundry service, Sauna, Indoor pool, Bar/lounge, Room service, Business services, Fitness facilities.

★★★

Residence Inn By Marriott
1775 Andover St
Tewksbury MA 01876
(978) 640-1003
$119 - $199
SAVE –B&P Discount Available

Pet Policy: Pets allowed, $100 per stay cleaning fee.

Features: Handicapped parking, In-room accessibility, Dry cleaning/laundry service, Number of rooms: 130, Number of floors: 3, Coffee in lobby, Parking, Free newspapers in lobby, Business center, Meeting rooms (small groups), Outdoor pool - seasonal, Tennis on site, Fitness facilities.

★★★

Towneplace Suites By Marriott
20 International Place
Tewksbury MA 01876
(978) 863-9800
$89. - $144
SAVE –B&P Discount Available

Pet Policy: Pets allowed, $75 per stay cleaning fee.

Features: Business services, Dry cleaning/laundry service, Number of rooms: 95, Number of floors: 3, Elevator, Barbecue grill(s), Coffee in lobby, Parking (free), Outdoor pool - seasonal, Fitness facilities.

Wakefield

Also see the following nearby communities that have pet friendly lodging:
Woburn - 2 miles, Saugus - 4 miles, Peabody - 5 miles, Danvers - 7 miles, Revere - 7 miles, Somerville - 7 miles, Arlington - 8 miles, Cambridge - 9 miles.

★★★★

Sheraton Colonial Hotel
1 Audubon Rd
Wakefield MA 01880
(781) 245-9300
$125 - $195
SAVE –B&P Discount Available

Pet Policy: Pets up to 80 lbs accepted, no additional fee. Sheraton Sweet Sleeper Dog Bed Available

Features: Business Center, Conference Room(s), Bar/Lounge, Restaurant(s), Hair salon, Number of rooms: 280, Number of floors: 11, Parking (free), 24-hour front desk, Porter/bellhop, Wireless Internet, Sauna, Smoke-free property, Room service.

Waltham

Also see the following nearby communities that have pet friendly lodging:
Newton - 2 miles, Arlington - 5 miles, Needham - 6 miles, Brookline - 6 miles, Cambridge - 6 miles, Lexington - 6 miles, Somerville - 7 miles, Dedham - 7 miles, Framingham - 10 miles.

★★★

Courtyard by Marriott
387 Winter St
Waltham MA 02451
(781) 419 0900
$101 - $129
SAVE –B&P Discount Available

Pet Policy: Pets allowed, $50 cleaning fee.

Features: Business Center, Coffee in lobby, Accessible bathroom, Handicapped parking, Indoor pool, Dry cleaning/laundry service, Fitness facilities, Bar/lounge, Restaurant(s), Number of rooms: 117, Number of floors: 5, Conference room(s), Grocery, Parking (free), Free newspapers in lobby, Wireless Internet, Meeting rooms

★★★

Crescent Suites Hotel
287 Crescent Street
Waltham MA 02453
(781) 314-7900
$154 - $195
SAVE –B&P Discount Available

Pet Policy: Pets accepted in pet-friendly designated rooms. No fee, limit 2 per room.

Features: Accessible bathroom, Handicapped parking, Dry cleaning/laundry service, Fitness facilities, Elevator, Airport transportation (additional charge), Air-conditioned public areas, Patio, Barbecue grill(s), Grocery, Parking (free), Business center, Limo or Town Car service available, Smoke-free property, Wireless Internet.

★★☆
Extended Stay Deluxe
32 4th Ave
Waltham MA 02451
(781) 622-1900
$89 - $144
SAVE –B&P Discount Available

Pet Policy: One pet is accepted per guest room. The General Manager has the discretion to allow additional pets per room. Guests with a pet are charged a $25 a day (not to exceed $150) pet fee upon check-in. The guest room carpet is cleaned, all bedding is washed, and a professional exterminator treats the room after a guest with a pet checks out. Occupied guest rooms with pets are similarly cleaned monthly in the event of a long-term stay.

Features: Number of suites: 135, Number of floors: 3, Elevator, Business services, Patio, Barbecue grill(s), Parking (free), Wireless Internet, Handicapped parking, Laundry facilities, Outdoor pool, Coffee in lobby, Fitness facilities.

★★★
Hilton Garden Inn
420 Totten Pond Rd
Waltham MA 02451
(781) 890-0100
$119 - $219
SAVE –B&P Discount Available

Pet Policy: Pets up to 40 lbs, $25 per night.

Features: Smoke-free property, Area shuttle (free), Number of rooms: 148, Number of floors: 6, Parking (free), 24-hour front desk, Wireless Internet, Indoor pool, Dry cleaning/laundry service, Bar/lounge, Business center, Shopping on site, Conference room(s), Babysitting or child care, Room service (limited hours), Fitness facilities.

★★☆
Holiday Inn Express
385 Winter St
Waltham MA 02451
(781) 890-2800
$83 - $186
SAVE –B&P Discount Available

Pet Policy: Pets accepted, $50 per stay fee.

Features: Handicapped parking, In-room accessibility, Dry cleaning/laundry service, Number of rooms: 156, Number of suites: 2, Number of floors: 6, Coffee in lobby, Free breakfast, Parking (free), Business center, Wireless Internet.

★★★
Home Suites Inn
455 Totten Pond road
Waltham MA 02154
(800) 868-9218
$109 - $119

Pet Policy: Pets accepted, $50 per stay fee. Pets must be held, leashed or crated in public areas.

Features: Number of rooms: 117, Full hot breakfast, Wireless internet, Outdoor pool, Exercise room, Restaurant, Airport shuttle (additional charge).

★★
Homestead Boston Waltham
52 4th Ave
Waltham MA 02451
(781) 890-1333
$79 - $169
SAVE –B&P Discount Available

Pet Policy: We gladly welcome one pet per guest room. A $25 per day non-refundable cleaning fee (not to exceed $150) will be charged the first night of your stay. There are size and breed restrictions. Please contact hotel directly for approval and reservation.

Features: Wireless Internet (additional charge), Elevator, Barbecue grill(s), Coffee in lobby, Parking (free), 24-hour front desk, Laundry facilities.

Not Rated
Oakwood Waltham
40 Kings Way
Waltham MA 02451
(800) 259-6914
$159 - $214

Pet Policy: Pets accepted, $10 per day to a maximum of $300.

Features: Extended stay suites, Fully equipped kitchens, Weekly housekeeping, Minimum 30 days stay may be required.

★★★★
The Westin Waltham-Boston
70 Third Ave.
Waltham MA 02451
(781) 290-5600
$98 - $344
SAVE –B&P Discount Available

Pet Policy: Pets up to 40 lbs accepted without a fee, limit 1 per room. Pets must be attended to at all times.

Features: Dry cleaning/laundry service, Restaurant, Parking (valet – fee), Gift shop, Number of rooms: 346, Number of floors: 8, Health club, Porter/bellhop, Wireless Internet, Concierge, Meeting rooms, Doorman/doorwoman, Smoke-free property, Wedding services, Room service (24 hours), Bar/lounge, Indoor pool, Business center.

West Dennis
Also see the following nearby communities that have pet friendly lodging:
South Yarmouth - 2 miles, West Yarmouth - 4 miles, Hyannis - 7 miles, Barnstable - 8 miles.

Not Rated
Cape Cod Ocean Resorts
416 Main St.
West Dennis MA 02670
$140 - $279

Pet Policy: Dogs accepted, $10 per pet per night.

Features: Private beach, Fitness center, Putting greens, Indoor and Outdoor pools.

West Springfield
Also see the following nearby communities that have pet friendly lodging:
Chicopee - 4 miles, Springfield - 4 miles, Westfield - 5 miles, Holyoke - 7 miles, Enfield - 10 miles.

★★
Candlewood Suites
572 Riverdale St
West Springfield MA 01089
(413) 739-1122
$97 - $152
SAVE –B&P Discount Available

Pet Policy: Dogs are allowed with a nonrefundable fee of $25 per night and up to $150 for 7+ nights. Limit of 2 dogs per room weighing less than 60lbs per dog. Pet agreement must be signed at check-in. Up-to-date vaccinations required. We do not accept cats.

Features: Accessible bathroom, Handicapped parking, Dry cleaning/laundry service, Indoor pool, Gift shop, Number of suites: 71, Number of floors: 4, Business services, Patio, Barbecue grill(s), Parking (free), Free newspapers in lobby.

★★
Econo Lodge West Springfield
1533 Elm St
West Springfield MA 01089
(413) 734-8278
$72 - $89
SAVE –B&P Discount Available

Pet Policy: Pet accommodation: $25 per night, only in K and QQ rooms.

Features: Number of rooms: 65, Number of floors: 2, Parking (free), 24-hour front desk, Wireless Internet, Free breakfast, Business services.

★★★
Hampton Inn West Springfield
1011 Riverdale St
West Springfield MA 01089
(413) 732-1300
$126 - $159
SAVE –B&P Discount Available

Pet Policy: Pets up to 50 lbs accepted, no additional fee. Limit 2 per room.

Feature: Business services, Dry cleaning/laundry service, Number of rooms: 126, Number of floors: 4, Coffee in lobby, Free breakfast, Parking (free), Free newspapers in lobby, Nearby fitness center (free), Wireless Internet, Outdoor pool – seasonal.

★
Knights Inn West Springfield
1557 Riverdale Street
West Springfield MA 01089
(413) 737-9047
$48 - $65

Pet Policy: Small pets accepted, $10 per night per pet.

Features: Outdoor pool, Continental breakfast.

★★
Quality Inn West Springfield
1150 Riverdale St
West Springfield MA 01089
(413) 739-7261
Rates from $79
SAVE –B&P Discount Available

Pet Policy: Quality Inns charge a fee of $10 per night per pet a $50 refundable damage deposit. Quality Inns accept any well-behaved pets with a maximum of 3 per room, but dogs are limited to 50 pounds. They do not currently require a veterinarian certificate. Pets may not be left alone in the room unless in a cage.

Features: Restaurant, Room service (limited hours), Gift shop, Number of rooms: 114, Number of floors: 5, Conference room(s), Arcade/game room, Free breakfast, Parking (free), Free newspapers in lobby, Business center, Wireless Internet, Outdoor pool, Dry cleaning/laundry service, Fitness facilities.

★
Red Carpet Inn
560 Riverdale Street
West Springfield MA 01089
(413) 733-6678
$71 - $105

Pet Policy: Dogs allowed, $10 per dog per day. Must indicate bringing dog on reservation.

Features: Wireless Internet, Continental breakfast.

★★
Red Roof Inn West Springfield
1254 Riverdale Street
West Springfield MA 01089
(413) 731-1010
$64 - $84
SAVE –B&P Discount Available

Pet Policy: One well-behaved family pet is permitted unless they are prohibited by state law or ordinance. Service animals are always welcome. Pets must be declared during guest registration. In consideration of all Red Roof guests, pets must never be left unattended in the guestroom.

Features: Accessible bathroom, Handicapped parking, In-room accessibility, Wireless Internet, Number of rooms: 111, Number of floors: 2, Suitable for children, Air-conditioned public areas, Coffee in lobby, Parking (free), Free newspapers in lobby, 24-hour front desk.

★★
Regency Inn and Suites
21 Baldwin St
West Springfield MA 01089
(413) 781-2300
$118 - $199
SAVE –B&P Discount Available

Pet Policy: Dogs and cats accepted, $25 per night.

Features: Suitable for children, Air-conditioned public areas, Parking (free), Wireless Internet, 24-hour business center, Indoor pool, Number of rooms: 50, Number of floors: 2, Coffee in lobby, Free breakfast, Multilingual staff, 24-hour front desk, Accessible bathroom, Handicapped parking, Business center.

★★★
Residence Inn by Marriott
64 Border Way
West Springfield MA 01089
(413) 732-9543
$179 - $247
SAVE –B&P Discount Available

Pet Policy: Pets allowed, $75 per stay cleaning fee.

Features: Dry cleaning/laundry service, Wireless Internet, Business center, Indoor pool, Picnic area, Fitness facilities, Number of suites: 88, Number of floors: 4, Coffee in lobby, Free breakfast, Parking (free), Free newspapers in lobby, 24-hour front desk, Smoke-free property.

West Stockbridge
Also see the following nearby communities that have pet friendly lodging:
Stockbridge - 3 miles, Lee - 5 miles, Lenox - 5 miles, Great Barrington - 8 miles.

★★
Pleasant Valley Motel
42 Stockbridge Road
West Stockbridge MA 01266
(413) 232-8511
$112 - $125

Pet Policy: Pets accepted, $10 per day per pet.

Features: Outdoor pool, Parking (free), 24-hour front desk, Wireless Internet, RV and truck parking.

★★★
Shaker Mill Inn
2 Oak St
West Stockbridge MA 01266
(413) 232-4600
Rates starting at $18
SAVE –B&P Discount Available

Pet Policy: Pets accepted, $15 per stay. Guests must ensure that their pets do not disturb other guests, and that all droppings are discarded in the flip-top container outside your door. We recommend Debbie at 413-281-5825 for all types of pet sitting services. Guest will be responsible for any pet-related damages that occur.

Features: Number of rooms: 9, Free breakfast, Suitable for children.

West Yarmouth
Also see the following nearby communities that have pet friendly lodging:
South Yarmouth - 3 miles, Hyannis - 3 miles, West Dennis - 4 miles, Barnstable - 5 miles,

★
American Host Motel
69 Main Street
West Yarmouth MA 02673
(508) 775-2332
$65- $133
SAVE –B&P Discount Available

Pet Policy: Pets accepted with fee at check in.

Features: Free breakfast, Indoor pool, Number of rooms: 70, Number of floors: 2, Air-conditioned public areas, Parking (free), 24-hour front desk, Business center.

★★
Castle Dawn Motel
226 Route 28
West Yarmouth MA 02673
(866) 872-8600
$74 - $119
SAVE –B&P Discount Available

Pet Policy: Pets accepted, $10 per night additional fee.

Features: Outdoor pool, Number of floors 1, Parking (free), 24-hour front desk, Wireless Internet.

★★
Super 8 West Yarmouth
41 East Rte. 28
West Yarmouth MA 02673
(508)775-0962
$89 - $258
SAVE –B&P Discount Available

Pet Policy: Pets allowed, $20 per pet per night.

Features: Coffee in lobby, Free breakfast, Parking (free), Outdoor pool, Business center, RV and truck parking.

Westborough
Also see the following nearby communities that have pet friendly lodging:
Northborough - 3 miles, Southborough - 3 miles, Marlborough - 5 miles.

★★ 🐾
Extended Stay America
19 Connector Rd
Westborough MA 01581
(508) 616-0155
$79 - $99
SAVE –B&P Discount Available

Pet Policy: One pet is allowed in each guest room. A $25 per day non-refundable cleaning fee (not to exceed $150) will be charged the first night of your stay. Weight, size and breed restrictions may apply. Please contact the hotel directly with inquiries. Please Note: Signature rooms do not currently accommodate pets.

Features: Number of rooms: 92, Number of floors: 3, Business services, Air-conditioned public areas, Parking (free), Multilingual staff, Free newspapers in lobby, 24-hour front desk, Wireless Internet.

★★★ 🐾
Extended Stay Deluxe
180 E Main St
Westborough MA 01581
(508) 616-9213
$87 - $117
SAVE –B&P Discount Available

Pet Policy: One pet is allowed in each guest room. A $25 per day non-refundable cleaning fee (not to exceed $150) will be charged the first night of your stay. Weight, size and breed restrictions may apply. Please contact the hotel directly with inquiries.

Features: Number of rooms: 86, Number of floors: 3, Airport transportation (additional charge), Business services, Air-conditioned public areas, Barbecue grill(s), Laundry facilities, Free breakfast, Parking (free), Multilingual staff, Free newspapers in lobby, Picnic area, Wireless Internet, Fitness facilities.

★★★ 🏃
Residence Inn By Marriott
25 Connector Rd
Westborough MA 01581
(508) 366-7700
$114 - $199
SAVE –B&P Discount Available

Pet Policy: Pets allowed, $100 per stay cleaning fee.

Features: Dry cleaning/laundry service, Number of suites: 109, Number of floors: 3, Airport transportation (additional charge), Air-conditioned public areas, Grocery, Parking (free), Free newspapers in lobby, Picnic area, Meeting rooms (small groups), Smoke-free property, Outdoor pool - seasonal, Tennis on site.

Westfield

Also see the following nearby communities that have pet friendly lodging:
West Springfield - 5 miles, Chicopee - 8 miles, Holyoke - 9 miles, Springfield - 10 miles.

★★
Econo Lodge Inn And Suites
2 Southampton Rd
Westfield MA 01085
(413) 568-2821
$72 - $99
SAVE –B&P Discount Available

Pet Policy: Pet Accommodation: $20 plus tax for 3 nights. Additional $20 plus tax for each additional 3 night stay after first 3 nights . Maximum 2 pets per room. Pets may not be left unattended in room at any time.

Features: Restaurant, Number of rooms: 56, Floors: 2, Free breakfast, Parking (free), Free newspapers in lobby, 24-hour front desk, Outdoor pool - seasonal, Wireless Internet, Business center.

Not Rated
Elm Motel
50 Russell road
Westfield MA 01085
(413) 562-9727
$49 - $54

Pet Policy: Small pets accepted with advanced approval. Please contact motel directly for pet approval and reservations.

Features: Efficiencies with Kitchenettes, Wireless Internet, In room coffee makers.

Westford

Also see the following nearby communities that have pet friendly lodging:
North Chelmsford - 5 miles, Lowell - 7 miles, Billerica - 9 miles, Boxborough - 9 miles.

★★★ 🏃
Residence Inn by Marriott
7 Lan Drive
Westford MA 01886
(978) 392 1407
$189 - $229
SAVE –B&P Discount Available

Pet Policy: Pets allowed, $75 cleaning fee per stay.

Features: Handicapped parking, In-room accessibility, Indoor pool, Free breakfast, Number of rooms: 108, Number of floors: 3, Parking (free), 24-hour front desk, Wireless Internet.

Westminster
Also see the following nearby communities that have pet friendly lodging:
Fitchburg - 5 miles, Gardner - 6 miles, Leominster - 7 miles.

Rodeway Inn Westminster
183 Main Street
Westminster MA 01473
(978) 874-5951
$59 - $110

Pet Policy: Allows 2 large or 4 small dogs, $5 per dog per night.

Features: Mini fridge and microwaves in all rooms, Continental breakfast.

Westport
Also see the following nearby communities that have pet friendly lodging:
North Dartmouth - 6 miles, Somerset - 7 miles, Fairhaven - 9 miles, New Bedford - 9 miles.

Hampton Inn
53 Old Bedford Rd
Westport MA 02790
(508) 675-8500
$129 - $219
SAVE –B&P Discount Available

Pet Policy: Pets up to 75 lbs, $35 fee.

Features: Bar/lounge, Indoor pool, Restaurant(s), Room service (limited hours), Number of floors: 4, Elevator, Conference room(s), Air-conditioned public areas, Parking (free), Business center, Fitness facilities, Free breakfast, 24-hour front desk, Dry cleaning/laundry service, Area shuttle (additional charge), Tennis on site.

Woburn
Also see the following nearby communities that have pet friendly lodging:
Wakefield - 2 miles, Saugus - 5 miles, Arlington - 6 miles, Somerville - 7 miles, Peabody - 7 miles, Revere - 8 miles, Cambridge - 8 miles, Danvers - 9 miles, Billerica - 9 miles.

Best Western Plus New Englander
1 Rainin Road
Woburn MA 01801
(781) 897-0081
$109 - $130
SAVE –B&P Discount Available

Pet Policy: Pets allowed based on the availability of pet friendly rooms. Up to 2 dogs per room with an 80 pound weight limit. Additional pet types (cats, birds, etc.) may be accepted at the hotel's discretion. Pet rate is $20 per day with a $100 per week maximum. A refundable cleaning & damage deposit of $50 is required upon check-in. If damage occurs or excessive cleaning is needed, the deposit can become non-refundable and the hotel may charge additionally to cover the costs of repair/cleaning.

Features: Restaurant, Number of rooms: 99, Number of floors: 5, Elevator, Conference room(s), Air-

Best Western Plus New Englander
Continued from previous page

conditioned public areas, Wireless Internet, Parking (free), Multilingual staff, Free newspapers in lobby, 24-hour front desk, Porter/bellhop, Indoor pool, Smoke-free property, RV and truck parking, Dry cleaning/laundry service, Business center, Room service (limited hours), Free breakfast, Bar/lounge, Fitness facilities

★★★♩
Extended Stay Deluxe Boston - Woburn
831 Main St
Woburn MA 01801
(781) 938-3737
$109. - $119
SAVE –B&P Discount Available

Pet Policy: One pet is allowed in each guest room. A $25 per day non-refundable cleaning fee (not to exceed $150) will be charged the first night of your stay. Weight, size and breed restrictions may apply. Please contact the hotel directly with inquiries. Please Note: Signature rooms do not currently accommodate pets, with the exception of handicap accessible rooms.

Features: Wireless Internet- additional charge, Business services, Dry cleaning/laundry service, Number of suites: 100, Elevator, Patio, Barbecue grill(s), Fax machine, Parking (free), 24-hour front desk, Smoke-free property, Outdoor pool - seasonal, Coffee in lobby, Fitness facilities, Outdoor pool.

★★★★♩
Hilton Boston/Woburn
2 Forbes Rd
Woburn MA 01801
(781) 932-0999
$84 - $229
SAVE –B&P Discount Available

Pet Policy: Pets up to 75 lbs. Pet fee: $75

Features: Accessible bathroom, Handicapped parking, Dry cleaning/laundry service, Wireless Internet, Indoor pool, Bar/lounge, Business center, Restaurant(s), Gift shop, Number of rooms: 344, Number of floors: 7, Coffee in lobby, Library, Parking (free), Swimming pool - children's, 24-hour front desk, Meeting rooms, Parking garage, Wedding services, Fitness facilities, Room service.

★★★
Holiday Inn Select
15 Middlesex Canal Park
Woburn MA 01801
(781) 935-8760
$98 - $199
SAVE –B&P Discount Available

Pet Policy: Pets welcome - $50 per stay.

Features: Restaurant, Concierge, Gift shop, Number of rooms: 195, Number of floors: 4, Secretarial services, Air-conditioned public areas, Parking (free), Multilingual staff, 24-hour front desk, Porter/bellhop, Wireless Internet, Meeting rooms (small groups), Accessible bathroom, Handicapped parking, Indoor pool, Dry cleaning/laundry service, Bar/lounge, Business center, Room service Fitness facilities.

★★
Red Roof Inn
19 Commerce Way
Woburn MA 01801
(781) 935-7110
$89 - $119
SAVE –B&P Discount Available

Pet Policy: Red Roof's Pet Policy: One well-behaved family pet is permitted unless prohibited by state law or ordinance. Service animals are always welcome. Pets must be declared during guest registration. In consideration of all Red Roof guests, pets must never be left unattended in the guestroom.

Features: 24-hour business center, Self-parking, Indoor pool, Free breakfast, Wireless Internet, Dry cleaning/laundry service, Number of rooms: 159, Number of floors: 5, Coffee in lobby, Free newspapers in lobby, 24-hour front desk, Accessible bathroom, Handicapped parking, Business services.

★★★
Residence Inn By Marriott
300 Presidential Way
Woburn MA 01801
(800) 331-3131
$219 - $220
SAVE –B&P Discount Available

Pet Policy: Pets allowed, $75 per stay cleaning fee.

Features: Bar/lounge, Business Center, Accessible bathroom, Handicapped parking, Indoor pool, Dry cleaning/laundry service, Fitness facilities, Number of rooms: 149, Number of floors: 7, Conference room(s), Patio, Coffee in lobby, Grocery, Parking, Newspapers in lobby, Nearby fitness center (free), Wireless Internet.

Worcester
Also see the following nearby communities that have pet friendly lodging:
Auburn - 7 miles, Northborough - 10 miles.

★★
Quality Inn And Suites
50 Oriole Dr
Worcester MA 01605
(508) 852-2800
$119 - $159
SAVE –B&P Discount Available

Pet Policy: Pets up to 70 lbs, $10 per pet per night. Limit 1 pet per room.

Features: Gift shop, Number of rooms: 116, Number of floors: 3, Elevator, Business services, Coffee in lobby, Parking (free), 24-hour front desk, Outdoor pool - seasonal, Wireless Internet, Accessible bathroom, Handicapped parking, Free breakfast.

★★★
Residence Inn by Marriott
503 Plantation St
Worcester MA 01605
(508) 753 6300
$119 - $179
SAVE –B&P Discount Available

Pet Policy: Pets allowed, $100 per stay cleaning fee.

Features: Photocopy machines, Fireplace in lobby, Fax machine, Health club, Free newspapers in lobby, Smoke-free property, Accessible bathroom, Handicapped parking, In-room accessibility, Dry cleaning/laundry service, Wireless Internet,

Residence Inn by Marriott
Continued from previous page

Bar/lounge, Number of suites: 122, Number of floors: 4, Elevator, Air-conditioned public areas, Patio, Pool table, Grocery, Parking (free), 24-hour front desk, Meeting rooms (small groups), 24-hour business center, Barbecue grill(s), Indoor pool, Coffee in lobby, Area shuttle (free).

New Hampshire

Ashland

Also see the following nearby communities that have pet friendly lodging:
Campton - 9 miles.

Cheney House
82 Highland St
Ashland NH 03217
(603)-968-4499
$140 - $160
SAVE –B&P Discount Available

Pet Policy: Small dog or cat permitted. Owners have own pets on premises. Please call directly for pet reservations and any restrictions.

Features: Year Built 1895, Dry cleaning/laundry service, Number of rooms: 3, Fireplace in lobby, Parking (free), Wireless Internet, Smoke-free property, Library, Suitable for children, Free breakfast, Barbecue grill(s), Front desk (limited hours).

Comfort Inn
53 West St
Ashland NH 03217
(603) 968-7668
$99 - $179
SAVE –B&P Discount Available

Pet Policy: Pet accommodation: $20 per night per pet. Pet Limit: 2 pets per room.

Features: Business Center, Outdoor pool, Gift shops or newsstand, Number of rooms: 40, Number of floors: 3, Air-conditioned public areas, Coffee in lobby, Video library, Free breakfast, Parking (free), 24-hour front desk, Banquet facilities.

Glynn House Inn
59 Highland Street
Ashland NH 03217
(603) 968-3775
$158- $289
SAVE –B&P Discount Available

Pet Policy: Dogs accepted in 4 of the rooms, $25 per stay for 1 dog, $35 for 2. A pet welcome kit - with a water bowl, treats, clean-up bags plus canine beds - in different sizes to ensure your dog gets a good night's sleep too - will greet your best friend upon arrival. Pet reservations MUST be made by telephone directly to the Inn.

Features: Free Breakfast, Number of rooms: 13, Laundry facilities, Parking (free), Wireless Internet, Suitable for children.

Bartlett

Also see the following nearby communities that have pet friendly lodging:
Intervale - 4 miles, Jackson - 4 miles, North Conway - 6 miles

Nordic Village Resort
Route 16
Bartlett NH 03846
(603) 383-9101
Rates from $279
SAVE –B&P Discount Available

Pet Policy: Pets are accepted with nightly fee that varies by the unit selected. Fees may run as high as $100 per night so check with the resort directly when making a pet reservation. Pets shouldn't be left alone in their room. Even well-behaved pets do act up when their master leaves them alone. Pets should be kept on a leash when not in their room (unless, of course, you have a goldfish). When you walk your pet, please do your part to help keep our grounds clean. There are many areas to walk your dog at Nordic Village Resort. Take a stroll on our hiking trails.

When asked if we allow dogs at our hotel, here's what we generally reply: Dogs are welcome in this hotel. We've never had a dog that smoked in bed and set fire to the blankets. We've never had a dog that stole the towels, played the TV too loud or had a fight with his traveling companion. We've never had a dog that got drunk and broke up the furniture. So, if your dog can vouch for you, you're welcome, too!

Features: Indoor pool, Outdoor pool, Number of rooms: 225, Number of floors: 4, Air-conditioned public areas, Parking (free), Free newspapers in lobby, Picnic area, Front desk (limited hours), Sauna, Tennis on site, Suitable for children, Coffee in lobby, Barbecue grill(s), Ski storage, Arcade/game room, Pool table, Steam room, Concierge services, Fitness facilities, 'Wireless Internet, Gift shop.

The Bartlett Inn
1477 US Rte 302
Bartlett NH 03812
(800) 292-2353
$80 - $195
SAVE –B&P Discount Available

Pet Policy: The Bartlett Inn has a tradition of welcoming pets in our cottages so that the whole family can come along for vacation. This service is just $15 per pet per stay. Prior approval of the pet and a valid credit card imprint with signature is required.

Features: Number of rooms: 15, Fireplace in lobby, Parking (free), Wireless Internet, Wedding services, Free breakfast, Suitable for children.

Not Rated
Villager Motel
1126 Route 302
Bartlett NH 03812
(603) 374-2742
$69 - $345

Pet Policy: Dogs accepted, $15 per night. Please call the hotel directly for pet reservations. We ask that the dog you bring be fully house-broken. We ask that you never leave your dog unattended in a guest room or any public area at any time. This does include going out to dinner, skiing for the day etc. If your dog is left unattended in your room there will be a $100 fee. We ask that you keep your dog on a leash in all public areas of the motel. We ask that you pick up after your dog outside. If there are complaints from other motel guests due to any noise or disturbance caused by your dog, you may be asked to remove the pet from the motel - No Refunds. You will be held responsible for the cost of any repairs or commercial cleaning that may be necessary as a result of damage or soiling caused by your pet. If you need assistance in arranging dog-care please ask we will provide you with some names and numbers.

Features: Full breakfast, Jacuzzi and fireplace rooms, kitchenettes available.

Bretton Woods

★★★★ Omni Bretton Arms Inn at Mount Washington Resort
173 Mt Washington Hotel Drive
Bretton Woods NH 03575
(603)-278-1000
$119 - $314
SAVE –B&P Discount Available

Pet Policy: Dogs and cats up to 25 lbs accepted, $50 per stay per pet, maximum of $100 per stay.

Features: Year Built 1896. Fitness facilities, Number of rooms: 34, Number of floors: 2, Elevator, Fireplace in lobby, Free breakfast, Self-parking, Full-service health spa, Meeting rooms (small groups), Sauna, Wedding services, 3 Indoor pools, Restaurant(s), Outdoor pool, Supervised child care/activities, Concierge, Gift shop, Coffee in lobby, Ski storage, Clubhouse, Free newspapers in lobby, Picnic area, 24-hour front desk, Porter/bellhop, Security guard, Dry cleaning/laundry service, Medical assistance available, Beauty services, Massage - treatment room(s), Ski shuttle, Smoke-free property, Children's club, Poolside bar, Swimming pool - children's, Designated smoking areas, Creche (nursery), Media library, Wireless Internet, Accessible bathroom, Handicapped parking, In-room accessibility, RV and truck parking, Bar/lounge, Area shuttle (free), Golf course on site, Tennis on site.

★★★♥ 🎿
The Omni Mount Washington Resort
301 Mt Washington Hotel Rd
Bretton Woods NH 03575
(603) 278-3000
$289 - $349
SAVE –B&P Discount Available

Pet Policy: Dogs and cats up to 25 lbs accepted, $50 per stay per pet, maximum of $100 per stay.

Features: Bar/lounge, Room service (limited hours), Photocopy machines, Suitable for children, Fireplace in lobby, Fax machine, Garden, Clubhouse, Poolside bar, Coffee shop, Wireless Internet, Parking (free), Spa services on site, Free newspapers in lobby, 24-hour front desk, Security guard, Beauty services, Steam room, Sauna, Designated smoking areas, RV and truck parking, Restaurant(s), Number of rooms: 234, Number of floors: 4, Elevator with attendant, Computer rental, Patio, Piano, Pool table, Picnic area, Business center, Dry cleaning/laundry service, Limo or Town Car service available, Medical assistance available, Creche (nursery), Grocery/convenience store, Accessible bathroom, Swimming pool - children's, On-site medical assistance available, Area shuttle (free), Year Built 1902, Number of indoor swimming pools 3, Babysitting or child care, Outdoor pool, Supervised child care/activities, Shopping on site, Conference room(s), Air-conditioned public areas, Ski storage, Arcade/game room, Nightclub, Porter/bellhop, Doorman/doorwoman, Concierge desk, Full-service health spa, Massage - treatment room(s), Meeting rooms (small groups), Ski shuttle, Smoke-free property, Wedding services, Children's club.

Campton

Also see the following nearby communities that have pet friendly lodging:
Ashland - 9 miles

★★ 🎿
Days Inn Campton
1513 Us Route 3
Campton NH 03223
(800) 370-8666
$55 - $159
SAVE –B&P Discount Available

Pet Policy: Pets accepted, $20 first night, $10 each additional.

Features: Sauna, Indoor pool, Conference room(s), Business services, Air-conditioned public areas, Barbecue grill(s), Coffee in lobby, Laundry facilities, Free breakfast, Parking (free), Free newspapers in lobby, Wireless Internet, Concierge desk, Wireless Internet, Steam room.

Claremont

★★ 🐾
Claremont Motor Lodge
16 Beauregard Street
Claremont NH 03743
(603) 542-2540
Rates starting at $65
SAVE –B&P Discount Available

Pet Policy: Pets accepted, $25 per day pet fee.

Features: Self-parking, RV and truck parking, Number of rooms: 40, Number of floors: 2, Suitable for children, Air-conditioned public areas, Coffee in lobby, Laundry facilities, Free breakfast, Grocery, Multilingual staff, Free newspapers in lobby, 24-hour front desk, Wireless Internet, Business services.

★★★ 🐾
Common Man Inn & Restaurant
21 Water St
Claremont NH 03743
(603) 542-0647
$94 - $190
SAVE –B&P Discount Available

Pet Policy: Pets accepted in 5 rooms, $15 per night. They'll feel right at home with their own personal pet bed, water and food bowls, and special personalized treat at check in. Please do not leave unattended in room and keep leashed when in public areas.

Features: Restaurant(s), Total number of rooms 35, Number of floors 3, Air-conditioned public areas, Self-parking, Business center, Smoke-free property, Wedding services, Wireless Internet, , Bar/lounge, Fitness facilities, Room service (limited hours), Gift shops or newsstand, Suitable for children, Fireplace in lobby, Patio, Garden, Library, Free newspapers in lobby, 24-hour front desk, Accessible bathroom, Handicapped parking, In-room accessibility, Smoke-free property (fines apply).

★★ 🐾
Rodeway Inn Claremont
24 Sullivan St
Claremont NH 03743
(603) 542-9567
$59 - $89
SAVE –B&P Discount Available

Pet Policy: Rodeway Inns charge a fee of $10 per night per pet and require a $50 damage deposit, which is refunded if the room is in order at check out. Max of 2 pets per room. A veterinarian certificate that the pet is on a flea and parasite program and that they are free from parasites is required. Pets may not be left alone in the room unless in a cage.

Features: Wireless Internet, Dry cleaning/laundry service, Suitable for children, Air-conditioned public areas, Parking (free), Multilingual staff, Free newspapers in lobby, 24-hour front desk, Business center, Nearby fitness center (discount), Coffee in lobby, Free breakfast, Number of rooms: 21.

Concord
Also see the following nearby communities that have pet friendly lodging:
Manchester - 16 miles.

★★
Best Western Inn & Suites
97 Hall St
Concord NH 03301
(603) 228-4300
$95 - $249
SAVE –B&P Discount Available

Pet Policy: Pets allowed based on the availability of pet friendly rooms. Up to 2 dogs per room with an 80 pound weight limit. Additional pet types (cats, birds, etc.) may be accepted at the hotel's discretion. Pet rate is $15.00 per day with a $100 per week maximum.

Features: Wireless Internet, Laundry facilities, Indoor pool, Number of rooms: 46, Number of floors: 3, Elevator, Conference room(s), Air-conditioned public areas, Coffee in lobby, Free breakfast, Parking (free), Multilingual staff, Free newspapers in lobby, 24-hour front desk, Business center, Meeting rooms (small groups), Nearby fitness center (discount).

★★
Comfort Inn Concord
71 Hall St
Concord NH 03301
(603) 226-4100
Rates from $119
SAVE –B&P Discount Available

Pet Policy: Pet accommodation: $15/night per pet. Pet limit: Two pets per room. Dogs only

Features: Wireless Internet, Indoor pool, Number of rooms: 100, Number of floors: 3, Elevator, Air-conditioned public areas, Coffee in lobby, Laundry facilities, Free breakfast, Parking (free), 24-hour front desk, Meeting rooms (small groups), Sauna, Business services, Fax machine, Fitness facilities.

★★★
Residence Inn by Marriott
91 Hall St
Concord NH 03301
(603) 226-0012
$139 - $179
SAVE –B&P Discount Available

Pet Policy: Pets allowed, $100 additional cleaning fee per stay.

Features: Number of suites: 92, Number of floors: 4, Elevator, Parking (free), Business center, Swimming pool, Smoke-free property, Free breakfast.

Dover

Also see the following nearby communities that have pet friendly lodging:
Durham - 6 miles, Rochester - 8 miles, Portsmouth - 9 miles.

★★↗ 🐾
Comfort Inn And Suites Dover
10 Hotel Dr
(route 9 & 108)
Dover NH 03820
(603) 750-7507
$119 - $219
SAVE –B&P Discount Available

Pet Policy: Pet accommodation: $20/night. Dogs and cats only. Dogs must be on a leash in public areas at all times, cats in a carrier. Pets must not be left unattended.

Features: Gift shops or newsstand, Number of rooms: 96, Number of floors: 4, Elevator, Air-conditioned public areas, Coffee in lobby, Free breakfast, Parking (free), Free newspapers in lobby, 24-hour front desk, Meeting rooms (small groups), Wireless Internet, Fax machine, Laundry facilities, Indoor pool, Business services, Fitness facilities.

★★ 🐾
Dover - Days Inn
481 Central Ave
Dover NH 03820
(603) 742-0400
$87 - $159
SAVE –B&P Discount Available

Pet Policy: Pets accepted, $10 per night per pet plus $50 refundable deposit. Limit of 2 per room, no size restrictions.

Features: Accessible bathroom, Handicapped parking, In-room accessibility, Indoor pool, Dry cleaning/laundry service, Shopping on site, Conference room(s), Air-conditioned public areas, Coffee in lobby, Free breakfast, Parking (free), Free newspapers in lobby, 24-hour front desk, Business center, Wireless Internet, Concierge desk, Smoke-free property.

★★★ 🐾
Homewood Suites Dover
21 Members Way
Dover NH 03820
(603) 516-0929
$149 - $209
SAVE –B&P Discount Available

Pet Policy: Pets up to 50 lbs, $50 per stay.

Features: Fitness facilities, Number of suites: 82, Number of floors: 4, Elevator, Conference room(s), Coffee in lobby, Free breakfast, Parking (free), Business center, Wireless Internet, Smoke-free property, Indoor pool, Shopping on site, Barbecue grill(s), 24-hour front desk, Dry cleaning/laundry service, Area shuttle (free).

Durham

Also see the following nearby communities that have pet friendly lodging:
Dover - 6 miles, Portsmouth - 7 miles, Kittery - 10 miles, Exeter - 10 miles.

★★↗

Holiday Inn Express Durham
2 Main St
Durham NH 03824
(603) 868-1234
$129- $229
SAVE –B&P Discount Available

Pet Policy: Pets accepted, $50 per stay fee. Pets may only stay in first floor rooms and may not be left alone.

Features: Accessible bathroom, Handicapped parking, Dry cleaning/laundry service, Number of rooms: 68, Number of floors: 3, Business services, Free breakfast, Parking (free), Wireless Internet, Smoke-free property, Fitness facilities.

★★★↗

Three Chimneys Inn
17 Newmarket Rd
Durham NH 03824
(603) 868-7800
Rates from $135
SAVE –B&P Discount Available

Pet Policy: Limited pet friendly rooms are available. Please contact property directly for pet reservations.

Features: Restaurant, Room service, Number of rooms: 23, Number of floors: 4, Air-conditioned public areas, Fireplace in lobby, Parking, Concierge desk, Smoke-free property, Coffee in lobby, Picnic area, Free breakfast, Bar/lounge, Conference room(s), Wedding services, Business services.

Exeter

Also see the following nearby communities that have pet friendly lodging:
Hampton Falls - 7 miles, Durham - 10 miles.

Not Rated
Colonial Hearthside Inn
137 Portsmouth Avenue
Exeter NH 03833
(603) 772-3794
Rates from $110

Pet Policy: Pets accepted with advanced approval, $10 per pet per night. Please contact hotel directly in advance for pet approval.

Features: Number of rooms: 31, Number of floors: 3.

★★↗

Hampton Inn and Suites Exeter
59 Portsmouth Ave
Exeter NH 03833
(603) 658-5555
$138 - $214
SAVE –B&P Discount Available

Pet Policy: Pets up to 75 lbs accepted.

Features: Indoor pool, Air-conditioned public areas, Parking (free), Smoke-free property, Fitness facilities, Number of rooms: 111, Number of floors: 4, Elevator, Free breakfast, Meeting rooms (small groups), Wireless Internet, ***Continued on next page***

Hampton Inn and Suites Exeter
Continued from previous page

Accessible bathroom, Gift shop, Patio, Free newspapers in lobby, Dry cleaning/laundry service, Handicapped parking, 24-hour business center.

★★★★ 🛏
The Inn By The Bandstand
6 Front Street
Exeter NH 03833
(877) 239-3837
$148 - $189
SAVE –B&P Discount Available

Pet Policy: Small dogs accepted. Sorry, we cannot accept large pets. Dogs cannot be left alone in guest rooms and are not allowed to roam the inn unattended. Further, dogs are not permitted in any dining areas and must be leashed when outside the guest rooms. Dogs are only allowed in certain guest rooms. Any guest whose dog is barking excessively, in the opinion of management, will be told to remove that dog from the property after a warning is initiated.

Features: Smoke-free property, Business services, Number of rooms: 9, Wireless Internet, Year Built 1809, Free breakfast.

Gilford
Also see the following nearby communities that have pet friendly lodging:
Tilton - 11 miles.

★★★ 🎿
Fireside Inn & Suites Gilford
17 Harris Shore Road
Gilford NH 03249
(603) 293-7526
$149 - $168
SAVE –B&P Discount Available

Pet Policy: We welcome pets at the Fireside Resort Inn & Suites in selected rooms with additional $10 per day fee. Dogs must not be left unattended in the room and cannot be allowed into food service areas, conference facilities or the pool. Pets are not allowed in the suites or at area beaches.

Features: Gift shop, Number of rooms: 59, Number of floors: 2, Suitable for children, Coffee in lobby, Arcade/game room, Free breakfast, Free newspapers in lobby, 24-hour front desk, Smoke-free property, Outdoor pool - seasonal, Fireplace in lobby, Indoor pool, Ski storage, Patio, Barbecue grill(s), Fitness facilities, Self-parking, Wireless Internet.

★★ 🎿
TownePlace Suites by Marriott
14 Sawmill Road
Gilford NH 03249
(603) 524-5533
$139 - $239
SAVE –B&P Discount Available

Pet Policy: Pets up to 100 lbs allowed, $100 per stay cleaning fee. Limit 1 pet per room.

Features: Indoor pool, Number of rooms: 75, Number of floors: 3, Elevator, Air-conditioned public areas, Parking (free), Free breakfast.

Gorham

Not Rated
A Top Notch Inn
265 Main Street
Gorham NH 03581
(800) 228-5496
$99 - $149

Pet Policy: We love well-behaved and well-groomed small & medium size dogs 50 lbs and under. They too are welcome to stay with us as long as they adhere to the following policies. Pets are not allowed in Pinkham House, Country Rooms, Deluxe kings and Birches Suite (109 & 110). We ask that you walk your pet behind, or on the side of the motel. Please do not walk on the front lawn. Doggie doo-doo must be picked up and deposited into the dumpster behind the motel. Please do not leave your pet alone in the motel room. Do not attempt to give your pet a bath in the room! Keep your dog on a leash at all times. Please do not let dogs on the beds.

Features: Smoke-free property, hot tub, pool, open May through October.

Not Rated
Mt Madison Inn
365 Upper Main Street
Gorham NH 03581
(603) 466-3381
$91 - $128

Pet Policy: Pets welcome, $5 per pet per day. Pets are not allowed on the bed, furniture, blankets, sheets or pillows. Please do not bathe your pet in our tub or sink. Pets cannot be left alone in the room unless they are crated. Please pick up after your pet when walking them on the property. If we find that your pet has been lying on the beds, comforter, sheets, blankets or pillows we will charge your card $100 to clean all bedding. Our machines cannot handle pet hair so we must send all bedding out to be cleaned.

Features: Number of rooms: 32, Number of floors: 2, Microwave, Mini fridge, In-room coffee maker, Wireless Internet, Heated pool, Hot tub.

★★★✦
Town And Country Motor Inn
20 State Route 2
Gorham NH 03581
(800) 325-4386
$90 - $116
SAVE –B&P Discount Available

Pet Policy: Small pets accepted in designated pet friendly rooms, $6 per pet per night.

Features: Breakfast available (additional charge), Bar/lounge, Babysitting or child care, Fitness facilities, Indoor pool, Restaurant, Arcade/game room, Parking (free), 24-hour front desk, Sauna, Laundry facilities, Wireless Internet, Luggage storage.

Hampton Falls

Also see the following nearby communities that have pet friendly lodging:
Exeter - 7 miles.

★★♪ 🛏

Hampton Falls Inn
11 Lafayette Rd
Hampton Falls NH 03844
(603) 926-9545
$106 - $158
SAVE –B&P Discount Available

Pet Policy: Dogs only are accepted, 50 lbs or less. There is a $50 deposit per dog required plus a nightly fee of $10 plus tax each, Max of 2 Dogs. Designated pet rooms Smoking and non-smoking rooms available. Pet approval and advance reservations required. Room inspections will be done after 9:00 AM on the day of departure.

Pet Rules: Dogs must be on a leash at all times outside of the room. Dogs are not allowed in common areas (lobby, pool, restaurant) or other guest rooms. Please use rear entrance ONLY to when with your dog. Please walk your dog on grassy areas and pick up after your dog. Pets are never allowed in an unattended *room*.

Features: Coffee in lobby, Parking (free), Business services, Air-conditioned public areas, Free newspapers in lobby, Wireless Internet, Restaurant, Conference room(s), 24-hour front desk, Indoor pool, Arcade/game room.

Intervale

Also see the following nearby communities that have pet friendly lodging:
North Conway - 3 miles, Bartlett - 4 miles, Jackson Village - 5 miles, Jackson - 5 miles.

Not Rated 🎿

Swiss Chalets Village Inn
Route 16A
Intervale NH 03845
(603) 356-2232
$129 - $189

Pet Policy: Dogs up to 40 lbs and cats may be accepted, $15 per pet per night, limit 2 per room. Pet approval must be obtained before arrival so please make reservations directly with the Inn. We will allow some dogs, occasionally cats, etc. If we believe certain dog breeds are more of a threat to our guests and employees, then we may disallow them on our property. Be specific as to what type and size pet you will bring on your trip. We require that pets must be leashed when out of the guest room. Pets are not allowed in the main building. This includes the lobby, pool areas, hot tub, game room and breakfast area.

Town And Country Motor Inn
Intervale
Continued from previous page

We do have a no-barking and a no-biting rule. Violation will results in loss of room without refund. Ask front desk personnel about the appropriate areas to walk your dogs on our property. You must clean up after the dog relieves itself.

Pets must be washed and on flea medication prior to arrival. Provide evidence of updated vaccinations, so please bring records. Provide a nametag with identification and a current rabies tag to be worn by the dog/cat at all times.

Keep pet in a crate leaving the guestroom to avoid innocent employees from being bitten and the furnishings in the room from being destroyed. Housekeeping is not allowed to enter a guest room with a pet. If you would like to arrange a time for the housekeeper to service your room when the pet is not in it, please contact the front desk. We require that your pet not be left unattended for more than 1 hour, and never unattended at night. If at all possible, please leave a cell phone number with us, when your pet is left unattended.

Features: Wedding services, Suites with Fireplace and Hot Tub, Outdoor pool and Hot tub, Game room, Pool table, Continental breakfast, Discounted ski lift tickets at front desk.

Jackson

Also see the following nearby communities that have pet friendly lodging:
Jackson Village - 1 mile, Bartlett - 4 miles, Intervale - 5 miles, North Conway - 8 miles.

★★★
Christmas Farm Inn And Spa
3 Blitzen Way
Jackson NH 03846
(603) 383-4313
$99 - $169
SAVE –B&P Discount Available

Pet Policy: Pets accepted, $25 per night cleaning fee. Three of our cottages are designated 'Pet Friendly.' They are also used by non-pet owners and we have to ensure that the cottages, furniture, flooring and bedding are free of any trace of pets staying there. Any additional cleaning or repairs due to messes and damage caused by a pet will be charged to your account. Visiting pets must be in the control of their owners at all times and on a leash when walking around the estate and village of Jackson. In the interest of other guests, we do not allow pets in the main inn and restaurant area.
Continued on next page

Christmas Farm Inn And Spa
Continued from previous page

Please do not leave your dog unattended in the cottage and do consider bringing your own kennel for keeping the dog safe while they are alone. All dog droppings must be picked up and disposed of immediately. We hope you enjoy your stay with your pet and appreciate that you strictly follow our pet policies for the good of all.

Features: Restaurant, Free breakfast, 24-hour front desk, Beauty services, Full-service health spa, Smoke-free property, Wedding services, Bar/lounge, Fitness facilities, Gift shop, Multiple conference/meeting rooms, Suitable for children, Fireplace in lobby, Garden, Indoor pool, Outdoor pool - seasonal, Poolside bar, Parking (free), Steam room, Wireless Internet, Babysitting or child care, Ski storage, Dry cleaning/laundry service, Rooftop terrace, Luggage storage.

★★★
Nestlenook Farm Resort
Route 16
Jackson NH 03846
(603) 383-7101
Rates from $464

Pet Policy: Pets up to 15 lbs accepted in designated pet-friendly room, with security deposit (credit card imprint). Excessive barking and disturbing other guests are grounds for guest and / or pet being evicted from property.

Features: Smoke-free property, Adults only in Nestlenook Inn, Families welcome in Victorian Village.

Not Rated
Nordic Villate Resort
Route 16
Jackson NH 03860
(603) 383-9101
$209 - $449

Pet Policy: Pets are accepted with nightly fee that varies by the unit selected. Fees may run as high as $100 per night so check with the resort directly when making a pet reservation. Pets shouldn't be left alone in the room and should be kept on a leash when not in the room (unless, of course, you have a goldfish). When you walk your pet, please do your part to help keep our grounds clean. There are many areas to walk your dog at Nordic Village Resort. Take a stroll on our hiking trails. When asked if we allow dogs at our hotel, here's what we generally reply: Dogs are welcome in this hotel. We've never had a dog that smoked in bed and set fire to the blankets. We've never had a dog that stole the towels, played the TV too loud or had a fight with his traveling companion. We've never had a dog that got drunk and broke up the furniture. So, if your dog can vouch for you, you're welcome, too!

Nordic Villate Resort
Continued from previous page

Features: Full resort offers accommodations from townhouses, suites, penthouses, to a 4 bedroom chateau.

★★★ 🛏 🎿
The Snowflake Inn
95 Main St
Jackson NH 03846
(603) 383-8259
Rates from $170
SAVE –B&P Discount Available

Pet Policy: We welcome your well behaved, well-traveled dog, $25 per night fee. The Snowflake Inn has 2 King Suites that are set up for our 4 legged friends w/a Special Bed, Dishes & Treat! He/She cannot be left in the room for long periods of time, unattended. We are very strict about clean up outside (we provide the bags)!

Features: Continental breakfast, Library, Dry cleaning/laundry services, Smoke-free property, Parking,, Number of rooms: 20, Fireplaces in each room, bathrobes, jetted tubs in each room.

★★★ 🛏 🎿
The Whitney Inn at Jackson
357 Black Mountain Road
Jackson NH 03846
(603) 383-8916
Rates from $119
SAVE –B&P Discount Available

Pet Policy: We have 2 dog friendly cottages. Please contact Inn directly for pet reservations.

Features: Bar/lounge, Restaurant, Number of rooms: 5, Number of floors: 3, Air-conditioned public areas, Parking (free), Front desk (limited hours), Free breakfast, Fireplace in lobby.

★★★ 🎿
Village House
49 Main Street
Jackson NH 03846
(603) 383-6666
$185 - $250
SAVE –B&P Discount Available

Pet Policy: Pets welcome, $10 per pet per night. We are pleased to offer a selection of clean, flexible, pet friendly rooms and hope that our guests will do everything in their power to be responsible pet owners while staying with us. If you wish to take your dog out on a lead, there is a designated dog walk around the grounds of the Village House and if you would like to let your dog run free, there are 35 acres of town land behind the town hall across the street, in addition to several cross country ski trails and some pleasant fields. We regret that we cannot allow dogs to run free on the hotel the grounds.

Guests are permitted to leave their dogs in their rooms, though if you decide to leave your dog alone in your room, please make sure that he will not bark or be destructive to the room in any way. We happily thank all our former guests that have been responsible travellers with their pets. They have made it possible for our tradition to continue.
Continued on next page

175

Village House – Jackson
Continued from previous page

Features: Outdoor pool, Number of rooms: 13, Smoke-free property, Wireless Internet- additional charge.

★★★ (icons)
Wildcat Inn & Tavern
94 Main St
Jackson NH 03846
(603)-356-8700
Rates from $109
SAVE –B&P Discount Available

Pet Policy: Well behaved, well-groomed, flea free, dogs are welcome with an additional $30 per night deep cleaning fee. Guests traveling with dogs are only permitted to stay in those rooms that are dog friendly. Pets must be leashed at all times and are not allowed in our restaurant. Dogs are allowed in our Tavern and gardens.

Features: Number of rooms: 12, Fireplace in lobby, Conference room(s), Concierge services, Arcade/game room.

Keene

★★★
Best Western Plus Sovereign Hotel
401 Winchester St
Keene NH 03431
(603) 357-3038
$94 - $149
SAVE –B&P Discount Available

Pet Policy: Pets allowed based on the availability of pet friendly rooms. Up to 2 dogs per room with an 80 pound weight limit. Additional pet types (cats, birds, etc.) may be accepted at the hotel's discretion. Pet rate is $20 per day with a $100 per week maximum.

Features: Room service (limited hours), Barbecue grill(s), Free breakfast, Self-parking, Free newspapers in lobby, Business center, Wireless Internet, Handicapped parking, RV and truck parking, Indoor pool, Dry cleaning/laundry service, Bar/lounge, Restaurant, Number of rooms: 131, Number of floors: 2, Elevator, Coffee in lobby, Arcade/game room, Picnic area, 24-hour front desk, Meeting rooms (small groups), Fitness facilities.

★★★
Courtyard by Marriott
75 Railroad St
Keene NH 03431
(603) 354-7900
$104 - $189
SAVE –B&P Discount Available

Pet Policy: Pets allowed, $25 cleaning fee.

Features: Dry cleaning/laundry service, Number of rooms: 98, Number of suites: 2, Number of floors: 5, Wireless Internet, Smoke-free property, Free newspapers in lobby, Business services, Indoor pool, Parking (free).

★★
Days Inn Keene
3 Ash Brook Road
Keene NH 03431
(603) 352-9780
$63 - $104
SAVE –B&P Discount Available

Pet Policy: Pets accepted, $20 per stay fee.

Features: Free breakfast, Fitness facilities, Business center, Wireless Internet, RV and truck parking.

★★★↓
Holiday Inn Express Keene
175 Key Rd
Keene NH 03431
(603) 357 3619
$99 - $139
SAVE –B&P Discount Available

Pet Policy: Dogs under 50 lbs accepted, $25 per night per dog. Dogs may not be left alone in room.

Features: Handicapped parking, In-room accessibility, Gift shop, Number of rooms: 80, Number of floors: 2, Air-conditioned public areas, Free breakfast, Parking (free), Multilingual staff, Front desk (limited hours), Business center, Wireless Internet, Dry cleaning/laundry service, Fitness facilities, Indoor pool.

★★★
The Lane Hotel An Ascend Collection
30 Main Street
Keene NH 03431
(603) 357-7070
$99 - $189
SAVE –B&P Discount Available

Pet Policy: Pets accepted, $25 per pet per night plus $100 refundable deposit. Limit 2 per room.

Features: 24-hour front desk, Business center, Number of rooms 40, Free breakfast, Wireless Internet.

Lancaster

★★
Coos Motor Inn
209 Main St
Lancaster NH 03584
(603) 788-3079
$84 - $100
SAVE –B&P Discount Available

Pet Policy: Small to medium size pets are welcome in specific rooms for an additional charge of $15 per pet per night. Please notify us in advance if you will be bringing pets. Pets must be declared at check in.

Features: Self-parking, Gift shop, Number of rooms: 41, Number of floors: 2, Elevator, Business services, Suitable for children, Coffee in lobby, Laundry facilities, Library, Free breakfast, Nearby fitness center (free), Front desk (limited hours), Concierge desk, Wireless Internet, Microwave in lobby.

Lebanon
Also see the following nearby communities that have pet friendly lodging:
West Lebanon - 3 miles, White River Junction - 5 miles, Quechee - 9 miles.

★★
Days Inn Lebanon Hanover
135 Route 120
Lebanon NH 03766
(603) 448-5070
$91 - $114
SAVE –B&P Discount Available

Pet Policy: Pet Friendly, only in smoking rooms, $20 for up to 3 days

Features: Dry cleaning/laundry service, Number of floors: 2, Air-conditioned public areas, Parking (free), Free newspapers in lobby, 24-hour front desk, Business center, Wireless Internet, Free breakfast.

★★★
Residence Inn by Marriott
32 Centerra Pkwy
Lebanon NH 03766
(603) 643-4511
$139 - $199
SAVE –B&P Discount Available

Pet Policy: Pets allowed, $100 cleaning fee per stay.

Features: Handicapped parking, In-room accessibility, Dry cleaning/laundry service, Wireless Internet, Number of suites: 114, Number of floors: 3, Breakfast, Grocery, Parking (free), Free newspapers in lobby, Meeting rooms (small groups), Smoke-free property, Coffee in lobby, Business services, Indoor pool, Fitness facilities, Shopping on site.

Lincoln

★★★
Comfort Inn & Suites
21 Railroad Street
Lincoln NH 03251
(603) 745-6700
$139 - $219

Pet Policy: Pet accommodation: $15/night per pet, limit 2 pets/room.

Features: Indoor Pool, Whirlpool.

★★
Econo Lodge Inn & Suites
381 US Route 3
Lincoln NH 03251
(603) 745-3661
$79 - $109
SAVE –B&P Discount Available

Pet Policy: Pet Accommodation: $15 per night, per pet. Pet Limit: maximum 2 pets per room, up to 50 pounds.

Features: Number of rooms: 53, Number of floors: 2, Air-conditioned public areas, Patio, Free breakfast, Self-parking, Children's club, Fitness facilities, Picnic area, Outdoor pool, Indoor pool.

Not Rated
Kancamgus Motor Lodge
11 Pollard Rd
Lincoln NH 03251
(603) 745-3365
Rates from $99

Pet Policy: Dogs under 20 lbs accepted in 1 pet friendly room. No fee but responsible for any damage or additional cleaning needed. Pet must be crated if left alone in room. As there is only 1 pet friendly room, it is advised that you book directly with the lodge.

Features: Indoor pool, Game room, Number of rooms: 34, mini fridge, Steam bath in some rooms, Restaurant.

★★
Rodeway Inn Lincoln
417 Us Route 3
Lincoln NH 03251
(603) 745-2267
$64 - $165
SAVE –B&P Discount Available

Pet Policy: Rodeway Inns charge a fee of $10 per night per pet plus a $50 refundable damage deposit. Max of 2 pets per room. A veterinarian certificate that the pet is on a flea and parasite program and that they are free from parasites is required. Pets may not be left alone in the room unless in a cage.

Features: Outdoor pool, Number of rooms: 30, Number of floors: 2, Laundry facilities, Free breakfast, Business center, Parking (free), Wireless Internet, Fax machine, Self-parking, Picnic area.

Manchester
Also see the following nearby communities that have pet friendly lodging:
Merrimack - 9 miles.

★★★
Best Western Plus Executive Court Inn & Conference
13500 S Willow St
Manchester NH 03103
(603) 627-2525
$104 - $129
SAVE –B&P Discount Available

Pet Policy: Pets allowed based on the availability of pet friendly rooms. Up to 2 dogs per room with an 80 pound weight limit. Additional pet types (cats, birds, etc.) may be accepted at the hotel's discretion. Pet rate is $10 per day with a $100 per week maximum.

Features: Indoor pool, Airport transportation (free), Number of rooms: 136, Number of suites: 8, Number of floors: 4, Free breakfast, Business center, Wireless Internet, Fitness facilities, Accessible bathroom, Handicapped parking, Coffee in lobby, Parking (free), Laundry facilities, Arcade/game room, Room service.

★★★ 🐾
Clarion Hotel
21 Front St
Manchester NH 03102
(603) 669-2660
Rates from $79
SAVE –B&P Discount Available

Pet Policy: Pets up to 75 lbs, $50 per stay. Limit 2 per room.

Features: Restaurant, Bar/Lounge, Free breakfast, Outdoor pool, Fitness center, Small meeting rooms, Wireless Internet, Room service, Business services, Free airport shuttle, Free parking, Laundry facilities, Number of rooms: 118, Non –smoking property, Mini fridge and microwaves available.

★★★ 🐾
Comfort Inn Airport
298 Queen City Ave
Manchester NH 03102
(603) 668-2600
$89 - $139
SAVE –B&P Discount Available

Pet Policy: Pet Accommodation: $25/stay per pet. Pet Limit: 2 pets per room up to 60 pounds..

Features: Parking (free), Wireless Internet, Gift shops or newsstand, Number of rooms: 100, Number of floors: 5, Elevator, Meeting rooms (small groups), Laundry facilities, Free breakfast, Business center, Indoor pool, Fitness facilities.

★★ 🐾
Econo Lodge Manchester
75 W Hancock St
Manchester NH 03102
(603) 624-0111
$59 - $135
SAVE –B&P Discount Available

Pet Policy: Pets accepted, $10 per pet per night plus $100 refundable deposit.

Features: Wireless Internet, Number of rooms: 112, Number of floors: 5, Elevator, Free breakfast, Parking (free), 24-hour front desk, Laundry facilities.

★★★ 🐾
Four Points by Sheraton Manchester Airport
55 John Devine Dr
Manchester NH 03103
(603) 668-6110
$89 - $195
SAVE –B&P Discount Available

Pet Policy: Pets accepted, $75 per stay fee.

Features: Wireless Internet, Coffee in lobby, Conference Room(s), Bar/Lounge, Business center, Indoor pool, Elevator, Dry cleaning/laundry service, Airport transportation (free), Restaurant(s), Room service (limited hours), Number of rooms: 119, Number of suites: 1, Number of floors: 4, Air-conditioned public areas, Breakfast available (additional charge), Free newspapers in lobby, Nearby fitness center (free), 24-hour front desk, Meeting rooms (small groups), Smoke-free property.

★★★♪ 🏃

**Holiday Inn Express Hotel &
Suites Manchester Airport**
1298 S Porter St
Manchester NH 03103
(603) 669-6800
$88 - $267
SAVE –B&P Discount Available

Pet Policy: Pets accepted with $50 refundable deposit.

Features: Airport transportation (free), Gift shop, Number of rooms: 107, Number of suites: 24, Number of floors: 3, Conference room(s), Air-conditioned public areas, Coffee in lobby, Fax machine, Parking (free), Multilingual staff, 24-hour front desk, Business center, Wireless Internet, Concierge desk, Free Breakfast, Indoor pool, Accessible bathroom, Handicapped parking, In-room accessibility, Dry cleaning/laundry service, Area shuttle (free), Fitness facilities.

★★★ 🏃

Homewood Suites by Hilton
1000 Perimeter Rd
Manchester NH 03103
(603) 668-2200
$98 - $169
SAVE –B&P Discount Available

Pet Policy: Pets up to 75 lbs accepted, $100 plus $25 per night fee.

Features: Gift shop, Number of rooms: 124, Number of floors: 4, Elevator, Conference room(s), Business services, Suitable for children, Multilingual staff, Free newspapers in lobby, 24-hour front desk, Porter/bellhop, Wireless Internet, Meeting rooms (small groups), Accessible bathroom, Handicapped parking, Dry cleaning/laundry service, Business center, Free breakfast, Coffee in lobby, Barbecue grill(s), Fireplace in lobby, Airport transportation (free), Picnic area, Indoor pool, Grocery, Air-conditioned public areas, Fitness facilities, Shopping on site, Luggage storage.

★★★♪ 🏃

Radisson Hotel Manchester
700 Elm St
Manchester NH 03101
(603) 625-1000
$96 - $179
SAVE –B&P Discount Available

Pet Policy: Domesticated, crated animals accepted, $25 per stay.

Features: Restaurant(s), Gift shop Number of rooms: 250, Number of floors: 12, Breakfast available, Wireless Internet, Free newspapers in lobby, Porter/bellhop, Meeting rooms (small groups), Parking garage ($8 per day), Wedding services, Handicapped parking, In-room accessibility, Indoor pool, Dry cleaning/laundry service, Business services, Airport transportation (free), Bar/lounge, Room service (limited hours), Sauna, Smoke-free property, Fitness facilities, Airport transportation (free) available 24 hours.

★★★ 🛏 🐾
The Highlander Inn
2 Highlander Way
Manchester NH 03103
(603) 625-6426
$79 - $149
SAVE –B&P Discount Available

Pet Policy: Dogs up to 75 lbs and cats are accepted, $10 per stay, limit 1 pet per room. We have designated an area for you to bring your pet for exercise. The designated area is located outside of the Coldwell House behind the Gazebo. For our guests in the Inn, your designated area is located across from the horseshoe drive way. We do provide gloves, bags and water for your convenience. We have provided a water bowl and pet bed in your room. These items are for your pet's overnight accommodations and are not to be removed.

Some Pet Rules: Pets are not permitted in the restaurant or on the veranda for breakfast. Guests may bring their pet to the lobby and have breakfast by the fireplace. Pets must always be on a leash or in a cage while they are in any public or common place within the hotel. Pet owners must pick up after their pets ($50.00 cleanup fee). Canned and dried dog food is available for purchase at the front desk. Pet owners are responsible for the repair or replacement of any items that may be damaged by their pets. Housekeeping service will be provided only if the pet is removed from the room during the service.

Features: Wireless Internet, Number of rooms: 87, Air-conditioned public areas, Free newspapers in lobby, 24-hour front desk, Wedding services, Handicapped parking, In-room accessibility, Free breakfast, Dry cleaning/laundry service, Business services, Parking (additional charge), Conference room(s), Fireplace in lobby, Fitness facilities, Airport transportation (free) available 24 hours.

★★ 🐾
TownePlace Suites by Marriott
686 Huse Rd
Manchester NH 03103
(603) 641-2288
$90 - $169
SAVE –B&P Discount Available

Pet Policy: Pets allowed, $100 per stay cleaning fee.

Features: Business Center, Indoor pool, Dry cleaning/laundry service, Airport transportation (free), Number of rooms: 77, Number of floors: 3, Elevator, Air-conditioned public areas, Barbecue grill(s), Coffee in lobby, Parking (free), Picnic area, 24-hour front desk, Free breakfast, Fitness facilities.

Merrimack

Also see the following nearby communities that have pet friendly lodging:
Nashua - 7 miles, Manchester - 9 miles.

★★

Comfort Inn
242 Daniel Webster Hwy
Merrimack NH 03054
(603) 429-4600
$89 - $119
SAVE –B&P Discount Available

Pet Policy: Pet accommodation: $25/night per pet.
Pet limit: 2 pets per room / up to 25 pounds

Features: Free Breakfast, Number of rooms: 70, Number of floors: 2, Air-conditioned public areas, Coffee in lobby, Parking (free), Multilingual staff, Free newspapers in lobby, 24-hour front desk, Number of rooms: 68, Handicapped parking, In-room accessibility, Accessible bathroom, Business center, Airport transportation.

★★★

Residence Inn by Marriott
246 Daniel Webster Hwy
Merrimack NH 03054
(603) 424-8100
$115 - $184
SAVE –B&P Discount Available

Pet Policy: Pets allowed, $100 per stay cleaning fee.

Features: Business services, Dry cleaning/laundry service, Number of suites: 129, Number of floors: 3, Elevator, Conference room(s), Air-conditioned public areas, Patio, Barbecue grill(s), Parking (free), Free newspapers in lobby, 24-hour front desk, Meeting rooms (small groups), Outdoor pool - seasonal, Tennis on site, Free breakfast, Fitness facilities, Smoke-free property, Fax machine, Free reception, Suitable for children, Coffee in lobby, Wireless Internet, Fireplace in lobby, Designated smoking areas.

Moultonborough

★★

Rodeway Inn Moultonborough
340 Whittier Hwy
Moultonborough NH 03254
(603) 253-4314
$89. - $149
SAVE –B&P Discount Available

Pet Policy: Rodeway Inns charge a fee of $10 per night per pet plus a $50 refundable damage deposit. Max of 2 pets per room. A veterinarian certificate that the pet is on a flea and parasite program and that they are free from parasites is required. Pets may not be left alone in the room unless in a cage.

Features: Wireless Internet, Number of rooms: 28, Outdoor pool.

Nashua

Also see the following nearby communities that have pet friendly lodging:
Merrimack - 7 miles, North Chelmsford - 9 miles.

★★★
Courtyard by Marriott Nashua
2200 Southwood Dr
Nashua NH 03063
(603) 880-9100
$98 - $169
SAVE –B&P Discount Available

Pet Policy: Pets accepted, $100 cleaning fee per stay.

Features: In-room accessibility, Dry cleaning/laundry service, Bar/lounge, Elevator, Indoor pool, Restaurant(s), Room service, Concierge, Gift shop, Air-conditioned public areas, Coffee shop, Parking (free), Free newspapers in lobby, 24-hour front desk, Business center, Wireless Internet, Meeting rooms, Fitness facilities.

★★
Extended Stay America
2000 Southwood Dr
Nashua NH 03063
(603) 577-9900
$81 - $118
SAVE –B&P Discount Available

Pet Policy: One pet is allowed in each guest room. A $25 per day non-refundable cleaning fee (not to exceed $150) will be charged the first night of your stay. Weight, size and breed restrictions may apply. Please contact the hotel directly with inquiries.

Features: Laundry facilities, Number of rooms: 101, Number of floors: 3, Elevator, Business services, Parking, Nearby fitness center, Wireless Internet.

★★★
Hampton Inn Nashua
407 Amherst St
Nashua NH 03063
(603) 883-5333
$84 - $159
SAVE –B&P Discount Available

Pet Policy: Pets up to 75 lbs accepted, $55 per stay.

Features: Indoor pool, Number of suites: 1, Number of floors: 4, Currency exchange, Parking (free), Business center, Smoke-free property, Wireless Internet, Fitness facilities, Free breakfast, 24-hour front desk, Dry cleaning/laundry service.

★★★
Holiday Inn Nashua
9 Northeastern Blvd
Nashua NH 03062
(603) 888-1551
$90 - $159
SAVE –B&P Discount Available

Pet Policy: Small pets, $25 per stay cleaning fee.

Features: Restaurant, Concierge, Number of rooms: 208, Number of suites: 24, Number of floors: 4, Conference room(s), Parking (free), Free newspapers in lobby, Wireless Internet, Handicapped parking, In-room accessibility, Outdoor pool, Room service Business center, Bar/lounge, Fitness facilities, Dry cleaning/laundry service.

★★★
Radisson Hotel Nashua
11 Tara Blvd
Nashua NH 03062
(603) 888-9970
$74 - $149
SAVE –B&P Discount Available

Pet Policy: Pet friendly, no additional fee.

Features: Smoke-free property, Dry cleaning/laundry service, Restaurant(s), Room service (limited hours), Concierge services, Number of rooms: 336, Number of floors: 7, Elevator, Airport transportation (additional charge), Suitable for children, Air-conditioned public areas, Fireplace in lobby, Breakfast available (additional charge), Wireless Internet, Health club, Parking (free), Multilingual staff, Free newspapers in lobby, Picnic area, 24-hour front desk, Porter/bellhop, Doorman/doorwoman, Security guard, Limo or Town Car service available, Medical assistance available, Massage - treatment room(s), Meeting rooms (small groups), Outdoor pool - seasonal, Wedding services, Business center, Conference room(s), Steam room, Sauna, Indoor pool, Bar/lounge.

North Conway

Also see the following nearby communities that have pet friendly lodging:
Intervale - 3 miles, Bartlett - 6 miles, Jackson Village - 8 miles, Jackson - 8 miles.

Not Rated
Colonial Motel
2431 White Mountain Highway
North Conway NH 03860
(603) 356-5178
$105 - $259

Pet Policy: Dogs accepted, $10 per dog per night. No other pets accepted. Be sure to request pet friendly room with reservation. Pets should be on a leash at all times. Pets are not allowed on the furniture or beds. Do not leave your pet in the room or a car unattended. Please do not bathe your pet in the room. Your pet may go to the bathroom out back along the woods only. Please do not allow them to relieve themselves in the front. Please pick up after your pet. Guests will be held responsible for any actions or damage incurred by pet during their stay. There is a $200 cleaning fee for allowing your pet on the furniture, on the beds or for leaving an excessive mess.

Features: Mini fridge in all rooms, Wireless Internet, Outdoor pool, Picnic area.

Cranmore Mountain Lodge
859 Kearsarge Road
North Conway NH 03860
(800) 356-3596
$109 - $154
SAVE –B&P Discount Available

Pet Policy: Accepts dogs only, in 4 of the rooms, limit 1 dog per room. If very small, might consider allowing 2 if you talk to us directly. Pet fee is $15 per night. Pets must be crated when left alone in room. We can rent you a crate, if needed, for $5 per day. Dogs must be leashed when in public areas, and are not allowed in the pool area at any time. Please keep dog off the furniture (bed/sofa...). A laundering charge of $50 will automatically be charged on your credit card if it is necessary for us to launder the duvets/blankets/pillows/sofas etc... If your pet is a high shedder please let us know – you can have the option of paying the laundering fee or bringing your own blankets.

Features: Front desk (limited hours), Outdoor tennis court, Number of rooms: 20, Parking (free), Outdoor pool - seasonal, Library, Barbecue grill(s), Gift shop.

Hampton Suites North Conway
1788 White Mountain Hwy
North Conway NH 03860
(603) 356-7736
$160 - $367
SAVE –B&P Discount Available

Pet Policy: Pets allowed up to 75 lbs.

Features: Handicapped parking, In-room accessibility, Wireless Internet, Free newspapers, Wedding services, Coffee in lobby, Dry cleaning/laundry service, Arcade/game room, Babysitting or child care, 24-hour business center, Waterpark, Restaurant, Number of suites: 35, Number of floors: 4, Parking (free), Swimming pool, Smoke-free property, Fitness facilities, Breakfast.

Kearsarge Inn
42 Seavey Street
North Conway NH 03860
(603) 356-8700
$69 - $319
SAVE –B&P Discount Available

Pet Policy: Well behaved leashed dogs are welcome at an additional charge of $30 per night per pet.

Features: Year Built 1850, Number of rooms: 15, Parking (free), Smoke-free property, Wireless Internet, Wedding services, Coffee and juices provided in morning.

Mt. Washington Valley Inn
1567 White Mtn. Hwy
North Conway NH 03860
(603) 356-5486
$84 - $185
SAVE –B&P Discount Available

Pet Policy: Dogs up to 40 lbs accepted with $50 refundable deposit. Please carry your dog in hallways, or if too big, keep dog on a tight leash. Do not leave dog in room unattended. If any dog is found alone, the guests will be asked to check out immediately with no refund Please walk your dog in

Mt. Washington Valley Inn
Continued from previous page

the back field and use your pooper-scooper. Outside trash receptacles are located at each entrance. Dogs are not allowed on the beds or chairs. Do not give your dog a bath in the bathtub. If your dog is dirty, please contact the front desk for information regarding local dog grooming services. Dogs are not allowed in the pool area, Jacuzzi at any time. Also, please do not bring your pet into the lobby or reception areas. Please do not allow your dog to bark while inside the hotel. Your $50 dog deposit will be refunded if the above rules have been followed and a staff member has checked your room for damage. Your deposit will not be returned if the following conditions result from your stay in our room: dog hair on bed or furniture, soiled or torn carpet, soiled or torn bed linens, scratches on furniture, walls, or doors, excessive pet odor.

Features: Parking (free), Wireless Internet, Breakfast, Conference Room(s), Arcade/Game Room, Indoor pool, Number of rooms: 68, Number of floors: 3, Laundry facility, Free newspapers in lobby.

Not Rated
North Conway Motor Inn
2144 White Mountain Hwy
North Conway NH 03860
(603) 356-2803
$89 - $114

Pet Policy: Pets accepted, $60 per stay, limit 1 per room.

Features: Air conditioning, Wireless Internet.

Not Rated
Old Red Inn & Cottages
2406 White Mountain Hwy
North Conway NH 03860
(603) 356-2642
$122 - $173

Pet Policy: Well-behaved pets accepted with a $50 refundable damage deposit. Pets must be leashed when outside room, and may be left in cottage alone when owner is gone, provided pet remains quiet. A 10% discount is offered at the local store Four Your Paws Only upon showing your room key.

Features: Year built: 1810, Rooms and Cottages, Kitchenettes in some cottages, Free breakfast.

★★★
Red Jacket Mountain View and Indoor Water Park
2251 White Mtn. Highway
North Conway NH 03860
(603) 356-5411
$189 - $299

Pet Policy: Dogs welcome, cats may be accepted at discretion of front desk A $30 fee per pet, per night applies, with a maximum of two per room. Amenities for your pet vary by resort but may include bowls, bed and blanket, clean-up bags and a treat and welcome letter upon arrival. ***Continued on next page.***

Red Jacket Mountain View and Indoor Water Park
Continued from previous page

SAVE –B&P Discount Available

You'll find walking and hiking trails surrounding our North Conway pet-friendly lodging as well as sitters, dog walkers, and veterinary services. Pets should not be left alone in room for more than 2 hours and must be leashed when outside of room. Limited number of pet rooms so it is advised that you book pet reservations directly with the resort.

Features: 2 Restaurants, Swimming pool - children's, Outdoor pool - seasonal, Patio, Porter/bellhop, Meeting rooms, Indoor pool, Room service, Parking (free), Poolside bar, Coffee in lobby, Business center, Arcade/game room, Bar/lounge, Garden, Number of rooms: 160, Number of floors: 3, Elevator, Smoke-free property, Health club, Dry cleaning/laundry service, Rooftop terrace, Wireless Internet.

★★★
Residence Inn by Marriott,
1801 White Mountain Highway
North Conway NH 03860
(603) 356-3024
$180 - $403
SAVE –B&P Discount Available

Pet Policy: Pets allowed, $100 per stay cleaning fee.

Features: Babysitting or child care, Indoor pool, Concierge, Number of suites: 108, Number of floors: 4, Elevator, Fireplace in lobby, Coffee in lobby, Ski storage, Grocery, Parking (free), Newspapers in lobby, Meeting rooms, Smoke-free property, Wireless Internet, Accessible bathroom, 24-hour business center, Fitness facilities, Free reception.

Not Rated
White Trellis Motel
3245 White Mountain Highway
North Conway NH 03860
603-356-2492
$125 - $179

Pet Policy: Pets under 40 lbs accepted, $20 additional per night.

Features: Number of rooms: 22, 1 and 2 bedroom units, Mini fridge in most rooms, Designated smoking rooms.

Peterborough

Not Rated
Jack Daniels Motor Inn
80 Concord Street
Peterborough NH 03458
(603) 924-7458
$114 - $129

Pet Policy: Pets are welcome in designated rooms with prior written approval. We charge a pet cleaning fee. Please contact Inn directly for pet approval and reservation.

Features: Number of rooms: 17, Wireless Internet, Air conditioning, Coffee tea and juices in lobby, Refrigerators available.

Portsmouth
Also see the following nearby communities that have pet friendly lodging:
Kittery - 3 miles, Durham - 7 miles, Dover - 9 miles.

★★★⌐

Anchorage Inns And Suites
417 Woodbury Ave
Portsmouth NH 03801
(800) 370-8111
$122 - $150
SAVE –B&P Discount Available

Pet Policy: We are a pet friendly hotel and have a few pet rooms. Pet fee is $20 per night per pet plus $100 deposit. When traveling with your pet, we encourage our guests to check on availability and book in advance as our pet rooms are very popular.

Features: Number of rooms: 93, Number of floors: 3, Elevator, Air-conditioned public areas, Patio, Coffee shop, Parking (free), Picnic area, 24-hour front desk, Swimming pool, Wireless Internet, Meeting rooms (small groups), Conference Room(s), Business services, Dry cleaning/laundry service, Sauna, Free breakfast, Fitness facilities.

★★

Comfort Inn Portsmouth
1190 Lafayette Road
Portsmouth NH 03801
(603) 433-3338
$139 - $179
SAVE –B&P Discount Available

Pet Policy: Pets up to 25 lbs accepted, $25 per pet per stay. Limit 2 pets per room.

Features: RV and truck parking, 24-hour business center, Free newspapers, Dry cleaning/laundry service, Fax machine, Photocopy machines, Wireless Internet, Gift shops or newsstand, Number of rooms: 121, Number of floors: 6, Elevator, Parking (free), Meeting rooms, Indoor pool, Coffee in lobby, Free breakfast, Fitness facilities.

★★★

Hampton Inn Portsmouth
99 Durgin Ln
Portsmouth NH 03801
(603) 431-6111
$160 - $209
SAVE –B&P Discount Available

Pet Policy: Pets up to 50 lbs accepted, $50 per stay additional fee.

Features: Gift shops or newsstand, Designated smoking areas, Accessible bathroom, Handicapped parking, In-room accessibility, Area shuttle (free), 24-hour business center, Shopping center shuttle (free), Number of rooms: 126, Number of floors: 5, Elevator, Air-conditioned public areas, Fireplace in lobby, Coffee in lobby, Free breakfast, Parking (free), Free newspapers in lobby, Nearby fitness center (free), 24-hour front desk, Wireless Internet, Dry cleaning/laundry service, Indoor pool, Fitness facilities.

★★★
Homewood Suites Portsmouth
100 Portsmouth Blvd
Portsmouth NH 03801
603-427-5400
$160 - $259
SAVE –B&P Discount Available

Pet Policy: Pets up to 75 lbs, $100 per stay fee.

Features: Indoor pool, Number of suites: 108, Number of floors: 4, Free breakfast, Meeting rooms (small groups), Suitable for children, Free newspapers in lobby, 24-hour front desk, Convenience store, Handicapped parking, In-room accessibility, Dry cleaning/laundry service, Wireless Internet, 24-hour business center, Parking (free), Area shuttle (free), Fitness facilities, Reception.

★★★
Residence Inn by Marriott
1 International Dr
Portsmouth NH 03801
(603) 436-8880
$218 - $239
SAVE –B&P Discount Available

Pet Policy: Pets allowed, $100 per stay cleaning fee.

Features: Dry cleaning/laundry service, Indoor pool, Gift shop, Number of rooms: 90, Number of floors: 3, Parking (free), Free newspapers in lobby, Wireless Internet, Coffee in lobby, Fitness facilities.

★★★
Residence Inn by Marriott
100 Deer Street
Portsmouth NH 03801
(603) 968-5095
$198 - $254
SAVE –B&P Discount Available

Pet Policy: Pets allowed, $100 per stay cleaning fee.

Features: Free breakfast, Wireless Internet, Dry cleaning/laundry service, Number of suites: 90, Number of floors: 3, Indoor pool, Parking (additional charge).

★★★✦
Sheraton Portsmouth Harborside
250 Market St
Portsmouth NH 03801
(603) 431-2300
$189 - $486
SAVE –B&P Discount Available

Pet Policy: Accepts dogs only, up to 80 lbs, no additional fee, in deluxe rooms only. No dogs allowed in club rooms, condos or townhouses. Dogs may not be left unattended in rooms for any reason. We reserve the right to charge for additional cleaning or damage caused by the dog. If damage is found after checkout, the credit card on file will be charged.

Features: Wireless Internet, Sauna, Bar/Lounge, Accessible bathroom, Handicapped parking, Indoor pool, Dry cleaning/laundry service, Room service, Restaurant(s), Concierge, Gift shop, Number of rooms: 202, Number of floors: 5, Coffee in lobby, Free newspapers in lobby, Business center, Porter/bellhop, Security guard, Massage - treatment room(s), Meeting rooms (small groups), Smoke-free property, Doorman/doorwoman, Wedding services, Valet parking (additional charge), Fitness facilities.

Rochester

Also see the following nearby communities that have pet friendly lodging:
Dover - 8 miles.

★★ 🛏

Anchorage Inn of Rochester
13 Wadleigh Rd.
Rochester NH 03867
(603) 332-3350
$98 - $150
SAVE –B&P Discount Available

Pet Policy: We are a pet friendly hotel and have a few pet rooms. Rate is $15 per night per pet plus $50 deposit. When traveling with your pet, we encourage our guests to check on availability and book in advance as our pet rooms are very popular.

Features: Free Breakfast, Barbecue Grill(s), Number of rooms: 31, Number of floors: 1, Coffee in lobby, Parking, Free newspapers, Front desk (limited hours), Outdoor pool - seasonal, Fireplace in lobby, Wireless Internet, Business center.

★★★

Holiday Inn Express Hotel & Suites Rochester
77 Farmington Rd
Rochester NH 03867
(603) 994-1175
$107 - $219
SAVE –B&P Discount Available

Pet Policy: Pets allowed, $50 per stay cleaning fee. Pets may not be left alone in room. Limited number of pet friendly rooms available.

Features: Accessible bathroom, Handicapped parking, Number of rooms: 77, Number of suites: 32, Number of floors: 3, Business services, Free breakfast, Wireless Internet, Fitness facilities, Indoor pool.

Salem

Also see the following nearby communities that have pet friendly lodging:
Methuen - 3 miles, Lawrence - 6 miles, Andover - 7 miles,
Haverhill - 7 miles, Tewksbury - 9 miles, Lowell - 10 miles.

★★★

La Quinta Inn & Suites Salem
8 Keewaydin Dr
Salem NH 03079
(603) 893-4722
$81 - $125
SAVE –B&P Discount Available

Pet Policy: Cats and dogs up to 50 pounds are accepted in all guest rooms. Housekeeping services for rooms with pets require pet owner be present or pet must be crated. No fees or deposits are required.

Features: Accessible bathroom, Dry cleaning/laundry service, Number of rooms: 105, Number of floors: 4, Coffee in lobby, Free breakfast, Parking (free), Free newspapers in lobby, 24-hour front desk, Wireless Internet, Outdoor pool - seasonal, Nearby fitness center (discount), Business center.

★★
Red Roof Inn Salem
15 Red Roof Lane
I-93 at Pelham Road, Exit #2
Salem NH 03079
(603) 898-6422
$54 - $94
SAVE –B&P Discount Available

Pet Policy: Red Roof's Pet Policy: One well-behaved family pet is permitted unless they are prohibited by state law or ordinance. Service animals are always welcome. Pets must be declared during guest registration. In consideration of all Red Roof guests, pets must never be left unattended in the guestroom.

Features: Wireless Internet, Self-parking, Coffee in lobby, Business services, Number of rooms: 108, Number of floors: 2, Free newspapers in lobby, 24-hour front desk.

Sunapee

★★★

Dexter's Inn
258 Stagecoach Road
Sunapee NH 03782
(603) 763-5571
$109 - $150
SAVE –B&P Discount Available

Pet Policy: Pets are welcome by special advance arrangement with the understanding that the owners are responsible for their pet's behavior at all times and are responsible for any damages that occur. There is a charge of $10 per day per pet, plus tax.

Features: Supervised child care/activities, Number of rooms: 19, Fireplace in lobby, Library, Parking (free), 24-hour front desk, Wireless Internet, Outdoor pool, Free breakfast, Conference room(s), Billiards, Tennis on site.

Tilton
Also see the following nearby communities that have pet friendly lodging:
Gilford - 11 miles.

Not Rated
Anchorage At The Lake
725 Laconia Drive
Tilton NH 03276
(603) 524-3248
$87 - $269

Pet Policy: Pet friendly cabins available, $20 per pet per day. Strict pet policies. Call directly at 603) 524-3248 to reserve a pet friendly cabin.

Features: Cabin rentals, Kitchenettes in all cabins, BBQ grills.

★★
Rodeway Inn Tilton
788 Laconia Rd
Tilton NH 03276
(603) 524-6897
$79 - $209
SAVE –B&P Discount Available

Pet Policy: Rodeway Inns charge a fee of $10 per night per pet plus a $50 refundable damage deposit. Max of 2 pets per room. A veterinarian certificate that the pet is on a flea and parasite program and that they are free from parasites is required. Pets may not be left alone in the room unless in a cage.

Features: Number of rooms: 30, Parking (free), Wireless Internet.

★★
Super 8 Tilton Lake
7 Tilton Rd
Tilton NH 03276
(603) 286-8882
$63 - $229
SAVE –B&P Discount Available

Pet Policy: Pets accepted with small nightly fee.

Features: Number of floors: 2, Business services, Free breakfast, Parking (free), Wireless Internet.

Wakefield

Also see the following nearby communities that have pet friendly lodging:
Rochester - 18 miles.

Not Rated
Palmers Motel
3301 White Mountain Highway
Wakefield NH 03872
(800) 992-2694
$65 - $89

Pet Policy: Pets accepted, $10 per night per pet.

Features: Number of rooms: 6, Mini fridge and microwaves, Kitchenettes in some units.

West Lebanon

Also see the following nearby communities that have pet friendly lodging:
White River Junction - 2 miles, Lebanon - 3 miles, Quechee - 5 miles.

★★
Baymont West Lebanon
45 Airport Road
West Lebanon NH 03784
(603)-298-8888
$95 - $149
SAVE –B&P Discount Available

Pet Policy: Pets welcome, $10 per pet per night. Limit 2 pets per room.

Features: Number of rooms: 56, Number of floors: 4, Air-conditioned public areas, Coffee in lobby, Free breakfast, Parking (free), Nearby fitness center (free), Wireless Internet, Outdoor pool - seasonal, Dry cleaning/laundry service, Business center.

★★★ 🎿
Fireside Inn & Suites
25 Airport Road
West Lebanon NH 03784
(877) 258-5900
$99 - $159

Pet Policy: We welcome dogs at the Fireside Inn & Suites in selected rooms. There is a $10 per night, per dog fee. Dogs must not be left unattended in the room and cannot be allowed into food service areas, conference facilities or the pool.

Features: Number of rooms: 126, Indoor pool and Hot tub, Fitness center, Wireless Internet.

For best rates, book reservations at BedAndPet.com
Or call:
U.S. & Canada – 1-800-780-5733
Europe - 00-800-11-20-11-40
Please enter Promo Code 102350 when requested by phone

Rhode Island

Coventry
Also see the following nearby communities that have pet friendly lodging:
East Greenwich - 7 miles, Warwick - 9 miles.

★★★ 🎾🏃
Residence Inn Marriott
755 Center Of New England Blvd
Coventry RI 02817
(401) 828 1170
$130 - $190
SAVE –B&P Discount Available

Pet Policy: Pets allowed, $100 per stay cleaning fee.

Features: Accessible bathroom, Handicapped parking, Wireless Internet, Indoor pool, Number of suites: 100, Number of floors: 4, Coffee in lobby, Free breakfast, Parking (free), Free newspapers in lobby, Porter/bellhop, Meeting rooms, Smoke-free property, Fitness facilities, Room service, Business center, Dry cleaning/laundry service, Tennis on site.

Cranston
Also see the following nearby communities that have pet friendly lodging:
Providence - 1 mile, East Providence - 3 miles, Seekonk - 6 miles, Warwick - 7 miles, Smithfield - 9 miles.

★★
Days Inn Cranston
101 New London Ave
Cranston RI 02920
(401) 942-4200
$84 - $122.55
SAVE –B&P Discount Available

Pet Policy: Small pets accepted with fee. Please contact hotel directly for advanced approval.

Features: Business services, Coffee in lobby, Parking (free), Free newspapers in lobby, 24-hour front desk, Wireless Internet, RV and truck parking.

East Greenwich
Also see the following nearby communities that have pet friendly lodging:
North Kingstown - 5 miles, Warwick - 5 miles, Coventry - 7 miles.

★★
Extended Stay America
1235 Division Rd
East Greenwich RI 02818
(401) 885-3161
$81 - $96
SAVE –B&P Discount Available

Pet Policy: One pet is allowed in each guest room. A $25 per day non-refundable cleaning fee (not to exceed $150) will be charged the first night of your stay. Weight, size and breed restrictions may apply. Please contact the hotel directly with inquiries.
Continued on next page

Extended Stay America **East Greenwich** *Continued from previous page*	**Features:** Laundry facilities, Number of rooms: 104, Number of floors: 3, Elevator, Coffee in lobby, Parking (free), Free newspapers in lobby, Wireless Internet, Nearby fitness center (discount).

East Providence

Also see the following nearby communities that have pet friendly lodging::
Seekonk - 3 miles, Providence - 3 miles, Cranston - 3 miles,
Pawtucket - 4 miles, Warwick - 7 miles.

★★
Extended Stay America
1000 Warren Ave
East Providence RI 02914
(401) 272-1661
$86 - $106
SAVE –B&P Discount Available

Pet Policy: One pet is allowed in each guest room. A $25 per day non-refundable cleaning fee (not to exceed $150) will be charged the first night of your stay. Weight, size and breed restrictions may apply. Please contact the hotel directly with inquiries.

Features: Laundry facilities, Number of rooms: 100, Number of floors: 4, Parking (free), Front desk (limited hours), Wireless Internet, Nearby fitness center (discount).

Middletown

Also see the following nearby communities that have pet friendly lodging:
Newport - 4 miles.

★☆
Bay Willows Inn
1225 Aquidneck Ave
Middletown RI 02842
(802) 253-2905
$79 - $180
SAVE –B&P Discount Available

Pet Policy: Dogs and cats accepted with fee and deposit.

Features: Number of rooms: 21, Number of floors: 1, Airport transportation (additional charge), Free breakfast, Parking (free), 24-hour front desk, Porter/bellhop, Wireless Internet, Wedding services.

★★
Econo Lodge Middletown RI
1359 West Main Rd
Middletown RI 02842
(401) 849-2718
$84 - $194
SAVE –B&P Discount Available

Pet Policy: Pet Accommodation: $15/night per pet plus $50 refundable damage deposit. Maximum 2 pets per room. Owners must register pets at check in. Cannot leave pets unattended in room. Must be on leash in public areas and must clean up after pet. Pet rooms limited, please see room descriptions

Features: Outdoor pool - seasonal, Number of rooms: 55, Number of floors: 2, Coffee in lobby, Free breakfast, Parking, Wireless Internet.

★★
Howard Johnson Inn
351 W Main Rd
Middletown RI 02842
(401) 849-2000
$92- $249
SAVE –B&P Discount Available

Pet Policy: Pet friendly rooms, $10 per pet per night. Do not leave dogs alone in room.

Features: Bar/lounge, Babysitting or child care, Airport transportation (additional charge), Conference room(s), Coffee in lobby, Breakfast available, Arcade/game room, Parking (free), 24-hour front desk, Porter/bellhop, Wireless Internet, Dry cleaning/laundry service, Business center, Indoor pool, Sauna, Fitness facilities.

★★
Knights Inn Middletown
240 Aquidneck Avenue
Middletown RI 02842
(401) 324-6200
$99 - $179
SAVE –B&P Discount Available

Pet Policy: Pets accepted, $10 per night per pet.

Features: Number of rooms: 39, Number of floors: 2, Coffee in lobby, Free breakfast, Parking (free), Picnic area, 24-hour front desk, Smoke-free property, Concierge services, Handicapped parking, Suitable for children, Patio, Nearby fitness center (discount), Wireless Internet, Area shuttle (additional charge).

★★↲
Newport Inn and Whirlpool Suites
936 W Main Road
Middletown RI 02842
(401) 846-7600
$129 - $309
SAVE –B&P Discount Available

Pet Policy: Pets accepted, $20 per night additional, limit 2 per room. Pet rooms are limited and reservations should be made directly with the Inn.

Features: Indoor pool, Business center, Number of rooms: 77, Number of floors: 2, Elevator, Free breakfast, Parking (free), 24-hour front desk, Massage - treatment room(s), Barbecue grill(s), Spa services on site, Free newspapers in lobby, Picnic area, Beauty services, Wireless Internet, Limo or Town Car service available, Restaurant(s), Health club, Area shuttle (free).

★★★
Residence Inn by Marriott
325 W Main Rd
Middletown RI 02842
(401) 845-2005
$239 - $499
SAVE –B&P Discount Available

Pet Policy: Pets allowed, $75 per stay cleaning fee.

Features: Handicapped parking, In-room accessibility, Concierge, Parking (free), Smoke-free property, Convenience store, Number of rooms: 97, Number of floors: 4, Barbecue grill(s), Free newspapers, Dry cleaning/laundry service, Wireless Internet, 24-hour business center, Free reception, Indoor pool, Free breakfast, Bar/lounge, Coffee in lobby, Airport transportation (additional charge), Smoke-free property (fines apply), Fitness facilities.

★★
Rodeway Inn Middletown
31 W Main Road
Middletown RI 02842
(401) 847-2735
$65 - $175
SAVE –B&P Discount Available

Pet Policy: Rodeway Inns charge a fee of $10 per night per pet and require a $50 damage deposit, which is refunded if the room is in order at check out. Max of 2 pets per room. A veterinarian certificate that the pet is on a flea and parasite program and that they are free from parasites is required. Pets may not be left alone in the room unless in a cage.

Features: Wireless Internet, Fax machine, Number of rooms: 46, Number of floors: 2, Free breakfast, Parking (free), 24-hour front desk, Business center, Air-conditioned public areas.

Newport

Also see the following nearby communities that have pet friendly lodging:
Middletown - 4 miles, North Kingstown - 10 miles.

Not Rated
Beech Tree Inn & Cottage
34 Rhode Island Ave
Newport RI 02840
(401) 847-9794
$99 - $325

Pet Policy: 1 designated pet room, $25 additional cleaning fee.

Features: Year built: 1887, Air conditioning, Gardens, Fireplaces and Jacuzzi Tubs in many rooms, Full breakfast, Free parking, Full kitchen access.

★★★★
Forty 1 North
351 Thames Street
Newport RI 02840
(401) 846-8018
$505 - $725
SAVE –B&P Discount Available

Pet Policy: Accepts dogs only, up to 20 lbs, $150 per stay. Limit 2 dogs per room.

Features: Babysitting or child care, Parking (valet), Number of suites: 6, Number of floors: 3, Elevator, Conference room(s), Air-conditioned public areas, Fireplace in lobby, Patio, Garden, Library, Pool table, Wireless Internet, Room service (24 hours), Multilingual staff, Nearby fitness center (free), 24-hour front desk, Doorman/doorwoman, Security guard, Dry cleaning/laundry service, Limo or Town Car service available, Concierge desk, Porter/bellhop, Media library, Accessible bathroom, Handicapped parking, In-room accessibility, Meeting rooms (small groups), Smoke-free property, Wedding services, Bar/lounge, 2 Restaurant, Marina on site, Valet parking (additional charge).

★★★★♥
Hyatt Regency Newport
1 Goat Island
Newport RI 02840
(401) 851-1234
$249 - $529
SAVE –B&P Discount Available

Pet Policy: Pet friendly with $75 per stay fee.

Features: Sauna, Business Center, Accessible bathroom, In-room accessibility, Full-service health spa, Indoor pool, Outdoor pool, Dry cleaning/laundry service, Restaurant(s), Hair salon, Concierge services, Gift shop, Number of rooms: 264, Number of floors: 9, Elevator, Conference room(s), Secretarial services, Computer rental, Air-conditioned public areas, Parking (additional charge), Coffee in lobby, Breakfast available (additional charge), Wireless Internet, Multilingual staff, Room service, 24-hour front desk, Porter/bellhop, Meeting rooms (small groups), Wedding services, Bar/lounge.

★★★★
Pelham Court Hotel
14 Pelham Street
Newport RI 02840
(401) 619-4950
$299 - $349
SAVE –B&P Discount Available

Pet Policy: 1 dog or cat accepted per room, with advanced approval from manager. Please call Hotel directly for approval and pet reservations.

Features: Wireless Internet, Air-conditioned public areas, Free breakfast, Parking (free), Concierge desk, Smoke-free property.

★★★★
Vanderbilt Grace
41 Mary Street
Newport RI 02840
(401) 846-6200
$475 - $1050

Pet Policy: Pets under 25 lbs accepted, $50 per night, maximum of $100 per stay.

Features: Year Built - 1909, Health Club, Bar/Lounge, Conference Room(s), Garden, Indoor pool, Restaurant(s), Number of rooms: 33, Number of floors: 4, Elevator, Air-conditioned public areas, Room service, 24-hour front desk, Doorman/doorwoman, Swimming pool, Concierge desk, Steam room, Sauna, Parking (self and valet) $16-$25, Multilingual staff, Picnic area, Wireless Internet, Smoke-free property, Room service (limited hours), Concierge services, Porter/bellhop, Piano, Free breakfast, Shoe shine, Free newspapers in lobby, Massage - spa treatment room(s), Outdoor pool - seasonal, Designated smoking areas, Pool table, Accessible bathroom, Handicapped parking, In-room accessibility, Number of restaurants - 2, 24-hour business center, Conference center, Rooftop terrace, Luggage storage.

North Kingstown

Also see the following nearby communities that have pet friendly lodging::
East Greenwich - 5 miles, Warwick - 10 miles, Newport - 10 miles.

★★★ 🏃

TownePlace Suites
55 Gate Rd
North Kingstown RI 02852
(401) 667-7500
$219 - $240
SAVE –B&P Discount Available

Pet Policy: Pets allowed, $100 per stay cleaning fee.

Features: Fitness facilities, Indoor pool heated, Number of suites: 104, Number of floors: 4, Translation services, Coffee in lobby, Free breakfast, Free newspapers, Dry cleaning/laundry service, Wireless Internet, In-room accessibility, Area shuttle, 24-hour business center, RV and truck parking, Ferry terminal shuttle, Parking.

Providence

Also see the following nearby communities that have pet friendly lodging:
Cranston - 1 mile, East Providence - 3 miles,
Seekonk - 6 miles, Warwick - 7 miles, Smithfield - 9 miles.

★★★★

Dolce Villa
63 De Pasquale Plaza
Providence RI 02903
(401) 383-7031
$172 - $266
SAVE –B&P Discount Available

Pet Policy: Pets accepted, $75 per stay. Please contact hotel directly for pet reservations.

Features: Wireless Internet, Dry cleaning/laundry service, Concierge, Number of rooms: 14, Number of floors: 3, Parking (additional charge), Free newspapers, Meeting rooms, Smoke-free property, Business services, Room service (limited hours).

★★★★♥

Providence Biltmore Hotel
11 Dorrance St
Providence RI 02903
(401) 421-0700
$154 - $239
SAVE –B&P Discount Available

Pet Policy: Accepts pets up to 40 lbs, $75 per stay, limit 2 per room. No aggressive breeds!

Features: Year Built 1922, In-room accessibility, Restaurant(s), Number of rooms: 289, Number of floors: 18, Limo or Town Car service, Piano, Newspapers in lobby, Wireless Internet, 24-hour business center, On-site car rental, Room service, Porter/bellhop, Doorman/doorwoman, Beauty services, Concierge, Massage - treatment room(s), Meeting rooms, Full-service health spa, Dry cleaning/laundry service, Security guard, Bar/lounge, Parking (valet) $24 Per Day.

★★★☾
Providence Marriott Downtown
1 Orms St
Providence RI 02904
(401) 272 2400
$104 - $254
SAVE –B&P Discount Available

Pet Policy: Pets accepted, $49 additional cleaning fee.

Features: Babysitting or child care, Restaurant(s), Gift shops or newsstand, Number of rooms: 351, Number of floors: 6, Elevator, Conference room(s), Air-conditioned public areas, Parking (free), Multilingual staff, Free newspapers in lobby, Room service, 24-hour front desk, Business center, Smoke-free property, Bar/Lounge, Accessible bathroom, Handicapped parking, In-room accessibility, Concierge desk, Indoor pool, Outdoor pool, Dry cleaning/laundry service, Breakfast available (additional charge), Fitness facilities, Coffee shop, Beauty services, Full-service health spa, Currency exchange, Health club, Shoe shine.

★★★★♥
The Hotel Providence
139 Mathewson Street
Providence RI 02903
(401) 861-8000
$169 - $319
SAVE –B&P Discount Available

Pet Policy: Dog friendly. $75 per stay.

Features: Bar/Lounge, Conference Room(s), Concierge desk, Restaurant(s), Room service (limited hours), Number of rooms: 80, Number of floors: 7, Elevator, Breakfast available (additional charge), Free newspapers in lobby, 24-hour front desk, Business center, Porter/bellhop Wireless Internet, Meeting rooms (small groups), Smoke-free property, Dry cleaning/laundry service, Wedding services, Air-conditioned public areas, Parking (valet) $24/Day, Fitness facilities.

★★★★
The Westin Providence
1 W Exchange St
Providence RI 02903
(401) 598-8000
$149 - $279
SAVE –B&P Discount Available

Pet Policy: Dogs and Cats, up to 40 lbs accepted, $75 per stay fee.

Features: Concierge services, Number of rooms: 564, Number of floors: 25, Parking (additional charge), Currency exchange, Wireless Internet, Health club, Multilingual staff, Free newspapers in lobby, 24-hour front desk, Security guard, Massage - treatment room(s), Meeting rooms (small groups), Smoke-free property, Dry cleaning/laundry service, Airport transportation (additional charge), Room service, Porter/bellhop, Doorman/doorwoman, Number of restaurants 2, Bar/lounge, Sauna, Shopping on site, Indoor pool, Business center, Parking $23/Night, Accessible bathroom, Handicapped parking, Luggage storage.

★★★
Wyndham Garden Providence
220 India St
Providence RI 02903
(401) 272-5577
$119 - $179
SAVE –B&P Discount Available

Pet Policy: Pets up to 20 lbs, $75 per pet per day.

Features: Bar/lounge, Restaurant(s), Number of rooms: 136, Number of floors: 6, Elevator, Air-conditioned public areas, Patio, Coffee in lobby, Breakfast available (additional charge), Parking (free), Multilingual staff, 24-hour front desk, Wireless Internet, Room service (limited hours), Conference room(s), Smoke-free property, Business center, Fitness facilities, Dry cleaning/laundry service.

Smithfield

Also see the following nearby communities that have pet friendly lodging:
Cranston - 9 miles, Providence - 9 miles.

★★⯩
Hampton Inn and Suites
945 Douglas Pike
Smithfield RI 02917
(401) 232-9200
$126 - $199
SAVE –B&P Discount Available

Pet Policy: Pets welcome. We offer a Pet Welcome Gift Bag.

Features: Internet access - free, Fitness facilities, Indoor pool, Number of rooms: 101, Elevator, Air-conditioned public areas, Free breakfast, Parking (free), 24-hour front desk, Business center, Meeting rooms (small groups), Gift shops or newsstand, Dry cleaning/laundry service, Luggage storage.

★★⯩
Quality Inn Smithfield
355 George Washington Hwy
Smithfield RI 02917
(401) 232-9974
$119 - $129
SAVE –B&P Discount Available

Pet Policy: Pet accommodation: $25 per night per pet plus Pet deposit of $200 which may be refundable upon inspection of the room. Pet limit: 2 pets per room up to 40 pounds Unauthorized pets in the room will result in a $300 fine for cleaning of the room.

Features: Outdoor pool, Nearby fitness center (discount), Coffee in lobby, Air-conditioned public areas, Wireless Internet, Number of rooms: 116, Number of floors: 2, Free breakfast, Parking (free), Free newspapers in lobby, 24-hour front desk, Meeting rooms (small groups), Barbecue grill(s), Laundry facilities, Garden, Business center.

Warwick

Also see the following nearby communities that have pet friendly lodging:
East Greenwich - 5 miles, Providence - 7 miles, Cranston - 7 miles, East Providence - 7 miles, Coventry - 9 miles, North Kingstown - 10 mile.

★★★

Comfort Inn Warwick Airport
1940 Post Rd
Warwick RI 02886
(401) 732-0470
$89 - $150
SAVE –B&P Discount Available

Pet Policy: Pets accepted, $50 per stay.

Features: Restaurant, Room service (limited hours), Number of rooms: 196, Number of floors: 4, Elevator, Air-conditioned public areas, Free breakfast, Parking (free), 24-hour front desk, Wireless Internet, Meeting rooms (small groups), Dry cleaning/laundry service, Fax machine, Self-parking, Coffee in lobby, Conference room(s), Bar/lounge, Business services, Multilingual staff, Free newspapers in lobby, Nearby fitness center (free), Designated smoking areas, Accessible bathroom, Handicapped parking, In-room accessibility, Airport transportation (free) available 24 hours.

★★★★

Crowne Plaza Airport
801 Greenwich Ave
Warwick RI 02886
(877) 270-1412
$152 - $219
SAVE –B&P Discount Available

Pet Policy: Pets welcome with $50 damage deposit.

Features: Restaurant(s), Gift shop, Number of rooms: 266, Number of floors: 6, Conference room(s), Air-conditioned public areas, Health club, Parking (free), Multilingual staff, 24-hour front desk, Porter/bellhop, Wireless Internet, Meeting rooms (small groups), Accessible bathroom, Handicapped parking, In-room accessibility, Dry cleaning/laundry service, Fitness facilities, Bar/lounge, Concierge services, Sauna, Indoor pool, Business center, Airport transportation (free), Room service (limited hours).

★★

Extended Stay America Airport
245 W Natick Rd
Warwick RI 02886
(401) 732-2547
$76 - $86
SAVE –B&P Discount Available

Pet Policy: One pet is allowed in each guest room. A $25 per day non-refundable cleaning fee (not to exceed $150) will be charged the first night of your stay. Weight, size and breed restrictions may apply. Please contact the hotel directly with inquiries.

Features: Laundry facilities, Number of rooms: 104, Number of floors: 3, Coffee in lobby, Parking (free), Wireless Internet, Nearby fitness center (discount).

★★★✦

Hampton Inn and Suites Airport
2100 Post Rd
Warwick RI 02886
(401) 739-8888
$98. - $189
SAVE –B&P Discount Available

Pet Policy: Pets up to 45 lbs accepted.

Features: Indoor pool, Dry cleaning/laundry service, Bar/lounge, Airport transportation (free), Room service, Number of rooms: 173, Number of floors: 5, Conference room(s), Free breakfast, Parking (free), Free newspapers in lobby, Business center, Wireless Internet, Fitness facilities, Airport transportation (free) available 24 hours, Shopping on site, Designated smoking areas, Snack bar/deli.

★★★✦

Holiday Inn Express Hotel & Suites
901 Jefferson Blvd
Warwick RI 02886
(401) 736-5000
$102 - $171
SAVE –B&P Discount Available

Pet Policy: Pets welcome with $50 refundable damage deposit.

Features: Accessible bathroom, Handicapped parking, Dry cleaning/laundry service, Airport transportation (free), Parking (valet), Number of rooms: 147, Number of suites: 31, Number of floors: 4, Conference room(s), Coffee in lobby, Free breakfast, Free newspapers, Business center, Porter/bellhop, Limo or Town Car service available, Wireless Internet, Fitness facilities, Indoor pool.

★★

Homestead Providence Airport
268 Metro Center Blvd
Warwick RI 02886
(401) 732-6667
$86 - $106
SAVE –B&P Discount Available

Pet Policy: We gladly welcome one pet per guest room. A $25 per day non-refundable cleaning fee (not to exceed $150) will be charged the first night of your stay. Weight, size and breed restrictions may apply. Please contact the hotel directly with inquiries.

Features: Business services, Dry cleaning/laundry service, Number of suites: 94, Number of floors: 3, Parking (free), 24-hour front desk, Wireless Internet, Airport transportation (free), Coffee in lobby, Area shuttle (free), Fitness facilities.

★★★★

Homewood Suites by Hilton
33 International Way
Warwick RI 02886
(401) 738-0008
$113. - $179
SAVE –B&P Discount Available

Pet Policy: Pets up to 75 lbs, $75 per stay fee.

Features: Dry cleaning/laundry service, Free breakfast, Indoor pool, Business center, Fitness facilities, Number of rooms: 82, Number of floors: 3, Fireplace in lobby, Patio, Barbecue grill(s), Coffee in lobby, Wireless Internet, Parking (free), Free newspapers in lobby, 24-hour front desk, Meeting rooms (small groups), Shopping on site, Tennis on site, Luggage storage.

★★☆

La Quinta Inn & Suites Airport
36 Jefferson Blvd
Warwick RI 02888
(401) 941-6600
$75 - $109
SAVE –B&P Discount Available

Pet Policy: Small pets accepted with a security deposit.

Features: Accessible bathroom, Handicapped parking, Dry cleaning/laundry service, Airport transportation (free), Number of rooms: 115, Number of floors: 5, Translation services, Coffee in lobby, Swim-up bar, Free breakfast, Parking (free), Newspapers in lobby, Wireless Internet, Outdoor pool - seasonal, Business center, Fitness facilities.

★★★☆

NYLO Providence Warwick
400 Knight Street
Warwick RI 02886
(401) 734-4460
$109 - $140

Pet Policy: Dogs up to 50 lbs accepted, $50 each per stay, limit 2 per room.

Features: Dry cleaning/laundry service, Wireless Internet, Business center, Smoke-free property, Conference room(s), Bar/lounge, Fitness facilities, Restaurant(s), Self-parking (free), Airport transportation - drop-off (free).

★★★☆

Residence Inn By Marriott
500 Kilvert St
Warwick RI 02886
(401) 737-7100
$128 - $168
SAVE –B&P Discount Available

Pet Policy: Pets allowed, $100 per stay cleaning fee.

Features: Indoor pool, Number of suites: 98, Number of floors: 2, Air-conditioned public areas, Barbecue grill(s), Coffee in lobby, Laundry facilities, Parking (free), Free newspapers in lobby, 24-hour front desk, Wireless Internet, Smoke-free property, Tennis on site, Fitness facilities.

★★★☆

Sheraton Airport Hotel
1850 Post Rd
Warwick RI 02886
(401) 738-4000
$95 - $189
SAVE –B&P Discount Available

Pet Policy: All pets are welcome with no maximum weight limit. A cleaning fee of $50 is required. Sheraton Sweet Sleeper Dog Beds are available upon request. Guests traveling with pets must be noted in the reservation.

Features: Health Club, Coffee in lobby, Bar/Lounge, Indoor pool, Dry cleaning/laundry service, Restaurant(s), Number of rooms: 206, Number of floors: 5, Free newspapers in lobby, Wireless Internet, Meeting rooms, Gift shop, Parking (free), Medical assistance available, Wedding services, Accessible bathroom, Handicapped parking, 24-hour business center, Smoke-free property, Conference center, Fitness facilities, Airport transportation (free) available 24 hours, Room service.

Vermont

Arlington
Also see the following nearby communities that have pet friendly lodging:
Manchester - 6 miles, Shaftsbury - 7 miles.

★★★ 🛏
Arcady At Sunderland Lodge
6249 Historic Route 7A
Arlington VT 05250
(802) 362-1176
$85 - $165
SAVE –B&P Discount Available

Pet Policy: Pets accepted, no fee. Limit of 1 pet per room.

Features: Number of rooms: 15, Wireless Internet, Suitable for children, Barbecue grill(s), Free breakfast, Parking (free), Outdoor pool - seasonal, Hot Tub.

Bellows Falls
Also see the following nearby communities that have pet friendly lodging:
Claremont - 16 miles.

★★
Everyday Inn
593 Rockingham Rd
Bellows Falls VT 05101
(802) 463-4536
$94 - $129
SAVE –B&P Discount Available

Pet Policy: Pets accepted, $15 per night.

Features: Outdoor pool - seasonal, Free breakfast, Parking (free), Wireless Internet.

Bennington
Also see the following nearby communities that have pet friendly lodging:
Shaftsbury - 8 miles.

★★
Americas Best Value Inn
357 Us Route 7 S
Bennington VT 05201
(802) 442-2322
$65 - $98
SAVE –B&P Discount Available

Pet Policy: Pets welcome, $10 per pet per night. Limit 2 per room.

Features: Free breakfast, Parking (free), Outdoor pool, Air-conditioned public areas, Business center, Wireless Internet.

★★
Autumn Inn Bennington
924 Main Street
Bennington VT 05201
(802) 447-7625
$80 - $89
SAVE –B&P Discount Available

Pet Policy: Small pets accepted if booked in advance, with fee at check in. Pets should not be left alone in rooms.

Features: Outdoor pool, Number of rooms: 32, Number of floors 2, Parking (free), Wireless Internet.

★★
Bennington Motor Inn
143 Main St
Bennington VT 05201
(877) 784-6835
$101 - $120
SAVE –B&P Discount Available

Pet Policy: Dogs and cats accepted, $20 per pet per night.

Features: Number of rooms: 16, Number of floors: 2, Parking (free), 24-hour front desk, Number of Free breakfast, Wireless Internet.

★★
Knights Inn Bennington
693 Us Route 7 S
Bennington VT 05201
(802) 442-4074
$63 - $99
SAVE –B&P Discount Available

Pet Policy: Pets allowed, $9 per day fee.

Features: Internet access, Number of floors: 2, Business services, Air-conditioned public areas, Parking (free), 24-hour front desk, Free breakfast.

★★★
Paradise Inn
141 W Main St.
Bennington VT 05201
(802) 442-8351
$103 - $148
SAVE –B&P Discount Available

Pet Policy: Pets accepted in limited rooms, $5 per pet per night additional.

Features: Wireless Internet, Tennis on site, Fitness facilities, Conference room(s), Air-conditioned public areas, Patio, Laundry facilities, Parking (free), Massage - treatment room(s), Meeting rooms (small groups), Ski shuttle, Outdoor pool – seasonal.

★★
The Vermonter Motor Lodge
2968 West Road
Bennington VT 05201
(802) 442-2529
$75 - $105
SAVE –B&P Discount Available

Pet Policy: Pets accepted, $10 per pet per night additional.

Features: Coffee in Lobby, Number of rooms: 28, Number of floors: 1, Parking (free), Free newspapers in lobby, 24-hour front desk, Business center, Wireless Internet, Free breakfast, RV and truck parking.

Bolton Valley

Also see the following nearby communities that have pet friendly lodging:
Stowe - 8 miles.

★★☞ 🛏 🐕

Black Bear Inn
4010 Bolton Access Rd
Bolton Valley VT 05477
(800) 395-6335
$119 - $340
SAVE –B&P Discount Available

Pet Policy: We are a pet-friendly inn, and have select pet-friendly rooms available at a charge of $20 per night. These include two Standard Rooms, numbers 2 and 8, a Super Deluxe room, number 4, and the Mountaintop Suite (these rooms are noted on our online availability tool). Feel free to relax with your pet in the lobby in front of the fire, or take them for a walk just out our front door! Guests may leave their dogs unattended in their rooms, if they are expected to remain quiet. Please be aware that housekeeping will not enter rooms, however, if a pet is not crated.

Features: Restaurant, Gift shop, Number of rooms: 27, Parking (free), Wireless Internet, Smoke-free property, Outdoor pool - seasonal, Free breakfast, Video library, Wedding services, Suitable for children, Fireplace in lobby, Library, Front desk (limited hours).

Bondville

Also see the following nearby communities that have pet friendly lodging:
Londonderry - 6 miles, Manchester - 9 miles.

★★★ 🛏 🐕

Bromley View Inn
522 VT Route 30
Bondville VT 05340
(802) 297-1459
$109 - $140
SAVE –B&P Discount Available

Pet Policy: Pets accepted in limited rooms, $25 per day per pet with maximum of 2 pets per room. Pets must be well behaved, on a leash or in a kennel at all times, and dogs must not bark. Pets are not to be left alone in the room while you leave for the day. Please let the Innkeepers know that you will have a pet prior to arrival. Innkeepers reserve the right to ask that misbehaved pet be removed from the premises without notice or refunds.

Features: Number of rooms: 17, Parking (free), Wireless Internet, Bar/lounge, Barbecue grill(s), Fireplace in lobby, Free breakfast, Suitable for children, Front desk (limited hours).

★★★ 🎿
Stones Lodge under Mt. Stratton
1 River Road
Bondville VT 05340
(802) 297-3622
$214 - $286
SAVE –B&P Discount Available

Pet Policy: Pets accepted, $20 per stay cleaning fee. If your pet damages or destroys any or our property, you will be charged a proportionate fee to the damage cost and replacement fee.

Features: Free breakfast, Self-parking, Room service, Airport transportation (additional charge), Parking (free), Multilingual staff, Smoke-free property, Wedding services, Bar/lounge, Restaurant(s), Number of rooms: 124, Number of floors: 2, Business services, Pool table, Wireless Internet, Gift shops or newsstand, Ski storage, 24-hour front desk.

Brattleboro

Also see the following nearby communities that have pet friendly lodging:
Marlboro - 7 miles.

★★
Americas Best Inns Brattleboro
959 Putney Rd
Brattleboro VT 05301
(802) 254-4583
$62 - $86
SAVE –B&P Discount Available

Pet Policy: Pets accepted, no fee and no size limit.

Features: Barbecue Grill(s), Coffee in lobby, Number of rooms: 46, Number of floors: 2, Free breakfast, Wireless Internet, 24-hour front desk, Outdoor pool - seasonal, Handicapped parking, In-room accessibility, Dry cleaning/laundry service, Business services, Parking (free), Multilingual staff, Limo or Town Car service available, Grocery/convenience store, 24-hour business center, RV and truck parking, Computer station, Luggage storage.

Not Rated
Colonial Motel & Spa
889 Putney Road
Brattleboro VT 05301
(802) 257-7733
$65 - $145

Pet Policy: Pets accepted, $10 per pet per night.

Features: Number of rooms: 68, Indoor heated lap pool, Spa facilities with sauna and steam rooms, Outdoor hot tub, Continental breakfast, Coffee & Tea in lobby, Restaurant, Bar/lounge.

★★
Econo Lodge Brattleboro
515 Canal St
Brattleboro VT 05301
(802) 254-2360
$59 - $109
SAVE –B&P Discount Available

Pet Policy: Pets up to 30 lbs accepted, $10 per pet per night. Limit 2 per room.

Features: Wireless Internet, Laundry facilities, Free breakfast, Business services, Number of rooms: 42, Number of floors: 2, Parking (free), 24-hour front desk, Outdoor pool – seasonal.

★★
Quality Inn
1380 Putney Road
Brattleboro VT 05301
(877) 784-6835
$69 - $159
SAVE –B&P Discount Available

Pet Policy: Pet accommodation: $10/night per pet. Pet limit: 1 pet per room 20 lbs or less.

Features: Wireless Internet, Restaurant(s), Number of rooms: 103, Number of floors: 2, Parking, Newspapers in lobby, Wireless Internet, Sauna, Outdoor pool - seasonal, Dry cleaning/laundry service, Game room, Indoor pool, Business center, Fitness facilities..

★★
Super 8 Brattleboro
1043 Putney Rd
Brattleboro VT 05301
(802) 254-8889
$62 - $89
SAVE –B&P Discount Available

Pet Policy: Pets accepted, $25 additional fee.

Features: Free breakfast, Business services, Free newspapers in lobby, 24-hour front desk, Parking (free), Wireless Internet, RV and truck parking.

Burlington

Also see the following nearby communities that have pet friendly lodging:
South Burlington - 2 miles, Colchester - 3 miles, Essex Junction - 6 miles, Shelburne - 6 miles, Williston - 7 miles.

★★★★
Hilton Burlington
60 Battery St
Burlington VT 05401
(802)658-6500
$135 - $289
SAVE –B&P Discount Available

Pet Policy: Pets up to 75 lbs, $50 per stay.

Features: Business Center, Bar/Lounge, Airport transportation (free), Restaurant(s), Room service, Gift shop, Number of rooms: 258, Conference room(s), Internet - fee, Newspapers in lobby, Porter/bellhop, Indoor pool, Dry cleaning/laundry service, Parking (fee), Fitness facilities.

Chittenden

Also see the following nearby communities that have pet friendly lodging:
Mendon - 5 miles, Rutland - 9 miles, Killington - 9 miles.

★★★
Mountain Top Inn & Resort
195 Mountain Top Road
Chittenden VT 05737
(802) 483-2311
$235 - $1600

Pet Policy: We invite you to bring your pet and stay with us in one of our five mountain cabins or select private home rentals with the following guidelines:

Your pet will receive a dog bed, bowls for food and water and a welcome treat. When outside of their

**Mountain Top Inn & Resort
Chittenden, VT**

Continued from previous page

guest room, pets must be on a leash and owners are expected to clean up after them. Pets are permitted on designated cross-country ski trails (15km) and hiking trails. There is a pet fee of $30 per pet, per night.

Pet sitters are available with 3 days advance notice. Sitters will care for, feed, exercise and entertain your pet while you are enjoying the resort and the surrounding area. When left alone in the cabin, we request that your pet be crated for the safety of both your pet and our housekeeping staff. Pets are not allowed in any of the guest rooms of the Main Lodge or the Dining Room, Highlands Tavern, Lobby Areas, Den and Porches.

Features: Year built: 1873, Accommodations range from rooms and suites to cabins, Fireplaces, Microwaves, Refrigerators, Breakfast and afternoon refreshments included.

Colchester

Also see the following nearby communities that have pet friendly lodging:
Burlington - 3 miles, Essex Junction - 4 miles, South Burlington - 4 miles, Williston - 7 miles, Shelburne - 10 miles.

★★
Days Inn Burlington Colchester
124 College Pkwy
Colchester VT 05446
(802) 655-0900
$67 - $174
SAVE –B&P Discount Available

Pet Policy: Dogs only, $10 per day per dog. Must book in smoking rooms.

Features: Indoor pool, Laundry facilities, Free breakfast, Fitness facilities, Business center, Multiple small meeting rooms, Elevator, Air-conditioned public areas, Coffee in lobby, Free newspapers in lobby, 24-hour front desk.

★★★
Hampton Inn Burlington
42 Lower Mountain View Dr
Colchester VT 05446
(802) 655-6177
$109 - $259
SAVE –B&P Discount Available

Pet Policy: Large pets accepted, up to 165 lbs. Pets cannot be left unattended in guest rooms.

Features: Bar/lounge, Airport transportation (free), Indoor pool, Restaurant(s), Number of rooms: 188, Number of suites: 10, Number of floors: 5, Laundry facilities, Parking (free), Free newspapers in lobby, Business center, Smoke-free property, Fitness facilities, Free breakfast.

★★
Quality Inn
84 South Park Drive
Colchester VT 05446
(802) 655-1400
$83- $199
SAVE –B&P Discount Available

Pet Policy: Pets accepted up to 50 lbs, $10 per pet night per pet plus $50 refundable damage deposit, limit 3 per room. Pets may not be left alone in the room unless in a cage.

Features: Handicapped parking, In-room accessibility, Number of rooms: 117, Number of floors: 3, Free breakfast, Parking (free), Meeting rooms, Computer station, RV and truck parking, Coffee in lobby, Fitness facilities, Wireless Internet, 24-hour business center, Free newspapers, Outdoor pool - seasonal, Dry cleaning/laundry service.

★★★
Residence Inn by Marriott
71 Rathe Rd
Colchester VT 05446
802 655 3100
$198 - $259
SAVE –B&P Discount Available

Pet Policy: Pets allowed, $100 cleaning fee per stay.

Features: Parking (free), Smoke-free property, Number of rooms: 108, Number of floors: 4, Business services, Coffee in lobby, Laundry facilities, Free breakfast, Free newspapers, Wireless Internet.

Corinth

Also see the following nearby communities that have pet friendly lodging:
Fairlee - 7 miles.

Not Rated
A Special Place
1258 Camp Munn Road
Corinth VT 05039
(505) 250-3805
$180 - $350

Pet Policy: Pets allowed.

Features: Fully furnished 6 bedroom vacation home and guest house, Sleeps up to 13, On 30 acres, Swimming pond, 2 fully equipped kitchens, Wood burning stove, Central heat, Air conditioning, Wireless Internet.

Danby

★★★
Silas Griffith Inn
178 S Main St
Danby VT 05739
(888) 569-4660
$149 - $299
SAVE –B&P Discount Available

Pet policy: Dogs and cats welcome, $25 additional cleaning fee charged. For safety reasons, we ask that you not leave your pet unattended for extended periods either in your room or in your car. All common rooms of the Inn are strictly off-limits to our pet visitors.

Silas Griffith Inn - Danby
Continued from previous page

Since we don't require a security deposit, we only ask that you agree to pay for any cleanup or damage that may result from pet misbehavior. Special Rules for Dogs Your dog must always be on leash outside of your room during your stay with us. Please clean up after your pets. Plastic bags are available at the front desk if you need them. Please dispose of them in the dumpster. Special Rules for Cats We strongly recommend that you transport your cat in a pet carrier. You must provide and maintain a sanitary litter box in your room at all times.

Features: Library, Restaurant(s), Concierge services, Gift shops or newsstand, Number of floors: 3, Air-conditioned public areas, Coffee in lobby, Free breakfast, Parking (free), Picnic area, 24-hour front desk, Meeting rooms (small groups), Smoke-free property, Outdoor pool - seasonal, Wireless Internet, Video library, Bar/lounge, Fireplace in lobby, Business services.

Essex Junction
Also see the following nearby communities that have pet friendly lodging:
Colchester - 4 miles, Williston - 4 miles, South Burlington - 5 miles, Burlington - 6 miles.

★★
Handy Suites - Essex
27 Susie Wilson Road
Essex Junction VT 05452
(802) 872-5200
$81 - $91
SAVE –B&P Discount Available

Pet Policy: Accepts dogs with advanced approval, $25 per day. Please contact hotel directly for approval.

Features: Wired (high-speed) Internet access - free, Elevator, Parking (free), Picnic area, Meeting rooms (small groups), Designated smoking areas, Conference room(s), Laundry facilities, Business center, Barbecue grill(s), Free breakfast, Air-conditioned public areas, Indoor pool.

★★★★
The Essex Resort and Spa
70 Essex Way
Essex Junction VT 05452
(802) 878-1100
$239 - $279
SAVE –B&P Discount Available

Pet Policy: Pets welcome, $25 per night. Not only do we accept pets, we go all out to make them feel as welcome as our human guests. Pet treats and a nice, cold bowl of water will be waiting, and we even offer dog-walking and pet-sitting services with advance notice. All we ask is that if Spot happens to, well, leave something behind outside, please pick it up. Disposal bags are available at our Front Desk.
Continued on next page

The Essex Resort and Spa
Continued from previous page

Our pet-friendly accommodations include traditional rooms, fireplace rooms, mini-suites, studios, and one-bedroom suites.

Features: Bar/Lounge, Accessible bathroom, Handicapped parking, Garden, Dry cleaning/laundry service, Airport transportation (free), Room service (limited hours), Gift shop, Number of rooms: 120, Number of floors: 3, Elevator, Air-conditioned public areas, Fireplace in lobby, Patio, Coffee in lobby, Parking (free), Free newspapers in lobby, 24-hour front desk, Porter/bellhop, Smoke-free property, Outdoor pool - seasonal, Babysitting or child care, Indoor pool, 3 Restaurants, Suitable for children, Ski storage, Poolside bar, Health club, Shoe shine, Beauty services, Full-service health spa, Massage - treatment room(s), Meeting rooms (small groups), Steam room, Sauna, Wireless Internet, Pick up service from train station, RV and truck parking, Golf course on site, Tennis on site, Library, Wedding services.

Fairfax
Also see the following nearby communities that have pet friendly lodging:
St Albans - 8 miles.

★★★
The Inn At Buck Hollow Farm
2150 Buck Hollow Rd
Fairfax VT 05454
(802) 849-2400
$110 - $130
SAVE –B&P Discount Available

Pet Policy: Pets accepted, $20 per pet per day additional fee.

SHOTS: All pets must bring documentation that their shots are current.

CRATES: We are willing to have owners leave their pets for a few hours while out. However, they (the pets) must be crated during those times.

BEDS: We cover all beds with handmade quilts, some of which are antique. Therefore guests are asked to keep pets off our beds at all times. We do have doggie beds available at no charge. Please ask.

DAMAGES: Our daily fee of $20.00 per pet will cover the ordinary expenses resulting from having pets. However, in the event of expenses out of the ordinary, such as quilt dry cleaning when a pet has been on the bed, we reserve the right to impose additional costs. We hope never to do so.

The Inn At Buck Hollow Farm	**Features:** Outdoor pool, Gift shops or newsstand,
Continued from previous page	Number of rooms: 4, Patio, Coffee in lobby, Free breakfast, Wireless Internet, Business services, Parking (free)

Fairlee

Also see the following nearby communities that have pet friendly lodging:
Corinth - 7 miles.

★★ 🛏

Silver Maple Lodge & Cottages
520 US Route 5 South
Fairlee VT 05045
(802) 333-4326
Rates starting at $89
SAVE –B&P Discount Available

Pet Policy: Well-behaved pets are welcome in our cottage rooms. Dogs may be left in room alone if they do not disturb others.

Features: Free Breakfast, Parking (free), Year Built 1790.

Killington

Also see the following nearby communities that have pet friendly lodging:
Mendon - 5 miles, Rutland - 9 miles, Chittenden - 9 miles.

★★★ 🐾

Cascades Lodge
58 Old Mill Rd.
Killington VT 05751
(800) 345-0113
$115 - $180

Pet Policy: Pets accepted with advanced approval, pet fee of $50 per pet per night for first 2 nights, $25 per pet per night for additional nights. Please contact property directly for pet approval.

Features: Number of rooms: 46, Indoor heated pool, Whirlpool/sauna, Sundeck, Restaurant, Bar/lounge.

★★★ 🐾

Cortina Inn and Resort
103 US Route 4
Killington VT 05751
(802) 773-3333
$94 - $109
SAVE –B&P Discount Available

Pet Policy: Dogs and cats accepted, $25 per night. Limit 2 pets per room.

Features: Sauna, Indoor pool, Restaurant, Number of floors: 2, Elevator, Air-conditioned public areas, Fireplace in lobby, Ski storage, Parking (free), Multilingual staff, Smoke-free property, Free breakfast, Front desk (limited hours), Wireless Internet, Smoke-free property (fines apply), Luggage storage.

★★ 🐾
Hillside Inn Killington
375 Killington Rd
I-89 At Exit #13
Killington VT 05751
(802) 315-0039
$54 - $69
SAVE –B&P Discount Available

Pet Policy: Pets up to 80 lbs accepted, $25 per day (maximum of $75) plus $100 damage deposit. Limit 1 pet per room.

Features: Airport transportation, Accessible bathroom, Ski shuttle, Area shuttle, Ski storage, Coffee in lobby, Airport transportation (additional charge), Parking, Free Internet, Arcade/game room, Meeting rooms, In-room accessibility, Free breakfast, Number of rooms: 93, Number of floors: 3.

★★ 🛏 🐾
Kokopelli Inn
4337 VT Route 4
Killington VT 05751
(802) 422-9888
$80 - $95
SAVE –B&P Discount Available

Pet Policy: Pets accepted in two rooms, $10 per pet per day. Please call inn directly for pet reservations.

Features: Number of rooms: 16, Wireless Internet, Fireplace in lobby, Free breakfast.

★★★ 🛏 🐾
Mendon Mountainview Lodge
78 Us Route 4
Killington VT 05751
(802) 773-4311
$79 - $129
SAVE –B&P Discount Available

Pet Policy: Pets allowed. $25 per night

Features: Free breakfast, Accessible bathroom, Handicapped parking, In-room accessibility, Restaurant(s), Number of floors: 3, Elevator, Parking (free), Wireless Internet, Outdoor pool - seasonal, Ski storage, Fireplace in lobby, Arcade/game room, Bar/lounge, Sauna, Room service, Rooftop terrace.

Londonderry

Also see the following nearby communities that have pet friendly lodging:
Bondville - 6 miles.

★★★★ 🛏 🐾
Frog's Leap Inn
7455 Route 100
Londonderry VT 05148
(802) 824-3019
$135 - $260
SAVE –B&P Discount Available

Pet Policy: Pets well-adapted to travel and well-socialized are welcome. Pet fee of $10 per pet per day is charged. Respect for others also enjoying their vacation is expected. Aggressive and noisy animals are strictly prohibited. Proper restraints are a must. Pet owners accept full responsibility for behavior and damages caused by pets. It is highly advised that you contact the Inn directly for pet reservations as pet-friendly rooms are limited.

Features: Fireplace in lobby, Wireless Internet, Restaurant(s), Free breakfast, Wedding services.

★★ 🏃

Magic View Motel Londonderry
3806 VT Route 11
Londonderry VT 05148
(802) 824-3793
$65 - $79

Pet Policy: Pets accepted with advanced approval. Please contact motel directly for approval, conditions and pet reservations.

Features: Ski storage, Coffee shop, Smoke-free property, Wireless Internet, Parking (free), Room service.

Not Rated 🏃

Snowdon Motel
4071 RT 11
Londonderry VT 05148
(802) 824-6047
$89 - $100

Pet Policy: Pets accepted up to 35 lbs, $10 per night fee. Only 1 pet-friendly room so please contact motel directly to reserve.

Features: Number of rooms: 35, Number of floors: 2, No elevator, Restaurant, Wireless Internet, Non-smoking rooms.

Ludlow

Not Rated 🏃

All Seasons Motel
112 Main Street
Ludlow VT 05149
(888) 228-8100
$99 - $142

Pet Policy: Pet friendly, but details have not been provided so please contact the property directly for more information and reservations.

Features: Stay & Ski packages for two or more days, which include room and two daily lift tickets for Okemo Mountain, Nonsmoking property, Number of rooms: 17, Number of efficiencies: 6, Mini fridge and coffee maker in each room, Free Shuttle in season.

★★ 🛏 🏃

The Combes Family Inn
953 East Lake Rd
Ludlow VT 05149
(802) 228-8799
Rates from $134
SAVE –B&P Discount Available

Pet Policy: Five units are attached to the main house. pets are allowed in these units.

Features: Year Built 1880, Free Breakfast, Library, Fireplace in lobby, Number of rooms: 11, Conference room(s), Barbecue grill(s), Smoke-free property, Video library.

Manchester

Also see the following nearby communities that have pet friendly lodging:
Bondville - 10 miles.

★★★★♥ 🏌
The Equinox Resort & Spa
3567 Main St
Manchester VT 05254
(802) 362-4700
$233 - $754
SAVE –B&P Discount Available

Pet Policy: Pets under 80 lbs, $125 pet fee per stay. Pets to be on leash at all times. Pets are not allowed in dining areas with the exception of Service Dogs. Please let housekeeping know when pet is out of the room so the room may be serviced.

Features: Coffee in lobby, Bar/Lounge, Indoor pool, Full-service health spa, Garden, Meeting rooms (small groups), Wireless Internet, Area shuttle (free), Golf course on site, Babysitting or child care, Restaurant(s), Hair salon, Shopping on site, Number of floors: 4, Health club, Parking (free), Room service, 24-hour front desk, Business center.

★★★★ 🛏 ♥ 🎾
Wilburton Inn
257 Wilburton Dr
Manchester VT 05254
(802) 362-2500
$200 - $235
SAVE –B&P Discount Available

Pet Policy: Pets are accepted in a few rooms but must be approved in advance. Please contact Inn directly if you wish to bring a pet.

Features: Free Breakfast, Outdoor pool, Restaurant, Number of rooms: 30, Smoke-free property, Suitable for children, Tennis on site, Bar/lounge, Gift shop, Garden, Parking (free), Rooftop terrace.

Marlboro

Also see the following nearby communities that have pet friendly lodging:
Brattleboro - 7 miles.

Not Rated
Golden Eagle Motel
5383 RT 9
Marlboro VT 3544
(802) 464-5540
$56 - $100

Pet Policy: Pets accepted, $20 per night pet fee.

Features: Game room with pool table, Exercise facilities, Refrigerator and Microwave in lobby for guest use.

Mendon

Also see the following nearby communities that have pet friendly lodging:
Killington - 5 miles, Chittenden - 5 miles, Rutland - 6 miles.

★★ 🏃

Econo Lodge Killington Area
51 US Route 4 E
Mendon VT 05701
(800) 992-9067
$49 - $69
SAVE –B&P Discount Available

Pet Policy: Pet accommodation: $15/day. Limit: 2 pets Pet Policy: Credit card required with pet stay. No dogs to be left in room unattended.

Features: Wireless Internet, Self-parking, Outdoor pool - seasonal, Pool table Number of rooms: 30, Number of floors: 2, Free newspapers, Ski shuttle, Free breakfast, Library, Arcade/game room.

Middlebury

Not Rated 🏃
Middlebury Inn
14 Court Square
Middlebury VT 05753
(802) 388 4961
$139 - $244

Pet Policy: Pets are welcome in our Annex section only. $25 per stay. Please be sure to confirm that your arrival includes a pet when making your reservation. There are plenty of trails in the area perfect for exploring with your dog.

Features: Year built: 1827, Number of rooms: 70, Wedding services, Wireless Internet, Afternoon Tea, Fitness center privileges, Breakfast included.

Not Rated 🛏
Swift House Inn
25 Stewart Lane
Middlebury VT 05753
(802) 388-9925
$139 - $259

Pet Policy: Pets are accepted only in the Carriage House and subject to a pet fee. You must call the Inn directly to book a pet friendly room.

Features: Former governor's mansion, Number of rooms: 20, Full breakfast, Restaurant, Lounge with fireplace, Daily passes to Middlebury Fitness Club.

Montgomery Center

★★★★ 🛏 🏃
Phineas Swann Bed & Breakfast Country Inn
195 Main Street
Montgomery Center VT 05471
(802) 326-4306
$109 - $249
SAVE –B&P Discount Available

Pet Policy: Dogs welcome, no fee. No size or breed restrictions (we especially love bulldogs). Unlike other lodging properties that will only tolerate your dog, we will welcome you and your pet with genuine enthusiasm. At the Phineas Swann, we are DOG CRAZY!!!! and would love to have you and your dog as our guests. Pets may be left unattended in room but should be crated if likely to jump on bed.
Continued on next page

**Phineas Swann Bed &
Breakfast Country Inn
Montgomery Center VT**

Continued from previous page

If you are going to be gone for an extended period, the dog should be crated or taken with you. Dogs are invited to swim in the Trout River that borders our property and hike on nearby hiking trails Dog beds, food and water bowls, pet-sitting services, dog-walking services, special dog towels, and dog treats are available. Please tell us your needs when making your reservation so we can be prepared to accommodate your pet in regal style For an extra special vacation with your pet, consider our Deluxe Dog Spa Package, which includes accommodations in our luxurious Honeymoon Suite, dog-walking services every 3 hours, bed-sleeping permission, a bag of deluxe dog treats, and more! During the Winter, try our Pet Perfect Ski Package - this wonderful package includes lodging, breakfast (with a Doggie Bag treat for your pet), ski tickets to Jay Peak, dog-walking services, and a lot of TLC for your baby while you ski the slopes. Special pet packages should be booked directly with hotel.

Features: Garden, Number of rooms: 3, Number of floors: 2, Free breakfast, Fireplace in lobby, Coffee in lobby, Library, Music library, Media library, Wireless Internet, Computer station.

Montpelier
Also see the following nearby communities that have pet friendly lodging:
Barre - 6 miles.

★★
Econo Lodge Montpelier
101 Northfield St
Montpelier VT 05602
(802) 223-5258
$69 - $119
SAVE –B&P Discount Available

Pet Policy: Pets accepted, $10 per night.

Features: Number of rooms: 54, Free breakfast, Front desk (limited hours), Wireless Internet, RV and truck parking.

Quechee
Also see the following nearby communities that have pet friendly lodging:
White River Junction - 3 miles, West Lebanon - 5 miles, Lebanon - 9 miles.

★★★ 🛏 🐾
Inn at Clearwater Pond
984 Quechee-Hartland Road
Quechee VT 05059
(802) 295-0606
$175 - $295
SAVE –B&P Discount Available

Pet Policy: Pets up to 20 lbs are accommodated when possible. Please contact Inn directly for pet reservations.

Features: Number of rooms: 5, Number of floors: 2, Wireless Internet, Massage - treatment room(s), Video library, Free breakfast, Patio.

★★ 🐾
Quality Inn At Quechee Gorge
5817 Woodstock Rd
Quechee VT 05059
(802) 295-7600
$89 - $189
SAVE –B&P Discount Available

Pet Policy: Quality Inns charge a fee of $10 per night per pet plus a $50 refundable damage deposit. Quality Inns accept any well-behaved pets up to 50 lbs, with a maximum of 3 per room. They do not currently require a veterinarian certificate. Pets may not be left alone in the room unless in a cage.

Features: Parking (free), Wireless Internet, Restaurant, Free breakfast, Number of floors: 2, Fitness facilities, Indoor pool, Picnic area.

Rutland

Also see the following nearby communities that have pet friendly lodging:
Mendon - 6 miles, Chittenden - 9 miles, Killington - 9 miles.

★★ 🐾
Comfort Inn Trolley Square
19 Allen St
Rutland VT 05701
(800) 483-7187
$79 - $119
SAVE –B&P Discount Available

Pet Policy: Pets up to 50 lbs accepted, $35 per night per pet. Limit 2 pets per room.

Features: Restaurant, Number of rooms: 104, Number of floors: 3, Parking (free), Free newspapers in lobby, 24-hour front desk, Wireless Internet, Meeting rooms, Sauna, Dry cleaning/laundry service, Indoor pool, Bar/lounge, Free breakfast.

★ 🐾
Econo Lodge Killington Area
51 RT 4
Rutland VT 05701-9652
(802) 775-7077
$45 - $79

Pet Policy: Pet accommodation: $15.99/day, plus credit card imprint. Limit: 2 dogs per room max 40 lbs. No dogs to be left in room unattended.

Features: Continental Breakfast, Wireless Internet, Hot Tub, Outdoor pool – seasonal, In-room accessibility.

★★★ 🐾
Holiday Inn Rutland-Killington
476 Us Route 7 S
Rutland VT 05701
(802) 775.1911
$123 - $154
SAVE –B&P Discount Available

Pet Policy: Pets accepted, $27.50 per night. Pets may not be left alone in room if you are off the property.

Features: Handicapped parking, In-room accessibility, Restaurant, Gift shop, Number of rooms: 151, Number of floors: 2, Coffee in lobby, Parking (free), Free newspapers in lobby, Porter/bellhop, Wireless Internet, Sauna, Arcade/game room, Concierge, Indoor pool, Bar/lounge, Currency exchange, Babysitting or child care, Business center, Room service, Airport transportation (free), Fitness facilities, Ski storage, Dry cleaning/laundry service, Designated smoking areas, Luggage storage.

★★ 🎾🏃
Ramada Limited Rutland
253 S Main St
Rutland VT 05701
(802) 773-3361
$57 - $99
SAVE –B&P Discount Available

Pet Policy: Pets accepted without size restrictions, $27.50 per stay. Pets may not be left alone in room at any time.

Features: RV and truck parking, Indoor pool, Dry cleaning/laundry service, Nearby fitness center (free), Limo or Town Car service available, On-site car rental, Arcade/game room, Parking (free), Room service, Business center, Tennis on site.

★★↗ 🐾
Red Roof Inn
401 US Route 7 S
Junction Of US 4 And US 7
Rutland VT 05701
(802)775-4303
$69 - $98
SAVE –B&P Discount Available

Pet Policy: Red Roof's Pet Policy: One well-behaved family pet is permitted unless they are prohibited by state law or ordinance. Service animals are always welcome. Pets must be declared during guest registration. In consideration of all Red Roof guests, pets must never be left unattended in the guestroom.

Features: Sauna, Free Breakfast, Coffee in lobby, Indoor pool, Free newspapers in lobby, 24-hour business center, Laundry facilities, Arcade/game room, Wedding services, Wireless Internet, Number of rooms: 100, Number of suites: 1, Number of floors: 2, Elevator, Air-conditioned public areas, Parking (free), 24-hour front desk, Luggage storage.

★★ 🎿

Rodeway Inn Rutland
138 N Main St
Rutland VT 05701
(802) 775-2575
$49 - $69
SAVE –B&P Discount Available

Pet Policy: Rodeway Inns charge a fee of $10 per night per pet and require a $5 damage deposit, which is refunded if the room is in order at check out. Max of 2 pets per room. A veterinarian certificate that the pet is on a flea and parasite program and that they are free from parasites is required. Pets may not be left alone in the room unless in a cage.

Features: Number of rooms: 29, Number of floors: 2, Parking (free), Free newspapers in lobby, Outdoor pool - seasonal, Wireless Internet, Free breakfast.

★★ 🎿

Rodeway Inn Rutland
115 Woodstock Ave
Rutland VT 05701
(802) 773-9176
Rates from $59
SAVE –B&P Discount Available

Pet Policy: Rodeway Inns charge a fee of $10 per night per pet and require a $50 damage deposit, which is refunded if the room is in order at check out. Max of 2 pets per room. A veterinarian certificate that the pet is on a flea and parasite program and that they are free from parasites is required. Pets may not be left alone in the room unless in a cage.

Features: Self-parking, Wireless Internet, Number of rooms: 20, Number of floors: 2, Parking (free), 24-hour front desk, Outdoor pool - seasonal, Free breakfast, Laundry facilities.

★★ 🎿

Travel Inn
125 Woodstock Ave
Rutland VT 05701
(802) 775-4348
$69 - $93
SAVE –B&P Discount Available

Pet Policy: Pets accepted, $25 per day pet fee.

Features: Number of rooms: 37, Number of floors: 2, Air-conditioned public areas, 24-hour front desk, Coffee in lobby, Fireplace in lobby, Parking (free), Self-parking.

Shaftsbury

Also see the following nearby communities that have pet friendly lodging:
Bennington - 8 miles.

Not Rated
Governor's Rock Motel
4325 Historic Route 7A
Shaftsbury VT 05262
(802) 442-4734
$71 - $89

Pet Policy: Small pets accepted, $10 per night per pet.

Features: Wireless Internet, Continental Breakfast.

★★★ 🛏

Meadowood Farm
557 Bennett Hill Rd
Shaftsbury VT 05262
(802) 442-2440
$170 - $195
SAVE –B&P Discount Available

Pet Policy: There is a seasonally-dependent charge of $10 for a well-behaved dog. Some breeds are excluded. Horses may be boarded at a neighbors stable for $35 per night.

Features: Number of rooms: 3, Free breakfast, Suitable for children.

Shelburne

Also see the following nearby communities that have pet friendly lodging:
South Burlington - 5 miles, Burlington - 6 miles, Williston - 9 miles, Colchester - 10 miles.

★★

Econo Lodge Inn And Suites
3164 Shelburne Rd.
Shelburne VT 05482
(802) 985-3377
$69 - $129
SAVE –B&P Discount Available

Pet Policy: Pets accepted, $10 per pet per night.

Features: Number of rooms: 53, Number of floors: 1, Business services, Coffee in lobby, Parking (free), 24-hour front desk, Wireless Internet, Beauty services, Outdoor pool - seasonal, Free breakfast.

★★

Quality Inn Shelburne
2572 Shelburne Road
Shelburne VT 05482
(802) 985-8037
$89 - $159
SAVE –B&P Discount Available

Pet Policy: Pets accepted, $10 per night per pet.

Features: Sauna, Indoor pool, Conference room(s), Business services, Laundry facilities, Free breakfast, Health club, Parking (free), Wireless Internet, Number of rooms: 73.

South Burlington

Also see the following nearby communities that have pet friendly lodging:
Burlington - 2 miles, Colchester - 4 miles, Essex Junction - 5 miles, Shelburne - 5 miles, Williston - 6 miles.

★★★★

DoubleTree by Hilton Burlington
1117 Williston Rd
South Burlington VT 05403
(802) 658-0250
$101 - $279
SAVE –B&P Discount Available

Pet Policy: Large pets allowed, $75 per stay. Pets may not be left alone in room.

Features: Indoor pool, Restaurant, Gift shop, Number of rooms: 161, Number of floors: 2, Wireless Internet, Parking, Newspapers, Security guard, Meeting rooms, Room service, In-room accessibility, Dry cleaning/laundry service, Airport transportation, Bar/lounge, Business center, Fitness facilities.

★★★
Green Mountain Suites
401 Dorset Street
South Burlington VT 05403
(802) 860-1212
$206 - $269

Pet Policy: Small pets accepted, $25 per night, maximum 2 pets per room. Pets are not allowed in pool or dining areas.

Features: One and two bedroom suites, Fully equipped kitchens in all suites, Full hot breakfast buffet, Free social reception, Indoor heated pool, Jacuzzi, Wireless Internet, Laundry facilities.

★★★♪
La Quinta Inn & Suites
1285 Williston Rd
South Burlington VT 05403
(802) 865-3400
$88 - $145
SAVE –B&P Discount Available

Pet Policy: Cats and dogs up to 50 pounds are accepted in all guest rooms. Housekeeping services for rooms with pets require pet owner be present or pet must be crated. No fees or deposits are required.

Features: Coffee in lobby, Accessible bathroom, Handicapped parking, Number of rooms: 105, Number of floors: 3, Elevator, Free breakfast, Parking (free), Free newspapers in lobby, Wireless Internet, Outdoor pool - seasonal, Business services, Dry cleaning/laundry service, Fitness facilities.

★★
Rodeway Inn South Burlington
1016 Shelburne Rd
South Burlington VT 05403
(802) 862-6421
$79 - $149
SAVE –B&P Discount Available

Pet Policy: Pets accepted $10 per night per pet plus $50 refundable damage deposit. Max of 2 pets per room. A veterinarian certificate that the pet is on a flea and parasite program and that they are free from parasites is required. Pets may not be left alone in the room unless in a cage.

Features: Free breakfast, Wireless Internet, Coffee in lobby, Number of rooms: 53, Number of floors: 2, Business services, Laundry facilities, Parking (free).

★★★♪
Sheraton Burlington Hotel & Conference Center
870 Williston Rd
South Burlington VT 05403
(802) 865-6600
$155 - $317
SAVE –B&P Discount Available

Pet Policy: Dogs up to 80 lbs and house cats accepted without fee. Pets may not be left in the guest room unattended. Guests are responsible for any additional charges related to cleaning or disturbances and noise. A pet waiver must be signed at check-in. Special dog bed is available.

Features: Restaurant(s), Concierge services, Shopping on site, Number of rooms: 309, Number of floors: 4, Laundry facilities, Parking (free), Room service, 24-hour front desk, Swimming pool, Smoke-free property, Wireless Internet, Business center, Bar/lounge, Conference room(s), Fitness facilities.

Not Rated
Smart Suites
1700 Shelburne Road
South Burlington VT 05403
(802) 860-9900
$125 - $169

Pet Policy: Pets up to 25 lbs accepted, $25 per stay per pet. Limit 2 pets per room.

Features: Efficiencies and 1 bedroom suites, Buffet breakfast, Wireless Internet, Fitness center, Business center, 24 hour airport shuttle – free, Laundry facilities.

★★
University Inn
1 Dorset St
South Burlington VT 05403
(802) 264-4114
$109 - $110
SAVE –B&P Discount Available

Pet Policy: Dogs and cats accepted, $25 per stay.

Features: Indoor pool, Outdoor pool, Number of rooms: 89, Number of suites: 1, Number of floors: 2, Self-parking, 24-hour front desk, Business center.

Springfield
Also see the following nearby communities that have pet friendly lodging:
Claremont - 8 miles, Bellows Falls - 10 miles.

★★★
Holiday Inn Express Springfield
818 Charlestown Rd
Springfield VT 05156
(802) 885-4516
$119 - $180
SAVE –B&P Discount Available

Pet Policy: Pets welcome, $25 per night additional fee.

Features: Accessible bathroom, Dry cleaning/laundry service, Number of rooms: 88, Number of floors: 2, Conference room(s), Suitable for children, Coffee in lobby, Free breakfast, Parking (free), Free newspapers in lobby, 24-hour front desk, Business center, Wireless Internet, Fitness facilities, Indoor pool, Arcade/game room.

St Albans
Also see the following nearby communities that have pet friendly lodging:
Fairfax - 8 miles.

★★
Econo Lodge St Albans
287 S Main St
St Albans VT 05478
(802) 524-5956
Rates from $79
SAVE –B&P Discount Available

Pet Policy: Pet Accommodation: $20 per pet per night, one pet per room maximum stay of 2 nights. Limit one pet per room based on availability of pet friendly rooms.

Features: Free breakfast, Parking (free), Wireless Internet, Number of rooms: 30, Number of floors: 2, Free newspapers in lobby.

★★☆
La Quinta Inn & Suites
813 Fairfax Rd
St Albans VT 05478
802-524-3300
$114 - $150
SAVE –B&P Discount Available

Pet Policy: Dog friendly, no fee, but do need rabies certificate.

Features: Coffee in lobby, Gift shop or newsstand, Number of rooms: 63, Number of floors: 3, Conference room(s), Laundry facilities, Arcade/game room, Free breakfast, Free newspapers in lobby, Business center, Indoor pool, Accessible bathroom, Handicapped parking, Parking (free), Wireless Internet, Fitness facilities.

Stowe

Also see the following nearby communities that have pet friendly lodging:
Bolton Valley - 8 miles.

★★☆ 🐕
Commodores Inn
823 S Main St
Rte 100 South
Stowe VT 05672
(802) 253-7131
$98 - $128
SAVE –B&P Discount Available

Pet Policy: Join other dog owners and visit the Commodores Inn. Guests visit with their pets from all over to attend the annual 'Camp Gone to the Dogs', which is a week-long training camp for dogs and their owners. We have also hosted the National Retriever Championships, and your dogs are always welcome at our Inn.

Features: Bar/lounge, Indoor pool heated, Outdoor pool, Number of rooms: 72, Elevator, Suitable for children, Air-conditioned public areas, Fireplace in lobby, Patio, Coffee in lobby, Ski storage, Breakfast & dinner buffets (additional charge), Arcade/game room, Pool table, Parking (free), 24-hour front desk, Sauna, Ski shuttle, Smoke-free property, Outdoor pool - seasonal, Pool table, Handicapped parking, In-room accessibility, RV and truck parking, Number of spa tubs 3, Smoke-free Conference center.

★★★ 🎾🏃🐕
Golden Eagle Resort
511 Mountain Rd
Stowe VT 05672
802-253-4811
$134 - $199
SAVE –B&P Discount Available

Pet Policy: Well-mannered dogs and cats, any size, welcome, $25 per stay.

Pet Friendly Areas- Pets must be leashed or held in the arms of the owner in all common areas of the property. For your pet's safety, the trout ponds and swimming pool areas are considered out of bounds.

Continued on next page

Golden Eagle Resort
Continued from previous page

Leash Free Policy- Pets are allowed off-leash on the trails as long as they are under voice control. For other leash free areas and fun locations in the Stowe area please inquire at the front desk for directions.

Waste Disposal- Provided for your convenience are waste disposal bags for your use. Pet owners are responsible for picking up after their pet in and around the resort at all times. Please dispose of them in the proper receptacles that are located throughout the property.

Housekeeping- Housekeeping will enter your room, only if: (A) your pet is not present or (B) your pet is caged/crated. Please call the front desk and make arrangements when it's convenient to enter the room.

Features: Handicapped parking, In-room accessibility, Gift shop, Number of rooms: 94, Number of floors: 2, Airport transportation (additional charge), Air-conditioned public areas, Coffee in lobby, Video library, Pool table, Restaurant, Wireless Internet, Health club, Parking (free), 24-hour front desk, Massage - treatment room(s), Meeting rooms, Ski shuttle, Smoke-free property, Outdoor pool - seasonal, Library, Babysitting or child care, Business center, Supervised child care/activities, Arcade/game room, Concierge services, Sauna, Suitable for children, Indoor pool, Picnic area, Laundry facilities, Conference room(s), Barbecue grill(s), Fireplace in lobby, Tennis on site.

★★★
Hob Nob Inn & Restaurant
2364 Mountain Road
Stowe VT 05672
(802) 253-8549
$120 - $210

Pet Policy: Pets accepted with advanced approval, $20 per day. Limited number of pet-friendly rooms.

Features: Fireplaces and Kitchenettes available in some rooms, Restaurant, Full breakfast, Non-smoking property, Jacuzzi rooms available.

★★↙
Mountain Road Resort
1007 Mountain Rd
Stowe VT 05672
(802) 253-4566
$98 - $179
SAVE –B&P Discount Available

Pet Policy: Pets accepted, $10 per pet per night.

Features: Bar/lounge, Babysitting or child care, Indoor pool, Room service, Outdoor pool, Number of rooms: 32, Number of floors: 2, Elevator, Conference room(s), Laundry facilities, Game room, Parking, Newspapers in lobby, Porter/bellhop, Concierge, Sauna, Fitness facilities.

★★★✓ 🏃

Northern Lights Lodge
4441 Mountain Rd
Stowe VT 05672
(802) 253-8541
$68 - $138
SAVE –B&P Discount Available

Pet Policy: Pets can be accepted on a case by case basis. Please contact the lodge's manager directly for approval and pet reservations.

Features: Indoor pool, Restaurant, Outdoor pool, Number of rooms: 50, Arcade/game room, Pool table, Free breakfast, Meeting rooms (small groups), Sauna, Front desk (limited hours).

★★ 🏃 🏃

Stowe Motel
2043 Mountain Rd
Stowe VT 05672
(802) 253-7629
$90 - $140
SAVE –B&P Discount Available

Pet Policy: Pets accepted in only a few rooms, $10 per stay. Must book directly with motel for pets. We welcome a well behaved pet under the following guidelines: Only one pet per room is allowed; A dog must be kept on a leash outside; it cannot disturb other guests; a pet can never be left alone in the room unless in a kennel (and a number where you can be reached) and never be left alone if it barks.

Features: Number of rooms: 38, Number of suites: 4, Number of floors: 2, Fireplace in lobby, Barbecue grill(s), Coffee in lobby, Arcade/game room, Smoke-free property, Wireless Internet, Parking (free), Tennis on site.

★★★★★ 🏃 🏃

Stowe Mountain Lodge - Destination Hotels & Resort
7412 Mountain Road
Stowe VT 05672
(802) 253-3560
$298 - $1,109
SAVE –B&P Discount Available

Pet Policy: Dog-friendly rooms are in the main hotel and exclude the Front Four accommodations and Mountain Cabins. When your dog joins in on the fun, they'll receive: A plush dog bed; Vermont-inspired food and water bowl; A paw print mint ball toy to play with and freshen their breath; A bag of assorted all natural flavor treats; A lavender fresh spritz spray to freshen up after a hard afternoon of playing. For dog-sitting services, contact our Alpine Concierge.

Features: Dry cleaning/laundry service, Babysitting or child care, Restaurant, Supervised child care/activities, Number of rooms: 139, Number of floors: 3, Elevator, Airport transportation (additional charge), Air-conditioned public areas, Ski storage, Breakfast available (additional charge), Full-service health spa, Wireless Internet, Grocery, Shoe shine, Multilingual staff, 24-hour front desk, Business center, Security guard, Limo or Town Car service available, Medical assistance available, Ski-in/ski-out, Porter/bellhop, Concierge desk, Massage - treatment room(s), *Continued on next page*

Stowe Mountain Lodge
Continued from previous page

Meeting rooms (small groups), Steam room, Sauna, Ski shuttle, Smoke-free property, Children's club, Shopping on site, Wedding services, Fireplace in lobby, Bar/lounge, Beauty services, Room service (24 hours), Outdoor pool, Golf course on site, Parking (valet) $17 Daily, Doorman/doorwoman, Fitness facilities, Accessible bathroom.

★★★★
Stoweflake Mountain Resort & Spa
1746 Mountain Rd
Stowe VT 05672
(802) 253-7355
$259 - $929
SAVE –B&P Discount Available

Pet Policy: Stoweflake is a dog friendly property. Fee of $40 per night, per room is applicable for up to two (2) dogs. Maximum weight for any one dog cannot exceed 80 lbs, with a combined weight not to exceed 100 lbs for two (2) dogs. The number of dog friendly rooms is limited, therefore, reservations must be made directly with the hotel.

Features: Business Center, Health Club, Poolside bar, Sauna, Steam Room, 3 Restaurants, Number of rooms: 117, Number of floors: 2, Elevator, Suitable for children, Barbecue grill(s), Coffee in lobby, Piano, Wireless Internet, Self-parking, Room service (24 hours), Concierge desk, Massage - treatment room(s), Meeting rooms (small groups), Smoke-free property, Pool table, RV and truck parking, Bar/Lounge, In-room accessibility, Full-service health spa, Arcade/game room, Indoor pool, Outdoor pool, Dry cleaning/laundry service, Garden, Security guard, Fireplace in lobby, Golf course on site, Tennis on site, Babysitting or child care, Shopping on site, Airport transportation (additional charge), Computer rental, Air-conditioned public areas, Ski storage, Breakfast available (additional charge), Video library, Multilingual staff, Picnic area, 24-hour front desk, Porter/bellhop, Doorman/doorwoman, Limo or Town Car service available, Beauty services, Ski shuttle, Wedding services.

★★↗
Sun & Ski Inn And Suites
1613 Mountain Rd
Stowe VT 05672
(802) 253-7159
$119 - $189
SAVE –B&P Discount Available

Pet Policy: Pets accepted, $15 per night. Pets are not to be left unattended in rooms unless crated. Hotel reserves the right to request that pet be removed from the property if pet is disturbing other guests do to noise or aggressive behavior. A refund will not be issued for stay under these conditions.

Features: Wireless Internet, Coffee in lobby, Front desk (limited hours), Barbecue grill(s), Indoor pool, Fireplace in lobby, Outdoor pool, Shopping on site, Air-conditioned public areas, Patio, Ski storage, Free

Sun & Ski Inn And Suites
Continued from previous page

breakfast, Parking (free), Multilingual staff, Picnic area, Business center, Ski shuttle, Smoke-free property, Media library.

★★★ 🛏 🎿
Ten Acres Lodge B&B
14 Barrows Road
Stowe VT 05672
(802) 253-7638
$99 - $159
SAVE –B&P Discount Available

Pet Policy: Dogs are accepted only in rooms 21 and 25. Dogs must be crated or out of the room to receive housekeeping service

Features: Free Breakfast, Library, Outdoor pool, Number of rooms: 16, Parking (free), Wireless Internet, Smoke-free property, Barbecue grill(s), Conference room(s), Suitable for children, Video library, Sauna, Spa Tub.

Not Rated 🎿
The Riverside Inn
1965 Mountain Road
Stowe VT 05672
(802) 253-4217
$65 - $99

Pet Policy: Pets accepted, $5 per pet per night additional.

Features: Lodge and motel units, Fireplace lounge, Games area with pool table, Free parking, Stowe Trolley stops at Inn, Bar/lounge (seasonal).

★★★ 🎿
The Stowe Inn
123 Mountain Road
Stowe VT 05672
(802) 253-4030
$84 - $179
SAVE –B&P Discount Available

Pet Policy: Pets allowed in the motel (not the Carriage House), $15 per pet per night, limit 2 per room.

Features: Restaurant, Outdoor pool, Fireplace in lobby, Arcade/game room, Parking (free), Wireless Internet, Smoke-free property, Billiards, Free breakfast, Bar/lounge.

★★★★ 🎿
Trapp Family Lodge
700 Trapp Hill Road
Stowe VT 05672
(800) 826-7000
$270 - $369

Pet Policy: Dogs up to 50 lbs are welcome to stay in the Main Lodge - pet additional charge of 30% nightly fee is added. Enjoy 2,500 acres with our dog-friendly lodging accommodations. To help our canine guests feel at home, we provide LL Bean Dog Bed and Blanket, Trapp Treats and Trapp Lodge Dog Bowls, along with a Doggie Trail Pass and Map to the dog friendly area of our property. Please call us directly for reservations.

While staying with us, we ask that you kindly observe the following rules: Please... Dogs over 50 pounds are permitted at the discretion of the manager.
Continued on next page

231

Trapp Family Lodge
Continued from previous page

Dogs must be leashed at all times when outside your room. Use only dog-friendly paths, and avoid our groomed trails. Use scoop bags and deposit them in the container provided. Barking dogs must not be left in room unattended. Note that you are responsible for any damage caused by your pet.

Features: Number of rooms: 96, Guesthouse Chalets, Cross Country ski trails, Restaurant, wine tasting, Fitness center, Indoor heated pool, Massage facilities, Wedding services.

Vergennes

★★★
Basin Harbor
4800 Basin Harbor Road
Vergennes VT 05491
(800) 622-4000
Rates from $187

Pet Policy: We understand the importance of the family pet and know how it is to leave them behind so here at Basin Harbor, furry guests are treated to our exceptional service as well as their owners. Our pet amenities include Vermont made biscuits, pick up mitts and a welcome letter from the BHC Mascots, Piccolo, Ava and Fannie. Piccollo and Ava host a dog walk weekly with their owner, Pennie Beach and dog walking/dog sitting services are available. All well-behaved pets are welcome in cottage accommodations only, for an additional charge of $10 per day, per pet and do not have to be crated or caged when owners are absent. Dogs must be kept leashed at all times on property and kept away from the pool and waterfront areas. The woods surrounding Basin Harbor are ideal for walking in the cool cover of the forest and the Edgewater Trail has some great swimming spots. It is understood that owners are responsible for any damage their pets may cause and that owners will "pick up" after their dogs. Our "VIC" amenity is available for an additional $125 and includes a logoed dog bed, custom collar and leash. And kitties are not forgotten here...A "VIF" package is also available for felines with catnip chair, food dish and kitty bed.

Features: Private cottages, Restaurants, Olympic size pool, Bar/lounge.

Waitsfield
Also see the following nearby communities that have pet friendly lodging:
Warren - 5 miles.

Not rated
Weathertop Mountain Inn
755 Millbrook Road
Waitsfield VT 05673
(802) 496-4909
$119 - $139

Pet Policy: Welcomes Dogs only, must be at least 1 year old and must be neutered! No fee is charged but guests are responsible for any damage. During your stay, visiting dogs will have unrestricted access to most of the inn's common areas. Access to the commercial kitchen, other guest rooms and the innkeepers' quarters is prohibited. Pet access to the dining room during meal times "may" be allowed, depending upon our occupancy level and other guest preferences during your visit - please enquire upon arrival.

To avoid potential pet-to-pet confrontations, our normal policy is to allow only one guest with a pet on the premises at any given time. As such, our approval MUST be obtained when booking your reservation. Please book directly with the Inn. This policy may occasionally be waived for pets that have previously stayed with us, or for families traveling together with pets that are already familiar with one another.

You may not leave your pet unsupervised in your guest room while you go out for the day. On some occasions, we may allow a crated pet to be left in your guest room; however, this must be discussed with us PRIOR to your arrival.

Features: Number of rooms: 8, Restaurant, Game room with pool table, Lounge with fireplace, Hot Tub, Full breakfast, Sauna.

Warren

Also see the following nearby communities that have pet friendly lodging:
Waitsfield - 5 miles.

Not Rated
Deer Meadow Inn
3215 Airport Road
Warren VT 05674
(802)496-2850
Rates starting at $160

Pet Policy: Dogs welcome, $5 per night per dog, limit 2 per room. No size restrictions.

Features: Number of rooms: 3, Full breakfast, Non-smoking property.

Not Rated
Sugarbush Condos
2405 Sugarbush Road
Warren VT 05674
(802) 583-6100
$140 - $365

Pet Policy: Pet friendly units available, $35 per night additional.

Features: One through four bedroom condos, fully equipped kitchens, Fireplace or wood stove in many units, private sundecks, washer/dryers..

★★★★
The Pitcher Inn
275 Main Street
Warren VT 05674
(802) 496-6350
$350 - $575

Pet Policy: The Pitcher Inn understands that dogs are an extension of your family and we do allow our guests traveling with well behaved, four-legged friends in our dog friendly room, The Stable Suite at $75 per pet, per night.

Features: Full breakfast and afternoon tea included, Number of rooms: 11, 2 Two bedroom suites, Wireless Internet, Jacuzzi tubs in all rooms, Radiant floor heating, Wood burning fireplaces in most rooms, King beds in most rooms, Restaurant, Full service health spa, Relais and Chateaux Club memberships accepted.

White River Junction

Also see the following nearby communities that have pet friendly lodging:
West Lebanon - 2 miles, Quechee - 3 miles, Lebanon - 5 miles.

Not Rated
Comfort Inn
56 Ralph Lehman DR
White River Junction VT 05001
(802) 295-3051
$109 - $149

Pet Policy: Pets accepted, no additional fee. Limit of 2 per room, must use credit card to check in. Dogs may not be left alone in room.

Features: Indoor pool and fitness center, An official Dartmouth College Athletics hotel.

★★
Hotel Coolidge
39 South Main Street
White River Junction VT 05001
(802) 295-3118
$89 - $100

Pet Policy: Pets accepted, $100 per stay fee. Please call hotel directly for pet reservations.

Features: Year Built 1927, Fireplace in lobby, Wireless Internet, Laundry facilities, Number of rooms: 28, Elevator, Meeting and conference rooms, Wedding services, Parking, Non-smoking property.

★★ 🐾
Super 8 Motel
442 N Hartland Rd
White River Junction VT 05001
(802) 295-7577
$58 - $74
SAVE –B&P Discount Available

Pet Policy: Pets accepted, no fee, but advanced approval required. Please contact hotel directly for pet approval and reservation.

Features: Free breakfast, Business services, Air-conditioned public areas, Parking (free), 24-hour front desk, Outdoor pool – seasonal.

★★ 🐾
White River Inn and Suites
91 Ballardvale Dr
White River Junction VT 05001
(802) 295-3015
$74 - $99
SAVE –B&P Discount Available

Pet Policy: Pet Accommodation: $10/night, per pet, 2 pets per room.

Features: Gift shop, Number of rooms: 112, Number of floors: 2, Air-conditioned public areas, Arcade/game room, Parking (free), Multilingual staff, 24-hour front desk, Fax machine, Free breakfast, Indoor pool, Business services, Laundry facilities, Fitness facilities.

Williston

Also see the following nearby communities that have pet friendly lodging:
Essex Junction - 4 miles, South Burlington - 6 miles, Burlington - 7 miles, Colchester - 7 miles, Shelburne - 9 miles.

★★★ 🐾
Residence Inn by Marriott
35 Hurricane Ln
Williston VT 05495
(800) 679-5601
$144 - $269
SAVE –B&P Discount Available

Pet Policy: Pets allowed, $75 cleaning fee per stay.

Features: Number of rooms: 96, Number of floors: 2, Health club, Parking (free), Multilingual staff, Free newspapers in lobby, 24-hour front desk, Wireless Internet, Meeting rooms (small groups), Accessible bathroom, Handicapped parking, In-room accessibility, Dry cleaning/laundry service, Barbecue grill(s), Fireplace in lobby, Air-conditioned public areas, Indoor pool, Grocery, Business services, Coffee in lobby, Fitness facilities.

★★ 🐾
Towneplace Suites Burlington
66 Zephyr Rd
Williston VT 05495
(802) 872-5900
$149 - $209
SAVE –B&P Discount Available

Pet Policy: Pets allowed, $75 per stay cleaning fee.

Features: Indoor pool, Number of rooms: 95, Number of floors: 3, Elevator, Laundry facilities, Currency exchange, Parking (free), Free newspapers in lobby, Picnic area, 24-hour front desk, Business center, Wireless Internet, Fitness facilities.

.

www.ingramcontent.com/pod-product-compliance
Lightning Source LLC
La Vergne TN
LVHW051504080426
835509LV00017B/1908